NAMING LILAH

A Novel

NAMING LILAH

A Novel

MONA GIBSON JAMES
Author

Naming Lilah – A Novel
A Novel
ISBN: 978-1-958977-00-2
Print Version

All rights reserved. No part of this book may be reproduced or transmitted in any form or by any means, electronic or mechanical, including photocopying, recording or by any information storage and retrieval system without permission from the author, except for the inclusion of brief quotations in a review.

FIRST EDITION

Copyright © 2022 Mona Gibson James

First Printing 2022

Printed in the United States of America
Library of Congress Cataloging in Publication Data on file.

Published by

Circle Square Services
circlesquareservices.com

CIRCLE SQUARE

Dedicated to

my Mother, my Grandmothers, and my Great-Grandmothers

TOGETHER

A reflection carries the history of the one who gives it light.

As the name from which it begins leads the journey home, the name it's finally given is a creation of its own.

It may often stand alone, and it may also seek greater heights.

But the reflection that remains is the one it learns to love and the one it discovers

it has always truly known.

- Mona Gibson James

CHAPTER ONE
Lily

Endings Pursue Beginnings

The morning mist is captured by the ornate tapestry of Jacaranda blossoms woven across our backyard. They arrived early this Spring. Summer seems too soon, and the end of another school year will bring me one year closer to the empty nest I dread. When is the time when happiness lasts beyond a mere moment?

Today's a bakery Monday. Changing my office days from Monday and Wednesday to Tuesday and Thursday was the best change I made this year. Sundays are no longer burdened with Monday morning anxiety. And, free/flex day Fridays are now the start of an actual three-day weekend.

My morning respite is perfected by a warm cup of Sage Tea and a calming view of our backyard. Time slows with each brush of wind across my cheeks.

"What's going on?" I question after my calm is interrupted by the thunderous sounds spilling from inside our patio doors. Our largest Golden slides on all fours headfirst as he jolts towards the front door. The other two immediately follow his lead and join in on the craze caused by a simple doorbell ring. We've researched and tried every dog training technique we could find to stop their over-the-top antics. Our two youngsters seem more willing to comply, but our old-school big guy refuses to learn new tricks. I know he's just testing me and being stubborn seems to be a thing for us both.

Adam restrains the racing mob and manages to answer the front door. The double doors framed like farmhouse picture windows allow much-welcomed light into our home, but the doors also allow visitors an unobstructed view into our home. Our foyer is simply decorated with a large painting gifted to us by Granna. She wanted to help a struggling young artist, and we were more than happy to house his art.

I am two steps behind Adam when he turns and points in my direction with his one free hand. His right hand and leg are being used to block our nosey canines.

"Lily Guillory? You've been served," I give Adam a firm swat with one hand and take the package from the delivery guy with the other. It is neither Valentine's Day nor my birthday so I'm not sure why Adam thinks staging a nerdy husband joke on a random Monday morning would be considered funny.

"Ouch!" Adam yells as the delivery guy makes his exit. "I've done nothing. You are really being served."

"Impossible," I say as I rip open the package. It's a large legal-sized envelope with no label. *"The Estate of Rosemary Cormier Romain versus Lilah Cormier Marchand, Lily Collins Guillory and Much Ado About Pecans, Inc.* "Who? What the Hell? Breach of Contract?" I read the words out loud without the ability to process their meaning. Someone is actually suing me!

The familiar feelings of being personally attacked and victimized return once again. "Wow, I'll have to remember these emotions and use them during my next trial," I speak to myself. "Well...Ha-ha! Looks like I'm probably going to be my next trial!"

After skimming through the entire package, I call Granna first. The lawsuit was filed by her deceased sister's family—family I have never met.

"Morning Granna...Rosemary Cormier?" I immediately ask. "If someone comes to your door, don't answer. They will have to stop at your guard station first anyway. I will call their attorney and let them know I'll accept service for you."

"Slow down, Lily," Granna responds, irritated. "What are you saying? What about Rosey?"

My shock led to my frantic call to Granna, but I know she does not allow room in her day for my theatrical protests. I take a deep breath and attempt to calm my tone before I speak again.

"Your sister's heirs are suing us," I speak as calmly as I can muster. "Do you know anything about her estate?"

"You're confused," Granna determines as she now begins to speak in a much louder tone than mine. "Rosey's been long gone."

"Yes, I remember. When was the last time you spoke to her children?" I inquire.

"She only has a daughter," Granna explains. "I haven't seen or spoken to her since our Rosey passed. Why are you asking about her?"

"Well, her daughter is suing us, that's why!" I respond as I grab my keys and throw the documents into my law office handbag. My Happy Monday is officially over. I was really looking forward to hanging out all day eating pastries fresh out of the oven. "I'm on my way to you, Granna."

"Suing us for what?" Granna questions with an even more elevated tone. "Don't be silly. How would they even know anything about us to sue— sue for what in Heaven's sake?"

Granna has been our only parent for over eighteen years and having her close by has allowed me to survive many dark days without mom. She helped Mom pick my name, Lily, because Granna's parents loved the beauty of flowers and wanted their children to appreciate their own beauty. It's why I named my daughter Lydia—*the beautiful one.*

I'm an orphan. Adam always tries to correct me when I say as much, but I looked it up, and technically, anyone who has lost their biological parents is an orphan. That's me. I'd lost both parents before my twenty-seventh birthday. My younger brother, Luke, was, at the time, a twenty-four-year-old medical student. He's now devoted himself to caring for victims of cancer.

Cancer took Mom from us far too early. Cancer robs, kills, and destroys not only its victim but entire families. My dad left us first— a heart attack. The stress of caring for his deteriorating wife took too great a toll on his health. He insisted on doing it all on his own and refused our help. We were helpless to do anything differently.

I am still angry and demanding an answer to my "why" questions. I've lost more than I ever allowed myself to imagine. I hide behind a cloud of grief, and my brother hides behind his work—helping others fight cancer. At least one of us is choosing to do something productive.

I arrive at Granna's on autopilot with lawsuit in hand and adrenaline on overload. I again remember to take a breath. Granna is in her 90's, and I don't want to be responsible for sending her over the edge. The guard waves me in, and I cautiously drive down the winding road adorned with meticulous beds of flowers framing each residence. I make complete stops at each turn to ensure that I do not collide with any of the seniors enjoying their morning walk. Behind these gates, retirement is seductive.

"Granna, it's that stupid television spot," I announce before giving her a proper greeting. "I know you're thinking I just need to stop and take a moment before I jump out and do stuff. This time you are correct. The new labels and marketing package we picked for our pecan pie and pecan butter campaign uses the photo of you as a child sitting in your front yard under a Pecan Tree. The picture is included with the lawsuit as an exhibit. They obviously recognized you in the photo."

A three-minute morning show appearance I prayed and begged over a year to secure was supposed to help promote our products and increase company sales, not set us up for a corporate takeover. Having our company sued by 'family' is a road bump none of us could have imagined, but I once again feel like I've failed my family. My bakery office wall is covered with flow charts detailing the steps needed to bring our products to store shelves. Not one bubble or line item includes the word "Lawsuit."

"*The Estate of Rosemary Cormier Romain versus Lilah Cormier Marchand,*" Granna reads. Her pocket doors are closed, but the view of the neighboring mountains is still inviting. She's seated in her favorite chair with feet stretched out on the matching ottoman, resting under a fluffy blanket, with her tea in hand. She's dressed in a jogging suit that I think is too young for her, and her hair and makeup are both perfect. Granna's style is always hard to outmatch.

"I missed my morning walk because of you," Granna scans the documents and hands them back to me tentatively.

I'm not sure if she's worried, angry, or strategizing. I also don't know much about her "White Family," as she calls them. Until recently, I had not even known that she grew up believing that she was White. Granna was raised by her White mother's family and did not meet her Black father until she was a newly married college graduate.

"I do not understand why this is happening, and I still cannot believe someone showed up at my door this morning and served me with a lawsuit?' I repeat out loud once again.

"Are they poor and need money?" Granna asks as if she may write them a check. "My sister is rolling over right now."

"I have no idea?' I reply. "I'm Googling them now, and it looks like her granddaughter is a Louisiana State Senator- Katherine

Tillerson Emory. She's the wife of Dr. Owen Emory and the daughter of Emma Tillerson and the late Dr. Edward Tillerson. They don't seem poor?"

"Well, what is it they want?" Granna asks. "Emma—that's Rosey's baby girl."

"They are claiming that the use of our recipes and packaging is a contract violation. Allegedly, we are simply repackaging their products using a different name," I explain. "It's ridiculous. Recipes are not intellectual property, and it is impossible that our recipes are some kind of secret recipe developed by your sister."

"Yes! Impossible, and it's not true," Granna laughs. "Rosey never baked a thing. I baked with Mother and Mrs. Ada. Have I told you about her? She is my grandmother, who worked in our home my entire life, and I was never told by any of them until after her passing. Rosey was also busy tagging along behind our father. You do not have to worry about this foolishness. Everything I make I learned from my mother and from Mrs. Ada—they definitely can't claim ownership to anything I know."

"Yes. I remember, and I pray you are right, Granna!" I say. "I need to call and warn Uncle. He should also be served soon as well. He is listed as our company's registered agent. After that, I'll work on picking a Louisiana attorney."

"I really never imagined that they were still in the pecan business," Granna ponders. "When Rosey sold the farm, she only mentioned the land, and I didn't ask any questions. I had opened my bakery by then and was doing fine."

"It looks like when they sold the farm, the rights to market and sell 'all' pecan products was included—but there's a royalty provision," I explain. "Your sister's family is still receiving royalty payments from the buyer. Granna, did your sister ever mention getting royalty payments? You should also be receiving payments. Our counterclaim will get answers."

"Rosey gave me money from the sale but nothing after that," Granna confirms. "I wasn't told anything about any royalty. Well, call me when you know more. I'll be here hiding from the law."

"You're safe," I laugh along with Granna. "Go and take your walk. I'll check on you again on my way home from the office."

The lawsuit was filed in New Orleans Federal District Court, which is appropriate and not surprising. Granna opened her first bakery in 1958—*Marchand's Sweet Tooth* in New Orleans East. After *Hurricane Katrina*, Granna did not reopen her original location. Our flagship location is now *Much Ado About Pecans* in the New Orleans French Market. Its opening was our last big family celebration— June 1, 2000, before mom's cancer had returned for the third time.

Granna had often talked about a French Market location and was not bothered by any of our objections as to cost. Her weekend trips to the market as a young mother planted her dream of one day having a French Market bakery. We were told stories of Granna's first summer in New Orleans and how the French Market was her favorite place to visit every Saturday. She would spend the day eating beignets for breakfast, strolling through art displays, shopping for handcrafted jewelry and crafts, and enjoying gelato in the afternoon. She would leave with bags of fresh fruit, vegetables, and homemade spreads she would use to create new recipes.

Mom was especially excited to help Granna realize her dream. *Much Ado* was a dream they began to share. Together they came up with the name and created the format and business model. Granna wanted her new bakery to start out as a family venture that would be owned and grown by us all. Mom wanted to make Granna proud. Many times, we all felt we were falling short of her high expectations.

As usual, Granna's business instincts were correct. Our family's joint efforts made us all equally invested and proud of what we were able to start together. The French Market is full of an eclectic variety of foods, arts, and crafts. A Pecan Shop/Bakery fit perfectly. Locals and tourists both love our walk and carry bags of roasted pecans, our bite-sized treats, and Pecan Butter Gift Baskets.

With both hands gripping my steering wheel, I drive without thinking until I reach the entrance to our office parking garage. I park and turn off my car. Each day typically begins with me taking time to get quiet, pray and meditate, but on law office days, I also stop and say another prayer before exiting my car. I kick off my ballet flats and slip into heels. I don't know why heels make me feel more powerful. Maybe it's the extra height?

The ride up to the twenty-first floor provides another moment for me to breathe. When the elevator doors open, I'm ready.

Our office speaks in money and power. The walls are a shade of light gray and covered with paintings meant to inspire wonder and fear.

No one is quiet or still. Finola appears and welcomes me with a needed embrace. "Anastasia Carver is a good idea," Finola approves. Finola was my second call after Granna. I needed to make certain that we officially scheduled a time for us to discuss the lawsuit.

As we walk towards my office, an unexpected rush of relief and comfort fills me. Today, I like this place. My career dreams were realized in this office. I'm grateful to be here for the first time in recent memory—it's been over two years of complex emotions. I still feel the weight of embarrassment and the pain of failure and disappointment. But today, those were not my first thoughts when I entered the doors. The legal resources I have will give us an advantage most small family businesses would not otherwise have available. A lengthy litigation battle can be a financial crusher for most.

Finola and I started working with the firm the same day. I was a transplant from Texas, and she was a transplant from Illinois. "I'll work with Anastasia and her team. We can trust her, but this is personal. I will oversee the case," Finola proclaims.

"Agreed, this will be a team effort," I offer in support. "Anastasia will throw her red bottom shoes at anyone who dares to try anything deceptive, and you will not let one fact go unchecked. This case is already won," I joke, but only because we've all witnessed Anastasia do as much many times, and Finola is a Rottweiler—she never eases up on her bite.

Within these walls, Finola and I only trust each other. We both now accept that it may always be difficult for us to effectively serve within this space.

Because of *Much Ado*, I've been able to start practicing law part-time. I loved this firm and excelled beyond my expectations until the slippery hands of Daniel, my managing partner, changed things for too many of my once eager-to-serve co-workers and me.

First, my administrative assistant came forward after an international trip to Japan. I led a team of three junior attorneys and four admins. It was a dream trip for us all. Daniel was our senior partner and a sloppy drunk. He was traditionally useless by the time we finished our evening team dinners, but we were all used to his routine.

Next, my junior associate came forward with similar grievances. I was a corroborating witness who should have spoken up sooner for the females on my team. I saw his slippery hands, and I regrettably made myself believe he would not take things further. He was happily married to a beautiful attorney fifteen years his junior. I made excuses in my head to not see the tragic truth. Daniel was a predator. I was their supervising attorney. I failed them.

No one outside this firm knows of its licentiousness. My speaking up, while ultimately helping to bring justice, I still judge as disappointingly late. I was excelling, applauded for my wins, and paid generously. I feared ending it all. I feared speaking up and causing the collapse of our glass house.

Stepping back to focus on my healing has helped me better understand why I feared speaking out—even if speaking out required me to speak against a boss I had once admired. I was trained to speak up against power. I'm a Dragon Slayer. Because I lived for a good courtroom debate, the fear I felt when I needed to speak out against authority was surprising and shameful. I knew my success and promotions were because of my hard work. I didn't understand my resistance—why I feared the truth. I still do not.

The glass walls crashed in on many more than first suspected. The harmed were promoted and given unspeakably large bonuses for their silence. After the bad apples were removed, those who remained were polished and placed on a pedestal for all to view.

We now all mostly avoid eye contact so as not to see another truth we fear may be hiding amongst the residue. Outside these walls, no one knows our anguish. No one knows my truth—not Adam, not Granna. I hide behind the story I tell even to myself… *"I'm stepping back a bit to help my Granna bake."*

Many of my hopes remain here with us all, but my dreams are now invested in *Much Ado*.

"Anastasia's firm also has an office in Houston with Louisiana licensed attorneys—correct?" Finola asks directing my attention back to the present. "We need Louisiana folks as well."

"They do," I confirm. "We should take the Louisiana Bar one day." We both revel at the thought but acknowledge that committing the time to study for another bar exam can be put to better use, especially when a *Pro hac vice Motion* will get us a seat at the litigants' table if needed.

    I am excited to again work with Anastasia. Our firms have worked together on a few other large cases whenever our legal team needed extra muscle and brains. Our joint efforts are five wins and zero losses.

    The three of us have known each other since meeting at a young lawyers networking luncheon our first year in Los Angeles. If Anastasia tells you she'll meet you at Noon, she'll be there at 11:55 AM. If she says, 'I'll call you back in ten minutes,' she's on your line in nine minutes. No excuses, no 'something came up,' no exaggerations, no pandering… she's someone I can always trust to do exactly what she promises.

    This is the first case we've taken on together since our firm's scandalous reorganization. Hopefully, Anastasia won't pick up on any apprehensions or the smell of toxic air floating around.

"Looks like we get to hang out in *NOLA*," Finola boasts. "We need *Saints* tickets and rooms at the *Plaza* on *Canal*." Finola has traveled to New Orleans twice, and now she's an expert. Her help is needed, and I'm pleased to see her excitement. Even if I wanted to handle this case personally, I know I cannot handle this case alone. I don't admit it out loud, but I will get whatever tickets Finola wants. I also never forget the common adages I share with all my clients…*"Physician Heal Thyself"* and *"A Person Who Represents Themselves Has a Fool for a Client."* I can neither heal myself, heal this situation nor represent us. We need to hire an attorney that's not me.

I read the petition once again as I replay the events of my morning. "Lily Guillory? You've been served," I see my name on the petition, but... I'm still not convinced it's meant for me. The number of citations I've requested and the defendants I've served are too many to count. And, never not once have I considered the feelings of the recipient of those citations. Today it's me, and now I suddenly care about feelings.

Trying to grow our business and take our products national has become my new full-time job, and it's a job I do not intend to lose because of a lawsuit filed by Granna's hateful long-lost family. I have lost enough.

CHAPTER TWO
Lilah

*"Proceed great chief, with virtue on thy side
thy every action let the goddess guide"*
- Phillis Wheatley

The evening of my eighteenth birthday was the day I learned my truth. Our home often served as host for Bible study groups and Deacon meetings, but tonight everyone had gathered for me. I was not surprised to see that most wore their finest Sunday attire. Mother set the standard each Sunday with her two-piece tailored dress suits, matching kitten heels, and handbags. Most also wore similar fitted dresses in bright spring colors, while only a handful arrived wearing dresses made from fabric with flower prints or shapes of plaid.

Earlier that day, I received my first birthday gift from Mrs. Ada— a white silk A-line dress covered by a handmade soft pink lace brocade. Mother objected to my wearing the dress until she saw the finished product. There was no issue to be found. My dress was just as exquisite as any of the department store dresses adored by the ladies now huddled around Mother.

Mrs. Ada's youngest sister delivered the dress to me the day before my birthday. The large white box was secured by a lace pink bow— matching the lace used to make my dress. I had seen the unfinished shell twice before when Mrs. Ada had me try it on for fittings. A handwritten note was included.

My Dear Lilah,
Watching you grow into a beautiful, loving
and smart young lady is one of the
greatest joys of my life. I know God has a great plan for your life.
Lovingly, Mrs. Ada

Two weeks before my birthday, Mrs. Ada had unexpectedly passed. She was fine the day before, baking with Mother and helping father with deliveries. Later that night, one of her sons came by our home to give us the news— a heart attack.

I had never cried more. I did not attend her service at the Black Baptist church. Father went for us all. We had a separate memorial service at the farm. Our pastor led a service for our family and all our workers, most of whom were related to Mrs. Ada. We had a plaque carved in her honor and nailed it onto her favorite tree—the large oak tree next to the barn. We both loved sitting under her tree. Its oversized branches stretched out in four different directions like an octopus.

My dress was the talk of the evening. Everyone asked my mother where she had found it. Mother only smiled and said, "It was a gift."

As tradition required, I received many new linens and household wares, but some ladies came bearing new clothing which was contrary to tradition. Mother had mentioned that my first choice for life after high school was to attend college instead of getting married like most girls in St. Francis. The church ladies didn't know what to make of my decision, so they did the Christian thing—smiled while bringing the customary items for my *Eighteenth Birthday Hope Chest*.

"Lilah is so thankful to you all for coming this evening," Mother expressed. "We are so proud of the young lady she has become. Please continue to pray for her as she starts her next journey in life. Whatever she decides, we trust that the Lord will always be with her, lighting the way."

I was the first young lady, as far as I had been told, who decided to go off to college. Not many girls, White or Black, chose college over a wedding. Most of the gifts I received that day were the same types of gifts received in preparation for a new life as a wife and mother.

As our last guest made her way down our drive, Mother and Father began sorting through the table covered with the gifts I had received. Rosey and I enjoyed one more slice of pecan pie in the kitchen after we cleared the dishes from our dining room.

We finished cleaning our serving trays first, and Rosey returned them to the dining room cabinet. She then quickly returned and was followed by Mother. Mother stared strangely at us both and turned to rejoin Father in the dining room.

"Mrs. Ada is your grandmother," Rosey whispered to me as she handed me a kitchen towel to dry the dessert plates I had just finished washing. "I wasn't going to say anything right away, but Mother just walked in and out without saying a word to you like nothing at all had just happened. I know she saw me listening. I don't think Mother ever plans on telling you the truth, so I guess it's my duty to say something?"

Rosey was three years old when our parents adopted me. I've always known I was adopted, but I had never asked about my "real parents," I was told an unwed young lady from another Parish needed a loving Christian home to take her child. As the head deacon of our church, my father had helped other families place unwanted children. When I came along, it was my parents' time to adopt. Rosey was an only child, and our mother had tried many times to have other children. "You were a blessing sent from above," my parents often proclaimed.

"What are you talking about?" I responded, confused by her statement.

"I overheard Mother telling Father about how proud she is of you," Rosey explained. "Then Mother mentioned Mrs. Ada and how proud she would be of you. I couldn't imagine why they were talking about Mrs. Ada?"

"When did you hear this?" I continued questioning, mostly wanting to know how long she had been able to keep a secret. I didn't imagine she had known very long, but I was still surprised by how little time it took for her to repeat what she had overheard without a bit of hesitation.

"Just now!" she confirmed. "I was going to help finish clearing your gift table. They probably thought I was in here helping you with the dishes. Mother turned around, and she saw me standing there."

"Rosey, just now?" I yelled. "How could you? Mother and Father probably didn't know you were snooping, and you run in here to repeat what you think you overheard?"

"They saw me," she declared. "And, I'm sure what I heard. You know Mother is not happy about you wanting to move away and go to college. I now see why she blamed Mrs. Ada's meddling as the reason."

"So that makes her my grandmother?" I said, confused. "Mrs. Ada cared for us both. You got married one month after your high school graduation. That's what you wanted. You could not wait to leave the farm and Mother's rules."

"Mother asked Father if she should tell you about Mrs. Ada and explain to you why you should not listen to her advice," Rosey attempted to reason. "She doesn't want you getting caught up in the dreams of an old lady."

"Because Mrs. Ada thought I was smart and talented; she's my grandmother?" I again questioned. "Grandmother—Rosey, do you know what you are saying?"

"Oh, yes," Rosey replied. "You are not as lily white as you look. Sorry, it's just so shocking to me as well. Mrs. Ada's sons are also as mixed-up as you. Look at them. Everyone knows she was favored by Mr. Parker. Remember him? He owned the general store, and he was always hanging around the farm pretending to want to buy pecans for his store?"

"Rosey, you're now a married woman," I reprimanded. "Why would you say such things about Mrs. Ada? What if I started rumors about you and your husband? You need to watch your tongue."

"Think Lilah," she admonishes. "One of her sons must be your real father? She didn't have daughters."

"You're trying to have a baby of your own," I reminded. "When are you going to grow up and act like an adult? And, stop picking on me like we are still little children. I'm your younger sister, and soon I will also be a woman living on my own—I'm not your competition. This is the most hateful thing you have ever done."

Without thinking, I take one of the recipe books from the kitchen shelf—I pick the heaviest of the bunch and throw it directly towards her head. Rosey's quick, but the odds were on my side. She gets a good smack across the side of her head. I'm sure she's hurt, but she doesn't dare give me the satisfaction of seeing her pain.

"Father!" she yells as she grabs the side of her head.

"You don't know what you heard—you're such a liar!" I convicted. Rosey and I always looked and acted differently, but so do many sisters. We all also knew I was adopted, so our differences were not unexpected. All sisters argue and compete with each other. It never bothered me, but her attacks on Mrs. Ada and me had crossed the line.

"You should be happy I was snooping," she defended. "You could have lived your entire life, and Mother would never have said a word. I just felt the Lord say to me, 'go and tell your sister the truth. It's time for her to know.' Mother was never going to tell you that her baby sister had a baby with the help, and they adopted you."

"Baby sister, the help!" I screamed as I ran towards her. "Liar!"

"I'm not a liar," she continued to assert. "I may tell everything

I know, but it is all true. I have no reason to ever lie about anything." We both run towards the dining room, yelling, and crying hysterically.

"You're lying now," I accused. "Your tears are fake, and you are a liar."

"I loved Mrs. Ada too," Rosey said. "I cried just as much as you when she passed. She took care of us both."

"What are you saying?" I hesitated while trying to hide my rising fears. "You don't know what you're talking about. Not another word from you."

"Look at what your perfect child has done," Rosey shouted. "She hit me with a book."

Our parents stood silent—I imagined, trying to understand why we were both so upset. The dining table was cleared except for a tray of tea cookies our parents had been enjoying.

"Sorry to ruin your evening," I offered—startling them both. "Rosey was standing outside the dining room earlier when she heard you talking about Mrs. Ada and me." Without another word, our mother stood from her chair and grabbed hold of our father's hand.

"Rosey, what have you done?" Mother cried out. "Why would you not come to me and ask about what you think you may have heard? Why would you run and blab about something you know nothing about? Why would you purposefully try to cause your sister and me pain?"

Mother grabbed hold of me, and we both sobbed as Father stood stoic.

"Rosey, come with me," Father ordered. He grabbed her hand and walked with her onto the front porch.

"Mother, it's fine," I consoled. "We all know you didn't give birth to me, but being my mother is something that always was and always will be."

As we both cried in each other's arms, Mother whispered, "We come from the same blood. You and I were meant for each other."

Rosey showed up bright and early the next morning to witness the aftermath of her betrayal. Mother was still resting, and Father and I were making her favorite biscuits for breakfast.

"Rosey, please behave today," Father instructed. "Let your mother speak to Lilah when she decides. It's not your truth to tell."

"Yes, sir," she spoke, almost sounding remorseful. "I just wanted to check on Mother and apologize to you all. Sorry."

"Sorry!" I yelled. "Sorry! Is that the best you can think to say?"

"I wanted you to know—I wanted you all to know that I understand why you are angry with me. I didn't cause this mess, but it's now my fault because I wanted you to know the truth."

"Rosey, I warned you," Father said with anger in his voice and agitation bellowing across his face. He again grabs Rosey's arm and leads her out the door.

"Father, I'm sorry Rosey has caused so much trouble," Blaming everything on Rosey was common for me. It was usually her fault things went wrong. Her busy mouth and wild nature caused much of our family drama. Getting her married quickly was a priority because a surprise pregnancy would have surely been on its way.

"My sweet Lilah, you have been a true blessing for your mother and me. We both wanted a house full of children. Because your mother suffered so many losses before and after Rosey, we always saw you as God's gift to us. We never thought twice about raising you," Father confessed as he leaned in to place a gentle kiss on my forehead. "Look at you—just beautiful inside and out. Your mother knew the moment she saw you that raising you was something meant for her to do."

"How could you be so sure?" I demanded to know. "Babies change. What if I changed?" I can feel the fear taking over— would I have been sent away?

"I'm going to tell you this only because Rosey has opened the door, and now the whole truth must be told," he asserted. "You looking so much like your mother is not by coincidence. Her sister, Daisy, was the young unwed mother in need of help."

"I don't understand?" I protested. "Why would this be kept a secret? Why wouldn't you tell me I'm related to mother by blood? Is it because my father is Black? That is it—isn't it?" I replied, unable to hold my tears. They did not want anyone to know that I was Black. "Who knows about Daisy?"

"No one," he confirmed. "Only me, your mother, Mrs. Ada, Daisy, and Franklin—Mrs. Ada's son. He worked on the farm, and Daisy wouldn't stay away. He's the son she seduced."

"Seduced?" I responded with concern.

"He was barely eighteen, and Daisy knew better," he continued. "She could have gotten that poor boy killed. Ada was terrified for anyone to know."

"I'm Black," I spoke out loud for the first time. Father gave me a surprised look as if he was miffed to hear those words come out of the mouth of his daughter.

"We didn't want you to be treated differently—Rose, Ada, and me," Father made known as he walks away. "No one else was ever told."

"What about my grandparents?" I asked.

"Daisy had left for New Orleans and only came back right before you were born," he answered. "She came to your mother for help. We all kept her secret."

"Was I born in this house?" my questions lingered. "I was born in this house, and no one ever said a word. Why?"

"Your mother helped birth many babies," he explained. "Daisy knew she would be safe. We had a doctor from New Orleans come by and check you both. Not my parents or Rose's parents knew."

"Mrs. Ada helped?" I questioned.

"Yes, Ada knew her son couldn't care for you," he replied. "She also wanted us to take you. When you came out looking just like your mother and Daisy, everyone knew what should be done." The words slip from Father's mouth before he realized. He did not ignore the shocked look on my face. "Not all of Ada's boys were for her husband. That was easy to see. The son who made you was obviously one of those slip-ups. Ada was first to ask your mother to take you. They came up with the story of a young teenage girl from another Parish that needed help."

As I listened to Father describe the day I was born, the tears again begin to flow uncontrollably.

Naming Lilah

"Mother's sister?" I continued. "She died when we were little?"

"Yes, not because of you," he assured. "She had pneumonia. Daisy was a free spirit like Rosey but even more rebellious. She went back to New Orleans and didn't return to St. Francis very often."

Neither of us could now bear to continue to look each other in the eyes. "Did she visit…" I couldn't finish my words.

"Daisy named you," he informed. "I don't think she ever thought your mother wouldn't take you? It was best for everyone—her, Ada, and the boy."

"Named me? I wondered. "Lilah or Flower?" Everyone called me Lil'flower. I thought it was because my mother's name is Rose, and my sister's is Rosemary.

"Your mother always called Daisy—Delilah," he disclosed. "Her wild nature and mischievous acts fit the name. When your mother discovered Daisy was pregnant, she and Mrs. Ada laughed about her being cut from the Bible— Delilah, the temptress. Good Christian people are not always the most forgiving," Father added with a smirk.

"Daisy made them promise to name you Lilah—her only request, and your mother honored it even though Ada and I complained," he said. "She thought that naming you Lilah would remind us all of Daisy and how you came to be."

"You told me Lilah means flower-like," I pondered, confused. "I was named after the temptress in the Bible. Just great—anymore I need to know?" My reaction brings a smile to Father's face. We both begin to laugh at the thought of it all. "Is that why you call me Lil'flower? Because you hated that they named me Lilah?"

"You are my Lil'flower," Father is now laughing so hard that we both are surprised by our reactions, but laughter is something we both needed. "Your mother added Grace because she knew you would need plenty of it. She has been so relieved that you have come into your own and that you have none of Daisy's wildness. She thinks it is all due to her prayers and because Grace is your middle name."

"How could no one else in Mother's family know about Daisy?" I wondered, seeking more confirmation that no one else in the town knew our family secret. I do realize that no one could possibly have known. I attended the White school and went anywhere else in the town without question.

Watching how some of our "Good Christian" church members treated the Black families in our town was nothing short of evil. The smugness I felt imagining the thoughts this town would have when they learned that this year's high school valedictorian was a Black child, that I was smarter than every other White student in this town, that they had welcomed me into their homes for dinner and to play with their children, left me uncomfortable. I also knew that as leaders in the church, my parents would be criticized for their deceit.

"Daisy left St. Francis, and their parents didn't fuss over her," he revealed. "They knew she could not be controlled. Everyone—our families and Mrs. Ada's family believed you were a baby from another Parish."

"Thanks for telling me," I offered. "It was time for me to know. I couldn't have left home without knowing."

"Well, you leaving is also something your mother is not accepting," he reminded. "But I want you to know that your mother was always grateful to Ada. Her remembering Ada last night was because she wished Ada could see you become all that we know you will grow into. Ada had so much hope for you."

"I always looked forward to our talks," I said. "I was curious to hear what she would tell me next. Her stories are one of the reasons I want to see the world, but Mother is also responsible. The poems and novels we read together—I want to experience some of what we've read. How could I not?"

"Ada also saw a bit of herself in you, and she knew a lot of the good in you came from her," Father continued. "Every time you won a prize or made all A's, Ada would remind us that you were born under a very bright star and that God's Light shines bright through you."

Mrs. Ada would sometimes talk to me about her six sons—three still lived in St. Francis, and three had moved North. We'd have long talks while baking or while working in Mother's flower garden. She often expressed how she wished she had a daughter. "Taking care of you and Rosey has been my pleasure—making dresses for you girls, putting your hair up in bows. I love you both like my own," she would always say to me... I can't remember her ever talking that way in front of Rosey or Mother? Knowing now that she knew I was her granddaughter and her saying nothing makes me wonder if I caused her pain?

I also had to admit that Rosey's thinking may have been right about one thing—Mrs. Ada taking me home would have caused unthinkable trouble for her and her sons.

Rosey is back again after dinner. She has her own husband to feed and should focus more on him than she does on me.

"Back so soon?" I joked. "Father is still pretty upset with you and Mother…"

"Don't be so selfish!" she reacted. "I am really sorry," she adds with a more sullen tone, but the fact that she still had the gall to admonish me at all is shocking. She really doesn't understand what she's done.

"You should just let things cool off and come back in a few days," I recommended. "Mother has not spoken all day, and Father is out back. He hasn't been in since lunch.

"I will!" she agreed. "Lilah, sorry. Truly."

"What else did you hear?" I asked without thinking about the dangers of asking Rosey to speak. "How long did you stand there listening?"

"I know Mother's still too upset—mostly at me, and you asking questions will just make it all worse," she responded. "I'll go. Just don't ask more questions before I can tell her how sorry I am."

Once again, Rosey was only thinking of herself. I felt sorry for her husband and her future children. I hoped she'd have a son for Father to spoil, but Rosey will probably still demand all the attention for herself.

"I won't bother Mother today," I agreed. "But, not for you. Don't look for me to help you. I am only concerned about Mother."

Mrs. Ada was Mother's best friend. She may not have described her as such, but it's an honest description. "Which son was Franklin?" I questioned. How could I find out more? Mother was not yet ready to talk, but my questions were growing. Why would Mrs. Ada not have told me? I want her to know I'm honored to be her granddaughter and hiding who I am was not how I would choose to live. Mother knows the answers to all my questions, but she had only said "Good Morning" to me. Waiting was my only option.

CHAPTER THREE
Kate

Bishops move diagonally any number of squares

*W*hy is this day finally here, I don't yet know, but I pray it brings me the results I've long been seeking? The Marchands will now and forever be a part of my life. My mother and brother, Ryan, have filed a lawsuit against the Marchands, and I need answers. A copy of the filing was provided to me by my legislative aide and not by my family.

I make the ride from my office in Metairie to my mother's. Our family home is adjacent to *Audubon Park*. It's a large home with perfect views of the treelined walkways surrounding the park and nearby universities. Selling the home will yield us a small fortune but doing so will not go over well with my mother especially considering her current condition.

"A lawsuit against family?" I ask as mom sits expressionless with her head down in an obvious effort to avoid answering my questions. "Have you always known that Grandma Rosey's sister is Black?"

Her hands begin to tremble as she reaches to pick up Snowball for comfort. If it wasn't for her cat, I doubt our visits would remain cordial. Mom has been on a steady decline for the past three years. First, she began repeating the same statements and questions without memory of our prior conversations. Then, friends' names and events were slowly forgotten. She now keeps a notebook by her side in which she records the events of her day—conversations, television shows she's watched, foods she has eaten.

The fear she feels is obvious, and it's becoming more difficult for her to hide behind her smile. I share her fears, but I feel ashamed to let anyone know how much fear I live with every day. I'm not ready to lose my mom, but I know my being ready or not means nothing.

"Certainly, I knew—I'm her daughter," my mom yells. "It matters to no one. It's one-hundred-year-old history. Why would I ever sit around and talk to you about someone you've never met?"

I shake my head in confusion as she continues to try and justify our family's omissions. We were told Grandma Rosey had a sister and that she was estranged from the family, but we were made to believe it was because she married a Black man. Her sister also being Black was no doubt a purposeful omission.

"You know their bakery is well known?" I say. "You suing them has made the news. Why would you file a lawsuit without speaking to me first? Did you even think about how this would affect my campaign?"

"You're always too busy," mom replies. "Your brother is here more. He answers when I call. You have your assistants screen my calls."

"Not true, and absolutely no reason for you to have him file a lawsuit without first speaking with me," I protest. "Ryan is money-hungry, and you know it. He smelled the cash and ran straight to your lawyer. How much are you paying for this?"

"I gave Ryan a check—I'm sure," mom says as she reaches for her notebook, which is in its assigned spot on the serving table next to the television remote. "You'll have to ask Ryan. I don't see it here. I don't think it was that much?"

"Yes, I will absolutely speak to Ryan, but first, please explain how she's Black?" I ask. "Who cheated?" I don't imagine that my White great-grandparents would have adopted a Black child in the 1930s.

"Don't ever say such a thing about our family—your grandparents," she says, visibly irritated. "You have no idea how they lived and what they sacrificed. That's my fault. Why should you respect your family when you know nothing about them? I allowed our life to be centered around you and your brother—such a silly mistake."

I attempt to measure my next words perfectly before speaking. Finding the proper words to use when speaking with my mom is a challenge. One day asking her about the weather is fine, and the next day, it may enrage her.

"I apologize," I offer while trying to think of another question to ask that may not upset her. "I'm truly not trying to annoy you. Can you please help me understand why after seeing an interview on television, you called Ryan and told him you saw your Grandma Rosey's sister on television? "

"I remembered seeing that photo on mama's bedroom dresser," she recalls. "The photo used for their packaging—it's where mama grew up. The barn in the background is the same barn used on their packaging."

Mom hands me a photo from her notebook. "Her sister was adopted, but they are blood-related—cousins. She is the daughter of your great-grandmother's sister and a Black man. Your great-grandparents raised her as their own. No one knew she was half Black."

"Ok, that's a lot," I admit. "Let me see if I follow. Mrs. Marchand's mother is the sister of my great-grandmother. We are related—cousins, correct? And, she is your cousin or aunt?"

"Yes, sure," mom answers. "I last spoke to her when mama passed. I think she was also living in New Orleans, but we never crossed paths."

"Why? Why have our families never met?" I ask as mom hands me more photos. I recognize a few, but I had never previously taken the time to study each one.

"Here they are as children," mom says as she hands me a photo of two young girls sitting under a large oak tree with hanging moss—a classic Louisiana photo like the ones you'd find in a history book. It's not surprising that the Marchands would also use these photos to promote their products. They're perfect.

"This is a stunning photo—they really all are, and they all appear to have a story to tell," I respond. "It will help them sell lots of pecan pies." Many of the photos are faded black and white images, but the beauty of the sisters and the richness of the time are clear. One girl is pale with long straight blonde hair. The other is the same, except she has long, wavy bronze-colored hair. They have similar joyful expressions, and one would imagine they are related—maybe not sisters but family.

"This is her—mama's sister," mom says as she points her out to me as if I didn't recognize which young girl was my grandmother. "She loved her sister and would talk about her a lot, especially after she lost my dad. I knew how much she hated living alone, but your father was not comfortable with her moving in with us."

"Why didn't Grandma Rosey move with her sister?" I ask, genuinely curious to understand why the families of two sisters who had once been so close had never met. "Why have you never mentioned her? You know she's still alive?"

Mom takes in a deep breath and exhales in exhaustion. She reveals that Grandma Rosey was her mother's only child, but she always wanted more. "They took on faith that because the baby was so fair, and she was after all her sister's child, that her race would not be questioned, and it never was. She was raised like any other White child in Louisiana. Back then, if you had French in your family line, a little color was not unusual. My grandparents were French—I'm sure."

"I don't understand?" I admit. "Grandma Rosey's sister was raised as White, but now she's not?"

"She's who she is," mom explains. "People see what they want to see. Her father is Black. Lilah has the right to live any way she wants—that's what mama would always say."

"I don't exactly know what you are trying not to tell me, but ok," I offer. "Do you know why they didn't keep in touch?"

"I don't know all the details, but it was a different time," mom says. "I only know she moved away and didn't visit much. I think they called each other often and kept in touch by telephone. They each had their own families to raise and lives to live."

"Well, now we'll be reunited with them in a horrible way," I remark. "I hope you know what you both have done. I wonder if her poor sister's children even knew we existed?"

"Probably not, but they do now," mom laughs. "I know I shouldn't laugh."

"It's ok, mom," I say. "It's a lot to process. Ryan should not have done this without talking to me first." Mom's always treated Ryan like the star of our family show. I'm older but still a minor supporting character at best. I really didn't need to ask why she called him and not me. I know exactly why.

Mom continues sorting through the stack of old family photos she has found and hands me another photo of the house and a barn.

"Mama sold the farm right after we moved to Lafayette," mom recalls. "I remember these flower gardens and all the Pecan and Oak Trees. I recognized right away the little girl on television. I'd seen that face many times in photos with mama. I knew that was her sister. Did I already tell you that?"

By the next morning, Ryan has arranged for me to meet with mom's lawyer. I need to hear for myself how Ryan convinced him to file this ridiculous lawsuit. Mom served as executor of Grandma Rosey's Estate, but since that time, mom has entered the early stages of dementia. I'm sure, if known, any court would question her mental capacity to sign legal documents.

The lawyer hired by Ryan is with the firm often used by our parents—a downtown New Orleans firm with offices overlooking the Mississippi River. I valet park, and I am then escorted by a building security officer. It wasn't necessary but having official *Louisiana Senate License Plates* does come with perks.

"Senator Emory, welcome. Please follow me," I make a quick turn and fling my hair dramatically, hoping to demonstrate my displeasure. We walk to the end of a long hallway, and one side of a double office door is opened. My brother stands to greet me.

"Ryan, what you have done to mom is unforgivable," I angrily announce. I want him to understand the harm he's done to mom and to me. "Why would you go as far as filing a lawsuit without speaking with me first?" Ryan has never cared to listen to my opinion. He was born to cause trouble for me and has never failed to accomplish his life's purpose.

"I told you as soon as I knew we had something, and mom called me," he responds. "You're just jealous she depends on me more than you. Mom was pretty upset when she saw that picture of her family on television." Ryan circles the room as we wait for his lawyer. His pacing is making me dizzy.

"Why can't you sit still?" I question. "What are you so anxious about? Guilt, maybe?"

"No, I'm fine, Kate," he says. "Trust me for once. When you receive your cut of millions, thank mom and me. You're not the only one that can do things!"

Their lawyer enters. He is a tall, thin man with a strong chin and gray hair. He looks legit enough, but I'm not sure if he's picked up on the fact that my brother is a complete wacko.

"Thanks for coming. I'm attorney Bob McNeil," he takes a seat, and Ryan finally sits down.

"We've pulled birth and school records and found that Lilah Cormier grew up in the same home as your grandmother and was represented as her sister," Mr. McNeil explains. "I found no official adoption records, but that's not uncommon for the time period. We found enough to support filing a claim on behalf of your grandmother's estate, but honestly, in my opinion—proving your case will be very difficult."

I clear my throat and gently place my hand at the center of my chest. My expressions seem to confuse both Ryan and his attorney because they both lean in and ask if I need a moment. I now think they are both wackos. Why would a lawyer file a lawsuit he didn't think he could win? Was it for the retainer? The why of this lawsuit is now more unclear. Suing my grandmother's sister seems like we are launching an attack without first finding out if we are enemies.

I'm given another copy of the lawsuit and family records. My name is not shown as a plaintiff, so maybe my campaign won't be affected. Being perceived as a money-grabbing parasite out to destroy my long-lost Black family is not going to be a good look.

"How much has our mother paid you to file this lawsuit?" I ask.

"Twenty-five thousand," he admits.

"Well, that seems like a waste. I'll review this with our mother and get back to you," I slide the documents into the envelope I was given and stand to signal an end to this meeting. I need time to digest everything before speaking to my campaign. "My district is diverse—you do realize that?"

"This is a good thing sis," he says as he gives me a devilish smirk. "Don't worry about anything. I will manage all the lawyer stuff. I just need you to calm mom and help her talk to the lawyer."

"Never!" My firm objection is received by them both. "Why would you think I would help you with mom? You need to call her doctor and her therapist. Go to one of her sessions. You should have done that first before seeing a lawyer and suing her aunt."

Ryan grabs me in a big bear hug before I am able to complete my protest. He takes my hand, and we make our way out of the lawyer's office and down the elevator without further discussion.

Before I'm allowed adequate time to process events, the lawyer calls and orders us to look through mom's papers for any letters or notes about Grandma Rosey's will. I want no part of this lawsuit, but I agree to help. I need to try and manage the fallout from my brother's destructive behavior, but most importantly, I need to protect those I love.

Ryan and I both drive straight to mom's. Her evening nurse has arrived, and mom is resting before dinner. Ryan and I start our search in dad's office. He's been gone for decades, but the room remains mostly unchanged. We sort through files and notebooks. I'm not sure if any of this will be of any help? Ryan and I don't know much about our grandmother's family, and mom's memory is too unreliable.

"I suggest you don't let mom see you tossing her stuff around," I say. "She may not know what's in that file cabinet, but she will worry for hours trying to rearrange everything back to some sort of familiar form."

"Stop hassling me," Ryan complains. "I'll put everything back. She won't know the difference."

"Tag everything you find about St. Francis, our grandparents, and especially the Pecan Farm and baking," I direct.

"You tag, and I'll copy," he says. "I brought extra ink for mom's printer. We can't take any of her notebooks out of this house. She'll lose it and wouldn't rest until she has found them all."

"I know," I reply. "Let's get this done quickly. She'll also not take it well that we are copying her notes."

"Have you noticed how she's starting to write smaller?" Ryan askes. "Her handwriting is getting more and more tiny."

The sweeping, flowing beauty of mom's handwriting has been replaced with tiny measured structured words. I'm not sure how she came up with the notebook idea—maybe her doctor or therapist?

If I simply ask about her day, she flips through the pages of her notebook in search of the answer. We joked with her about the notebooks in the beginning and would urge her to just tell us what she could recall. Now, her notebooks provide an increased level of confidence and comfort to not only mom but to us as well.

"This one has ten pages to copy," I say. "I have three more with only one page. We should be finished before she's up. If not, I'll ask her to fix us a snack before dinner, and you can help keep her distracted in the kitchen while I copy."

"I'm praying this works," Ryan responds. "She loves her notebooks more than she loves her grandchildren."

"Prayer may help, but if you stop moving like a slug, maybe we can finish before midnight," I propose in an attempt to help Ryan focus.

"Prayer helps!" Ryan informs. "Ever since dad died, your thinking has become whacked out. You only go to church for votes."

"Well, not true," I proclaim. "I just know that all prayers do not get a 'yes' little brother."

"Maybe for you because you don't ask," he adds. "My life is pretty great. I own a great bar. I party all night and sleep in late every day. I answer to no one. You are bossed around by your husband, rug rats, and the people who vote for you."

"Why are we talking about this?" I question. "Your life sucks, and you know it. Stop trying to pretend you are happy alone. That bar is all you have, and those people only love liquor — not you. They care nothing about you. Find a wife and grow up."

I give up trying to have an adult conversation with Ryan and just let him continue to speak. He's been a drunk since his college fraternity days. He lost his spot on the football team, and then dad's accident the following year sent him on a non-ending downward spiral.

Dad preferred to take long drives during the middle of the night— "less traffic," he always said. He left one evening before Thanksgiving to pick up Ryan from *LSU*, even though the weather was bad. He should have arrived to pick up Ryan just before dawn, but instead, we received a call about his accident. Everything after that was a blur. I don't remember how we made it through the first few years without dad.

Ryan was able to graduate from college, but he then spent the next year blowing through the money dad left him. He used mom's money to open his bar. I'm still bitter about that transaction. I understand he's a "Mama's Boy" but how far will mom go to please Ryan? I've told them both that if they lose all their money chasing Ryan's dreams, I'm not taking care of either of them.

Our mom's condition is obviously another reason Ryan has given up on himself. I understand his sadness and anger, but I don't understand why he's still unwilling to accept love from anyone other than mom. I really don't think he likes me, but I know he loves me. He has no choice.

"Ryan, how's Justine?" I decide to ask. "Mom and I truly like her. Does knowing that make you less likely to treat her well?"

"She's fine," he replies. "I don't like that her parents were friends with our folks. They constantly remind me of all the fun they had back in the day—it's annoying. It's also annoying that she has both her parents and could care less about either of them. I would give anything to have my dad here."

"People with parents don't get it," I say. "I've learned to ignore them."

"Yeah, I try to tell Justine she's being a jerk to her parents, but she takes it too personally and starts with the tears. I don't have the time for her tears," Ryan reasoned.

"Look at this file with old church records," I discover. "This stuff may help, but it's too much to copy. Do you think we can sneak the file out for a few days and return it before mom notices? Did you know our grandparents and great-grandparents were all leaders in the St. Francis Baptist Church? Our family is listed in this program as church founders."

"When was the last time I have been inside a church?" Ryan questions. "I really can't remember. Kate, you have to go. You're a politician. Getting any votes in Louisiana requires seeing the inside of a church every Sunday. Good thing no one knows you are still angry with God."

"I go because I love the Lord," I admit. "And, I'm not angry. I don't know why you keep saying that. You are still up from the night before, so going to church Sunday morning should be no problem for you. Most churches have an early morning service—just change out of your bar clothes and walk a few blocks to the closest church. Shock the Lord."

"Humph," he responds. "Maybe. I could go with Justine one Sunday. Her parents would love that."

I offer Ryan the biggest smile I can manage, but I say nothing. If I agree, he'll never go. If I really want him to consider going to the church, I should say nothing. I listen, pray and hope for a miracle. Prayer and letting God work never fails. We are certainly a product of our grandparents' service and faith.

"I think we're done with the copies," I say. "I'll sneak out the church file and make sure it gets back. Is there anything else we need? Did you copy these pictures?"

"I'll take everything to the lawyer," Ryan offers. "You stay until mom wakes up. I'm sure you want to talk about me behind my back and tell her what I said about Justine—FYI, I'm never getting married."

"Make sure you bring this file back just as we found it," I instruct. "Mom may forget some things, but I bet she knows exactly what's in this file."

"I will get it back—geez!" he replies. "Just relax and trust your little brother."

"You joke, but yes—I'll try and trust you," I say. "But you did just sue our family. You're pretty much pond scum."

"You're so strange," he laughs. "No one says that." Ryan grabs the file out of my hand and heads towards the back door making sure to avoid mom. I double-check that we have put everything back in its proper place before closing the office door.

I'm able to start dinner, and mom walks in just as I'm finishing the salad. "It's a good day for a grilled chicken Caesar salad with extra parmesan and loads of salad dressing," I say. "Your favorite."

"Should we have lemonade or iced tea?' mom asks.

"Lemonade!" I reply. Mom grabs the lemons and bag of sugar. Real sugar with real lemons is the only way to make a respectable Southern Lemonade.

"Mama wasn't the best cook," mom admits as she watches me toss the salad. "I learned how to cook real Cajun food from my mother-in-law, and I taught you."

"You taught me some things, but a Caesar salad is not really considered Cajun food," I laugh. "You did teach me how to make a pretty good jambalaya."

"I also taught you Gumbo and Étouffée," she corrects. "And, how do you think you know how to make that sweet pan cornbread you make every holiday? I taught you that."

"Well, I guess you did." I offer in agreement. "We need to start teaching my daughters. They're clueless in the kitchen. Maybe we'll come over one Saturday and cook everything you've taught me? We can take stuff to Ryan's bar and feed his crew. He'd love that."

"If Justine comes along, I'll do it." mom adds. "Your brother needs a wife. We can't take care of him forever."

"I've already told him the same earlier today," I say. "Maybe if we both pray, God will send help?"

"I have a direct line, you know," mom jokes. "Mama kept me in church. I failed you and your brother. It's no excuse for you both not serving in the church."

"At least I attend service," I respond. "Ryan doesn't even attend. Ask him when he last attended church."

"Never mind that," she exclaims, obviously trying to defend Ryan. "You two are city kids. Country kids like me go to church every Sunday."

"You are not a country kid," I correct. "How old were you when you all moved to Lafayette?"

"Ten or eleven," she says. "I'm a country kid. Lafayette was not citified like it is today, and it's nowhere as citified as you had growing up in New Orleans."

"Did you go back to St. Francis often?" I ask.

"Not much at all after mama sold the farm," she responds.

"Did Grandma Rosey's sister still live there when you all moved?" I continue. "Do you remember her at all?"

"I do not," she thinks out loud. "I only remember the photos. I can't picture her other than that."

We enjoy our salads and fresh Southern Lemonade. I try to capture and record every detail of this moment and the appearance of mom's face as she enjoys her favorite meal. As her memory fades, I am becoming more determined to never forget her laugh, the expressions she makes when telling a story, and the way she chews her food. It all seems to be changing daily right before my eyes.

Grandma Rosey's sister should now be in her nineties. I wonder what she still remembers. Lilah Cormier Marchand—will you tell your family we've met?

CHAPTER FOUR
Lily

Denial is Comfortable

As the slight brush of my hand begins to sway my rows of clothing meticulously arranged by seasons and color, the memories attached to each garment follow me. Safety and comfort exist within the walls of a closet.

I have always found this to be true. It was my favorite place to nap as a child. I would bring my favorite dolls and teddy bears and dream of a world filled with joy and magic. I've stopped bringing my dolls, but I still often sit on the floor of my closet. I immediately feel safe, and I am also reminded to dream.

My favorite pair of pink running shoes stare me straight in the eye, and I know putting them on will help to make my day much better. I slip them on, and I'm out the door. The morning chill provides a boost of energy, and I don't stop until I get in a good thirty-minute run.

My *"Tummy Alarm"* — the name I've given to the ever-familiar warm rush of anxiety-filled emotions I experience during any moment of despair, greeted me this morning, but it is now less angry. I now trust that it never fails to warn me of possible danger like *Robot* in *Lost in Space*..."Danger *Lily Guillory—Danger!*" Today, I won't try to quiet it too much. The extra adrenalin will help. It's a law office day, and today I will need to slay a few dozen dragons—off to work I go.

The view from the twenty-first floor is meant to distract us all from the bad choices we often make inside these walls.

I put on my classic smile and give my standard greeting. "Happy Monday, everyone." Finola pushes the conference room door open and gestures for me to sit. In an attempt to avoid eye contact, her focus immediately rests on the painting covering the wall behind me.

"Discovery responses are behind schedule," Finola whispers as her eyes seem to trace the stream of colors from the painting to the end of the long conference room wall and then back to me. We're in the large room today because Anastasia's team plans to join us.

"Our first round of discovery is not due until Friday," I offer. "Today is Monday. How are we behind?" Trial prep stress is nothing new for any of us, but because this case involves my family, the stress vibe is different. To break Finola's trance and cut the stress, I begin spinning myself around in the silken conference chair.

"Stop it." Finola laughs. "Being silly is not helpful. We cannot mess this up!"

"We'll send what we have and respond unavailable or none to missing info," I reply in a dismissive tone. "What's hard about that?"

"We are not working on Friday," she adds. In our minds, Friday is an off day; check your messages and leave at Noon. Having a tedious work project to complete is not allowed.

"You type, and I'll tab documents. We'll be done by Wednesday," I assure.

"The French Market location eventually replaced the original location—correct?" Finola asks.

"Yes. The French Market location had started bringing in double the business," I explain. "Closing shop in their old neighborhood was hard, but Granna decided to remain in Los Angeles after *Katrina*, so not reopening was best. Uncle worked full-time at the Farmer's Market, and Aunt Helen had been helping Granna at *Marchand's*. We all think Granna was ready to slow down. Baking all day was starting to become too much for her to maintain."

"Number forty asks about *Marchand's* closing documents." Finola read out loud.

"Do you think we can just send them photos of *Katrina*?" I ask sarcastically. "There's no paperwork."

"Well, that would answer the question—Why not?" Finola agrees. "I didn't think your grandmother was too formal with her paperwork before you came along."

"Nothing formal—just DBA's and a Tax ID. We completed corporate documents for *Much Ado*, but before that—nothing," I confirm. "Numbers forty through forty-five answer "None.""

"Ownership percentages—Mrs. Marchand owns fifty percent, and you and your uncle own twenty-five each?" Finola asks. "How did you get the entire twenty-five? That's your mother's—correct?"

"Yes, when Mom passed, her share went to Luke and me, but Luke wanted me to buy him out. He used the money to pay off his med school loans. He also bought a *Porsche*, but I didn't give him that much money, so he's probably still making payments on the *Porsche*." My joke was followed by an unexpected gasp that startled us both.

"Are you okay?" Finola questions as she extends her hand.

"Nothing," it surprised me that I was able to talk about my Mom and make a joke without skipping a beat. I stopped bringing up my grief to Finola a year ago. She would try to cheer me up, but I wasn't ready to let go of grief. Today was different. Is this Progress?

I'm not surprised that Finola easily picks up on my mood shift. I hope to be as supportive of her as she has always been to me. I've had many bad friends, co-workers, and bosses, but also, luckily, a few decent ones. Just as children promise to parent differently from their parents, I have always vowed to be a better version.

When it's hard to look me in the eye, and you're staring at the painting behind me, I see you, and I hear you. The work needed our attention, and I needed to provide more help. Remembering to listen and to "talk less, smile more" is a good motto I picked up—compliments of *Hamilton*.

"*Much Ado's* value will greatly increase if the frozen foods line takes off. Do you think Luke will want back in?" Finola questions.

"He may, but it will cost him," I joke. "Granna may sell him some of her shares if he comes up with the right number. You know she's tight with her money."

"So...*Marchand's Sweet Tooth* closed in 2005. *Much Ado* had opened in 2000, closed in 2005, and reopened in 2006 after *Hurricane Katrina*—correct? Finola asks while mapping out the timeline on our conference room dry-erase board. "Let's add Houston here. When did it open and close?"

"Houston opened at the end of 2003 and closed in 2005, opened for about eighteen months total," I explain. "I moved to L.A. in April 2005. Houston had closed that February—all before *Katrina*."

"I was a brand-new baby lawyer, just out of law school, and *Much Ado* became my first corporate client. Well...I had just started at a big Houston Law Firm that billed out my time at three hundred dollars per hour, so *Much Ado* was technically a free family hookup." I ramble as I take a trip down memory lane.

"Question?" Finola continues. "*Much Ado* still uses the *Marchand's* name on a few products?"

"Yes. Many of Granna's original customers still visit the Farmer's Market location looking for Mrs. Marchand. Uncle loves it. Keeping the family business legacy going is important to us all, but Uncle has always only worked in the bakery. He started when he was five years old. Its success is his legacy as well as Granna's. Uncle had hoped his only child, Will, would love the baking business, but my nephew is following my brother into medicine," I explain as I pause and consider my legacy. What will mine look like? Am I even going in the right direction?

"Last question?" she asks. "Why a kitchen in Los Angeles?"

"In 2015, we opened a kitchen in Los Angeles because my Granna could no longer keep up with the local demand for her pastries from her home kitchen. We once again took a chance and added a new location, but this time I was not the culprit," I joke. "Since arriving in the area after *Katrina*, Granna has been baking pies, croissants, yeast rolls, cookies, and brownies—all with and without pecans. She started off making small batches for church friends. They told their friends, and then someone had a specialty shop and put her stuff on the shelf, and then holiday requests, and then the need for a commercial kitchen and staff to handle the demand led to the birth of *Marchand's Originals*—online and local delivery only!"

"Got it—Perfect!" Finola offers. "You could moonlight as a PR Rep. If I ever need one, I know who to call first," she pauses before giving me a thumbs up. "That answers everything in this first set. Let's get this sent, and we are good for today. Hallelujah!"

"Thanks for your love and patience," I say. "You're the main reason I'm still working at this firm. We've been together within these walls since day one. You know...we should give more thought to building our own walls. We could build a safe place for us all to focus on the work we love.

"Just say the word," Finola responds. "When this trial is over, we can work on a plan. I would love to do more Poverty Law. I'm volunteering this weekend at the Food Bank. What's on your agenda?"

"We have a camping event," I say. Finola's look of confusion is familiar. I gave Adam the same look when he agreed to us taking our children. "I understand your confusion—don't judge. I'm not losing my mind. It's for charity. We went last year, remember? I'll fill you in later."

By Friday, it's finally an off day. Our team finished discovery production yesterday, and today, everyone is taking a well-deserved mental health day. I sleep in before joining other parents to prep for tomorrow's camping event. Volunteering at my kids' school most often doesn't feel like work. I enjoy seeing my kids in their element, and I enjoy socializing…gossiping with other parents. Also, volunteering for the setup team is the best. You've done your part, and you get to enjoy the event.

Saturday, we all awake excited for the day. This is our second year attending the kids' school's *Spring Fest Family Camp Out*. They attend a sixth through twelfth-grade private school, and its hefty tuition price is starting to drain the college fund we started when Lydia was two. We are now praying that scholarships will save the day.

Because I grew up poor, learning that a community filled with well-to-do families voluntarily choose to spend the evening camping overnight on the neighborhood soccer fields was a shock. There's a drive-in movie screen, campfires, s'mores, and over one hundred tents set up by parents who desperately want their children to have a childhood better than their own.

Luckily, I enjoy campfire food, and the ability to fall asleep on a whim is one of my superpowers. A warm sleeping bag, plush blanket, comfy chair, or even a slightly reclined car seat as I'm waiting in the school carpool pickup line all work for me. I made a promise after the last time I fell asleep in the carpool line, and one of the moms was kind enough to tap on my car window to awake me, that I would never allow myself to again embarrass myself in such a way. But, even with my best efforts—I fell asleep waiting in line many more times.

Lydia was in third grade, Josh in first grade, when I started napping during carpool, so I couldn't blame my behavior on infant sleep training. It took over a year of therapy before I was able to admit that my non-stop pursuit of perfection fuels anxiety and drains my brain of its energy.

Honestly, my brain is rarely allowed to rest, so any moment of calm results in my brain claiming the time for a moment of much-needed rest. Turns out that camping is also good for resting your brain.

"Who's ready for s'mores," I shout while making my way to the crowded s'mores station. It's my favorite, especially while telling camp ghost stories. The best storyteller wins a trophy. Of course, there are trophies. Rich people enjoy winning trophies to put on their mantles more than they like cash prizes—trophies are better than gold. That's why this is the school's largest charity fundraiser.

"I've been working on a story that's sure to top yours this year," Grant announces. "Noel told me you've been working on a good one. Forget about telling yours. I'm getting that trophy this year."

The four of us have been the best of friends since meeting when our kids started at the same preschool. Noel has become a true sister and my kids' favorite aunt—Luke does not seem interested in marriage, so other than Granna, Uncle, and Aunt Helen, our circle is thin.

"We've known each other over a decade, and you have lost how many challenges to the Guillory's?" I boast. "Give up now, Grant, and save yourself from embarrassment."

We all take off running in an effort to get the best spot up front. We're the best of friends, but we know that losing to the other will never be forgotten. Their oldest is a six-foot-tall track star, so he takes this victory, but we muscle in on the row next to them.

"Noel, stop Lily," Grant yells.

I begin to sing, *"What about ya' friends..."* as *TLC* eloquently worded. They both give us a "what about my friends" battle-prepared look. Let the trophy chase begin.

My story is fun. A few kids let out screams, and a few jumped. Grant's story was decent, but we both lose to a newcomer—a television writer with a sixth-grader. We should have protested her entry, but then many of us would be excluded from something. Every parent and child here have probably either taken professional music, dance, or acting lessons or has had professional athletic training, received an Ivy League or better education, or some other exceptional training. Why complain?

After our first loss, too many s'mores and grilled hot dogs, we receive our next marching orders. "Next game, Mom," Josh demands. The four of us run to the next station and continue our quest for victory. The night is young, and we don't plan to surrender until at least one challenge is conquered.

"There's an ice cream sundae eating contest—who's in?" Josh asks.

Adam raises his eyebrows in objection, but we all ignore him. Josh and I have a sugar addiction, and Josh is a kid. If he eats too many sweets, his stomach will suffer.

My truth is that I refuse to let go of sugar because I cannot bear the thought of experiencing another loss. Holding onto sugar is something my mind has decided I can control. The havoc sugar is inflicting on my body is within my ability to prevent, but ignoring this reality, and for now preventing another loss is more important. Also, Adam is not my father. I do not have to listen to him!

Josh and I eat until our sugar high is unbearable, but we have put forth a respectfully decent effort. Another almost win for the Guillory's.

Campfire songs and yard games continue throughout the night. We undertake as many challenges as possible.

As the first ray of sunlight casts its shadow across the campground, Adam and I take in the beauty of the morning. Our night under the stars was a great success. We won the second-place trophy for best trivia team, and I didn't win for telling the best ghost story—this year!

It's Sunday afternoon, and I haven't seen my family since arriving home this morning. I took a short nap, but now I'm up looking for something to occupy my mind. Is Googling movie spoilers a sign of a very troubling psychological problem? After person one hundred and one asked me why I ruin the pleasure of watching a story unfold, I paused, and after a long moment of deep reflection—I changed nothing. If an ending is a sad, disappointing disaster, why take the journey? Time is precious. I refuse to waste it watching a sad story that doesn't end happily.

"What's wrong with you today—exhausted from yesterday?" Adam asks.

"Nothing, the usual," I respond. "It's been an unbelievable week, and tomorrow's Monday. I want it to be as stress-free as possible— Stress-Free Sunday! Let's order a movie. Where's that ice cream I bought last week?" I ask while searching the freezer. "After spending my Saturday camping, I deserve another day of unlimited treats."

"I let Josh finish off most of it," he explains. "Sure, it tastes great, but did you read the label? You really shouldn't have eaten any of it."

"What are you talking about?" I ask. "We buy that flavor all the time." Adam hands me the nearly empty container and points to the label.

"Twenty-five grams of added sugar is the daily max," Adam claims. "This ice cream has 35 grams per serving, and you know you'll have way more than one serving."

Ever since his company required us to take that stupid Wellness Evaluation, Adam cares about what we eat. We've been eating trash forever. Is now really a time to change? I take another look at the label. What can I eat with "No Added Sugar"? That statement is so not what I thought it represented. "Hello, Sugar. I'm adding a teaspoon of you to my coffee." Nope, not what it means. If I never touch a cube of sugar, I still consume "Added" sugar with many of the things I put into my mouth. I checked the label again, tossed the container, and tried not to cry!

"What else do we have because this little bit of ice cream will not do the trick?" I ask. "What is hidden in your chocolate stash, Mr. No Added Sugar?"

"I'm just trying to help you." Adam jokes. "You are the one with the border line *A1C*. What was your last number?"

"Can we not talk about this today?" I argue. "If we were having a romantic evening, it's definitely off the table now."

"Don't hint at sex in order to gain access to my super-secret chocolate stash," he says.

"Do you hear yourself?" I ask. "You just used sex and chocolate stash in the same sentence. Get over here and give me some of your sweet chocolate."

"Come and get it if you have the strength," Adam responds as he darts out of the kitchen. I still want to eat the ice cream, but I'll let it go for now and play along this time.

CHAPTER FIVE
Lilah

"There is no charm equal to tenderness at heart."
- Jane Austen

The winding roads surrounding our farm perfectly framed our world. Homes with matching wrap-around porches supporting rocking chairs and nosey occupants were found along every bend. St. Francis was a quiet, friendly town in my eyes, but I'd never been on the side of St. Francis where Mrs. Ada lived. I'm not even sure how much of her family she had in town? I only knew of the family that worked on our farm. My St. Francis suddenly became less familiar.

From days forward, Mother's comforting stares and firm hugs never felt foreign. Finding out Mother was really my aunt did not bother me as much as I think Rosey had hoped. She's the dramatic one, and I know my ability to ignore her causes her to work that much harder to get my attention. Never was I the one to run around having crying fits the way she did. Even when I cut my leg on the fence and needed stitches—not a scream, not a tear.

The floorboard at the entrance to our kitchen groaned as I made my way across. Our home was unrecognizably quiet. Mother was still not speaking. The busyness of Mrs. Ada's morning prep work was gone forever. I wasn't sure what I should do with this new life?

As I stood waiting for inspiration, Mother's voice revived me.

"Lilah, I'm so sorry Rosey upset you," Mother finally spoke two days later. "You are my daughter and always will be. She's being hateful and repeating things she had no right hearing. Rosey should not have repeated a thing!"

I comforted Mother, who was more upset than I had been since Rosey blabbed.

"I know, Mother," I agreed. "Nothing has changed."

"Lilah, always know that you are my daughter," she affirmed. "My little sister was careless and wild. She hated growing up under the eye of our strict parents. The moment she was able, she left home. We helped her with money when we could."

"I know you did all you could to help," I offered in agreement.

"Daisy would be sure to come over whenever Franklin was working around the yard," Mother condemned.

"His name is Franklin?" I inquired before putting down the recipe book I was holding to better focus on her every word.

"They probably got into it all over the property!" Mother accused before covering her face in shame. "I knew something would happen. She just wouldn't stay away. Every time I saw him—there she was."

"Mother!" I couldn't hold my laugh. Her disapproval was obvious, but her loose words shocked us both.

"I would do anything for my sister and Ada," Mother admitted. "When you were born, it was obvious you could not be raised by Ada. There would be no way to explain her raising a

White baby. We all decided I should raise you. I couldn't carry another baby, and your father also wanted Rosey to have a sister."

"Why did Mrs. Ada never tell me?" I finally asked.

"She wanted you to have the best life," Mother explained. "There was no need to have the entire town know about her son. It would not have been taken well."

"How about the church? How much do they all know?" I continued.

"We're church leadership. Our actions aren't questioned," Mother responded. "Your father told everyone a young girl's family came to him for help. It wasn't uncommon. The Honeywell's had adopted twins the year before from a poor family in the next parish. People were always coming to the deacons for help."

"Mrs. Ada knew about her son?" I questioned. "What if I had looked more like him?" The words felt strange coming out of my mouth, but the thoughts would not leave.

"Franklin's name was never spoken except between us—Ada knew it was him," Mother confirmed. "We didn't know about you until the month you were born. Daisy kept her being pregnant hidden until the end. You were delivered in your own bedroom by Ada and me. Is this too much or too strange for me to say?"

"When did Daisy die?" I asked. "You don't talk about her much. Is that because you didn't want me to ask questions?"

"Daisy wanted me to raise you," Mother stated. "She knew I would love you as I loved her. She left for New Orleans three days after you were born. You had just turned two when we found out she had died of pneumonia. Our parents were unable to say goodbye.

"Did she ever see me again?" I wondered, saddened for her. "Do you think she thought of me?"

"You were such a beautiful baby," she said. "She wanted to visit, but she only did once—your first Christmas. We sent letters. She would write about how beautiful you were and how you didn't look at all like Franklin."

"I'm a unique beauty because I'm half and half," I replied while trying to not sound offended. "That's why everyone stares. They are trying to pinpoint what's different—what's unique. It's in my eyes. It was the first thing I noticed when I looked in the mirror last night."

"My sister is partly responsible for your independent spirit, and both are responsible for how beautiful you are," Mother agreed. "You are a product of two different bloodlines, and that makes you all the more remarkable to us all."

Mother is careful to not let me see her concern. Once again, I comforted her.

Rosey was married and living two miles away in her own home with her husband, but not much changed with her presence in our home. She was still around more than any of us liked. She still enters my room each morning like she's still sleeping on the other side of the wall. Her bedroom was as she left it, and she would have probably slept in her room if Mother had allowed it.

"I realized that you are really my cousin, but that doesn't matter," Rosey tried to explain. "Isn't that weird? We should have always known."

"Why?" I wondered. "How would things have been any different?"

"I've taken care of you your entire life—you're my little sister," Rosey leaned in and gave me her standard one-arm hug and a pat on the back. 'That's why you look so much like Mother and not at all like Father and me. Your real mother is Mother's sister. That just explains so much."

"It explains nothing!" I reacted, "Do you wish Mrs. Ada had taken me home with her?"

"Stop it, Lilah—Grow up," Rosey yelled. "Mrs. Ada could not have raised you. She couldn't take her White grandbaby home, now could she?" Rosey's smirk revealed more than her words.

"It's just a lot for me to take in," I admitted. "I wasn't able to sleep much last night. Sorry if I say strange things," I heard myself speak the words, but I wasn't sure why I was apologizing to Rosey.

"Mother and Father raising you as their own for sure helped prevent a lynching." Rosey seems to try and rationalize with a strange sounding tone of delight. She seems happy to be the one who set our family free from the burden of my family secret.

"Mrs. Ada made this quilt for me last Christmas," I reflected as I wrapped the quilt over my shoulders.

"She gave me handmade kitchen towels," Rosey said. "But I didn't complain. I was newly married, and I also knew you were her favorite. Ha-ha…you are her granddaughter, and you're…"

"Why'd you stop?" I asked, irritated. "What is it you were going to say? Colored, Negro, or is something more awful running through that disgusting head of yours?"

"There's no need for that kind of talk," Rosey protested. "I'm not like that, and you know it. I haven't told my husband, and I'm not sure when I will."

"I'm not concerned about him or his family," I replied. "Father told you his family weren't true Christians when he asked to marry you. The only reason he allowed you to marry him was because he joined our Church and let the pastor Baptize him."

"Now I understand why you have also always been everyone's favorite," she spoke as the tears began to flow. "I thought it was because they felt sorry for you because your mother didn't want you. You're mother's dead little sister's child."

"Rosey—our parents love us both the same," I proclaimed. "Stop allowing such thoughts into your head." We all knew Rosey was jealous of the extra time mother and I spent together. We loved baking and reading novels and poetry. I also helped Father with his books and payroll. Rosey was a tomboy who loved driving the tractor and running around the farm.

"I know I'm right," Rosey added.

"Mother was happy to have us both," I repeated. "It has nothing to do with favorites. What do you know about Mrs. Ada's sons?" I spoke without thinking. I should have waited until Mother was ready to tell me more.

"The youngest one and Daisy made you," she responded crassly and without giving it much thought. "I heard Mother say something about Daisy having her eye on Ada's youngest and how she warned Daisy to stay away."

The number of times White men took up with Black women creating mixed-race babies is too large a number to count. The reverse happened less, but even so; it was never as casually ignored. White fathers didn't raise their Black Children— the Black mother cared for her child. The White unwed mothers were often forced to give away their children—no matter the race. Having a child without a husband was a shame hidden at all costs.

I rested my head alongside the opened window of Father's truck as we made our way home. The warmth of a mild Summer Breeze captured my attention. Father was going on about the inventory forms he needed me to complete as my thoughts drifted forward.

As we entered our long driveway, I admired the view of our home accented by the shadows of the setting Sun. Mother is fussing over the flowerpots which lined our front porch. Her reassuring smile welcomed us home.

"What's all this you've brought home today?" Mother asked as I clinched hold of my findings. I was carrying stacks of books and handwritten pages of notes.

"More college stuff," I disclosed. "I think I want to leave Louisiana?" I knew this news would not please Mother, but I needed to tell her what my heart had decided.

"Is this because of Rosey and the hurtful things she said to you about Ada?" she questioned while taking off her gardening gloves and grabbing hold of me for a desperate hug.

"Mother, the news of Mrs. Ada is not hurtful," I admitted. "Don't worry about me. I know you think Rosey meant harm, and maybe she did, but I'm fine. Knowing the truth is a good thing—please don't worry."

"Then why would you want to leave?" Mother wondered. "Where would you go?"

"I'm not sure, but you will be the first person I tell," I assured her. "Do you think I should study literature or business? You know I love reading, and it will remind me of our time together exploring poetry and the many novels we've enjoyed."

"Business? What would you do?" she responded. "You are a very smart young lady, Lilah. You also love math and history. You could study anything. What about a nurse?"

"I don't think I could handle all the blood?" I replied, "I stopped helping you and Mrs. Ada with dinner the day you both wanted me to help cut a whole chicken. I can barely eat chicken without imagining it walking around in the yard. Somethings are not for me to see."

"Humph, I remember," she giggled. "We were so tickled. I was happy it didn't keep you away from baking.

"I would love to start a business like Father and help people," I said. "Maybe a bakery? I love baking. I could give people jobs and help feed my community."

"Where do you come up with such things? How would you manage a business? What if your husband doesn't want a bakery business? You should pick something you can do. What about literature or English?" Mother suggested. "You would make an excellent teacher. I would have made a great teacher, but I'm a great mother, so that's enough for me."

"You're an excellent mother," I confirmed. "And, you would have also made an excellent teacher. I would also make a great teacher. But I would make a better businesswoman." Mother's head drops, and she turns to walk away without another word. I can feel her sense of failure, but I'm not sure if she thinks it's because of something she did or if it's because I'm Daisy and Franklin's daughter?

"Teach kindergarten and I will be your classroom helper," she added as she turned back towards me. "We would make the best team. All the parents would want their children in our class."

"They would," I agreed. "No one misses our Sunday Bible class, but Rosey thinks it's because we bring cupcakes and cookies every Sunday."

"Rosey should help us teach and stop being so contrary," Mother laughed. "Those children love our class for the message, not just for the cupcakes and cookies."

The library soon became my favorite place to visit. If I couldn't get my answers from people, I hoped I could find answers within the pages of books. We were one of the first Parishes to establish our own library. Mother and her church friends made sure to raise money each year to help keep it open. The librarian was one of Mother's church friends, and her helper was a young Black girl barely my age. I'm not sure if she was also in school? Whenever I would visit the library, she was also there working.

"Good morning, Mrs. Harvey," I greeted. "I'm going to look around for a new novel. Any suggestions?"

"We have a few new selections," she responded. "Nora, show Lilah where you put the new novels we received yesterday." I followed Nora, and she pointed for me to sit at a long table behind the first shelf of books. She handed me two novels and placed another on the table.

"This one is my favorite," Nora replied with a curious look. "I have read most of the books in here. Are you surprised?"

"No, not at all," I said. "Aren't we about the same age? Are you still in school?

"I need to work, but I'm smart," she boasted. "I read better than most."

"That's wonderful," I supported. "I also love to read. There's much more to see beyond St. Francis. I'm going to college after high school." I proudly announced to my surprise.

"You are lucky," Nora admired. "Where will you go?"

"I'm not sure, but I think I will leave Louisiana," I continued. "I'm just not sure where I should go?"

"You can go anywhere," she answered. "If your parents let you and pay your way."

"If you could go anywhere, where would you go?" I asked purposefully, wanting to know the dreams of a young Black girl from St. Francis—a Black girl that could have been me.

"*Tuskegee!*" she responded with pride. "They are training Black pilots for the war, and I have family in Alabama. I'm saving my money to move there with my mama's sister. She works on the Army base, and she promised mama she'd get me a job there like hers."

"Alabama, that's not too far away," I inquired. "Do you think you will soon be able to go?"

"Maybe next summer," Nora continued. "I give my mama money to help with my brothers, so I don't have much saved, but I will, and then I'm going to Alabama."

When Nora was summoned away by Mrs. Harvey, I searched the library for anything I could find on Alabama and *Tuskegee*. When Mrs. Harvey asked questions, I explained that I was working on a research paper for school. She helped me search newspaper files, and we also found a picture book on Southern historical sites. Photos of Birmingham and Alabama were included.

I didn't ask Mrs. Harvey about *Tuskegee*, but a few of the books and newspapers we found included stories about *Tuskegee*. Nora was right; Alabama seemed like another world but not too far from home. Louisiana has flat lands with tons of waterways. Alabama looked different but still familiar. I became excited by the possibility of one day seeing Alabama for myself.

I found the school's address and mailed a letter, "attention admissions." My letter requested information on admissions and housing. I prayed they had rooms at least half as decent as my bedroom at home.

After a week had passed, I began checking the mail each day before Father was able to make his way to the mailbox. Some days I would leave the mail inside the box, so he didn't become curious about the amount of attention I began showing our mailbox. After another three weeks of checking, I received a large envelope filled with application forms—forms I'd use to change my life.

I applied to *Tuskegee* without saying a word to anyone. Explaining my actions to my parents would not have been easy. I filled out the applications and sign my father's name. I took another stamp from the bureau drawer and held onto the application until my next trip to the library. There was a mailbox outside the front library door. Our mailman didn't question the arrival of the large envelope with application materials, but I didn't want to chance him speaking to my father about an outgoing letter addressed to *Tuskegee*.

Three weeks later, to my joy and complete terror, I now needed to give details to my parents about why I applied to a Black school in Alabama and why my acceptance letter arrived in today's mail. I wasn't sure what would happen, and I didn't want to worry Mother. Not telling them I applied was the right decision even though I was still very unsure of the right decision now that I had been accepted.

"Father, I need to talk to you quietly," I whispered. Rosey was at her own home for once, and Father seemed rested. Mother's attention was consumed by her latest favorite novel, and I knew this was a good time to explain my actions to Father so he could help me justify what I'd done.

"Sure, my Lil'flower, what do you need?" he inquired with a loving smile. "Did you find out if you will be Valedictorian? Having a girl Valedictorian will really have this town talking."

"Not yet, but I've been accepted to college," I blurted out without giving it more thought. "I want to go to a Black college. It's the one that's training all the soldiers for the war. You've seen them in the paper."

"Lilah, why would you want to go there?" he asked, concerned. "You could go anywhere. Are you afraid that when you leave St. Francis, people will not see you as White?"

His question must have been something I had also been asking myself without realizing, but I wasn't sure? Was I worried? Mrs.

Ada always reminded me to be proud of myself and to love myself completely. I just thought she encouraged me because I had book smarts and was not the average St. Francis girl looking for marriage.

"Maybe, but I think that I should let people know that I am half and half," I said. "I know that means that I am Black, but I don't think that means that I will be a different person. People may treat me differently, but I don't care what people think. It didn't bother me when Mrs. Holliday told me to stop answering all the questions in class, or no boy would ever like me."

"No, you sure didn't," he laughed. "But, the world outside St. Francis is not so kind. I don't want you hurt."

"I know, but getting hurt is a part of every life," I explained. "I think that if you remain honest in whatever you do, you will have less pain in life, not more." I also somehow knew that trying to avoid pain is a waste of time. Pain's relentless pursuit is impossible to outwit and impossible to outrun.

"I love your courage," he responded. "You are strong like your mother. Let's hope she understands?"

I knew Mother would not understand, but I decided the dream of *Tuskegee* should not be ignored. Do most people know who they are, or do we all at some point wonder if the person we see in the mirror gives us the answer— I wondered?

Mother and I shared a love for poetry and studying fine art. Poetry taught me to always look beyond the obvious, but I realized I failed to do so when I needed to the most. I failed to look beyond the image of me created by my parents. Now, I examine everything with a more resolute curious eye— nothing is ever only as it appears. Layers of truth cover us all.

Naming Lilah

As a child, my days were filled with running around barefoot between our house and pecan tree orchards, walking to school with my sister, baking in the afternoons with Mother and Mrs. Ada, and church two nights a week and all day Sunday. The days I was allowed to enjoy were much different from the days I would have experienced if I had been born with a shade darker skin. I'm reminded of my truth with every memory of home.

"Granna, is something wrong?" Lily asks as she reaches out to hold my hand. "You had a strange frown on your face. Would you like a Tylenol? Is something hurting?"

"Stop your constant worrying about me," I scold. "I'm feeling fine," I know Lily worries because she has suffered too much loss. Losing me will again challenge her Faith and weaken her Spirit, but my leaving this world will happen one day.

Loss comes with Love. None of us can escape it, and no matter how much I want my grandbaby to not experience more pain, I know she will. I am trying to prepare her, but after all I've lost, I still don't know a good way to truly dilute most pain.

"Sorry, did you hear me ask about going to the kitchen tomorrow?" Lily says in a nervous tone, trying to lighten the mood. "We want you to try a few new recipes we've been working up for the *Santa Barbara Food Fair* next month."

"I'll come," I reply. "What time are we going? Don't you have work tomorrow, or are you taking off again? You must be a really good lawyer because your boss lets you miss a lot of days."

"I'm my own boss now," she answers. "I told you months ago that I switched to part-time. I work as needed. Our business is also doing well, and I have a husband who can pay the bills. I want to spend more time with my family and with myself!"

"Well, don't stop being a lawyer," I say. "We need people fighting for us. You're young and can handle both. When Lydia and Josh start college, you'll have more time, so don't forget how to be a lawyer."

"I can never forget," Lily asserts. "Law is a part of me, and my ability to effectively win any argument was a gift at birth. I take after you Granna. I've learned how to give people that look you make when you are trying to convince someone to follow your orders. You know that—'Do not say another word and just do what I say' look."

"Maybe, but I've been the boss for so long, I've lost patience with trying to explain myself," I say. "You just need to do what I ask and stop with the questions. Questions are annoying to ninety-year-olds. They became annoying by fifty now that I think about it. By fifty, you know what you know, and questions are less necessary."

"Well, great!" Lily adds. "So, when I'm fifty, you will no longer question me?"

"I'll be in Heaven then, but I'll send you a few signs to keep you going in the right direction." Just as the words came out of my mouth, I knew I should have kept them in. I can see the pain on my grandbaby's face. "Lily, I'm here now. Be happy!"

"Ok, Happy," she smiles.

The losses we've both suffered came before they should. I'm Lily's grandmother. She should still have her parents. I should still have my daughter.

"Lily, do you think I've done enough to help people?" I ask. "Have I done enough with my ninety plus years?"

"More than enough," Lily confidently states. "Your grandchildren are doctors and an attorney. Your son is a smart, talented businessman. Your daughter was a talented and successful educator."

"Everyone should do good by their children," I add. "Have I done enough to help others? I think I should do more." The concern on her face makes me laugh. She must be worried that I'll give away her inheritance.

"More?" she asks as I anticipated.

"Not more of your inheritance," I laugh. "I've been talking to our pastor about starting a business development grant to help young entrepreneurs. Well… I'm funding the grant, but you all will still have the bakery. I'm spending all my money as I please. You all have plenty of your own."

"It's your money," she agrees. "Don't pledge any shares of *Much Ado*. Uncle and I have the right of first refusal, and we refuse."

"One of my failures has been raising children who don't fight more for the less fortunate," I say. "Don't worry about our precious family business. I know you will keep it in the family. You're fighting off Rosey's children. I wouldn't dream of inviting others to the party."

"I'm taking the kids to the *Unity March* in D.C. this year," she responds. "We give back plenty. Don't count us as failures. And, don't discount our efforts. We're still young and have plenty of time left to save the world."

"Great, get busy and show me," I order. "The clock is ticking, young lady."

"How about I bring you your favorite macarons?" Lily offers. "Will that make you love me more? I'm going to New Orleans next week for work, and I'll stop by and get a few things done with Uncle at the bakery. Finola's coming. Oh! Did I also mention that I'm going to Detroit?"

"Lily don't cause trouble—I mean it this time," I say in protest. "There is no need for you to go to Detroit. Mrs. Ada's family knows nothing that can help us. I've told you that many times. Listen for once."

I wish my daughter was still here. It's exhausting trying to manage Lily alone. I wish I understood God's Plan. At my age, I still don't. Lily needs her mother, and I need someone to share this load. By now, I should know how to carry life's burdens and how to handle loneliness. Did I ever know? Maybe I've forgotten?

CHAPTER SIX
Lily

Love Quiets Anger

"Did you bring the kolaches," Finola yells as I enter the office. She has us in the large conference room again. We both love reclining and hiding within the extruding cushions of the oversized swivel chairs.

"Yes, and Good Morning to you!" I reply. Kolaches are a Texas thing and not traditionally available in the Los Angeles area. They opened a shop not far from my home a few months ago, and I stopped in one morning to pick up a few for our staff. Of course, they were a big hit, and now, I get requests for pickup far too often.

Finola grabs the kolaches and heads straight for the conference room. It looks like we'll be in this room most of today. Our snack buffet is stocked with popular favorites for munching. Sitting in a room all day asking and answering questions while being videotaped is not a thing I imagine anyone wants to endure, but the legal system has turned witness depositions into a standard litigation torture tactic.

"Thanks, Good Morning, and please give me the notes I need to review," Finola responds. "Why do you seem so calm, and what are you wearing? You know you're being videotaped?"

"I wanted something comfortable but professional," I explain. "Cardigan with a pencil skirt—stop hating."

"You look like a librarian when you need to look like a shark," she replies. "I have an extra blazer in my office— double-breasted with bronze buttons. You're changing. Anastasia would never go along with this outfit."

I pout, but I change as ordered. My deposition is not scheduled today, so I question what difference what I'm wearing really makes? Traveling between Los Angeles and New Orleans is a cost neither side wants to cover, so parties agreed to remote video depositions. This is not a Billion Dollar case—it will be a zero-dollar case for them because I don't intend to lose. They may end up owing us money in the end.

"Cousin Kate is up first. She's assumed the role of Good Cop to her brother Ryan's…Jerk!," I comment. "Do you think we should confirm that Ryan is not listening during Kate's deposition? I don't want him influencing her answers. He's the kind of jerk that also loves to bully anyone to get his way."

"You're only saying that because Kate has reached out to you," Finola replies. "I still cannot believe she actually called you to apologize. She's a true politician, for sure—working both sides of the aisle. She's trying to get on your good side so she can start picking you for info."

"Maybe, but I'm smart enough to know not to talk about the case," I respond. "She seems sincerely interested in getting to know us and trying to understand why we have been estranged."

"That's easy—you're literally the "Black" sheep of their Louisiana White Bayou family," Finola reminds. "Your grandmother blended in just fine, but your Black grandfather ended the "blending in" for the rest of you."

"Stop it!" I laugh. "You are probably right, but maybe there's another reason we were never invited to Thanksgiving?"

"Ok, think what you want, but don't start trusting Cousin Kate," Finola advises. "And, why is that the way you identified her on the schedule? One phone call, and now she's your cousin—you are such a strange mixed bag of emotions."

"That's just for us," I explain. "I want you all to keep the family connections in mind. Our dispute is over a one-hundred-year-old family recipe. Family and then, of course, money is what this mess is all about."

"Ok, family," she laughs. "Why is Ryan listed by his government name?"

"Ryan?" I pause. "Arrgghh! Let me show you this video he has linked to his bar's website. It's Ryan promoting his bar." As Finola watches, I immediately see the confusion covering her face.

Less than one minute in, she makes the same look of disgust I made while watching. Ryan is either drunk or just normally sloppy. The video is a promo piece highlighting the live band nights held at his bar. Ryan goes on about the changes in crowd size and 'type' during Mardi Gras, the Sugar Bowl, conventions, and large football games. His comments about "Locals" versus "Urban Populations" clearly reveals all anyone needs to know about his level of thinking.

"Wow, has no one told him this video is offensive?" Finola remarks. "He's using this to promote his bar. Well...I guess that's that?"

"My thoughts exactly," I say. "Kate seems more decent, but it could be a front because she's running for reelection. Look at her All-American Family campaign photo," I switch screens to reveal Kate's campaign site.

"Oh, I see why you call her cousin Kate." Finola giggles. "She looks like *Rachel* from *Friends*. Who wouldn't want to have her in their family— how fun?" We both take in the thought and continue scrolling through family photos of Kate and Ryan.

"WHY did I go on television and tell the entire world that our pecan products are based on a family recipe my grandmother has been using since she was a child?" I ask myself out loud once again. "I'm an experienced attorney. What was I thinking?" Finola does not bother to respond.

Anastasia and her team arrive fifteen minutes early, and we have everything set up and ready to go. Cameras are working on both sides, and Kate comes into view first, waving like she's in a parade.

"Good morning, everyone," Kate warmly greets. "Lily, good to see your face. When this is all over, we're going to have a big family Thanksgiving Dinner."

Finola's look of shock causes us both to slightly giggle, but she is unable to hold her outburst of laughter. She slides behind the camera and covers her mouth with both hands. Maybe they didn't notice?

"Good to see you as well," I respond. "Has your brother arrived?"

"Not yet— our lawyer told him to come right after lunch," she answers. "He's such a live wire. Sitting around and waiting is not for him."

"I'm sure there are a lot of things, 'Not for Ryan'— He's your brother," I joke.

"Yes, I have to put up with him," she agrees. "Give him a chance when this is all over. He has some good qualities. He owns a bar— that's something."

Their lawyer walks in and breaks up our family chat fest. We all immediately sit up straight as if our fifth-grade teacher had just entered the room. We turn on our professional battle-tested faces. We are now camera ready.

Anastasia covers the rules, includes housekeeping items, and then asks Kate her first question. "Mrs. Emory, please tell us your full name and why you believe you are here today?"

Kate's animated eyerolls make her aggravation undeniable, but her lawyer does his best to redirect her. He points to the camera, reminding her that she's being recorded. She quickly plasters on a big fake smile.

"I'm here because you want to ask me questions about our grandmothers and their family farm," she responds.

"Yes, that's correct," Anastasia replies. "But I'd like to know your understanding of the complaint filed by you, your brother, and mother."

"Not me," Kate answers. "I really knew nothing about this. It was all my brother's idea, and because of my mother's fading memory, she went along with him."

We all turn towards Anastasia and give her an off-camera thumbs-up. Their lawyer doesn't try to mask his displeasure. He's up with coffee in hand as he makes a quick stride towards the conference room door. "I have an emergency call," he states. "Give me a quick minute—let's go off the record."

Anastasia doesn't protest—we received our first win, and their lawyer obviously realizes the harm caused by Kate's comments will not be an easy fix.

We get through the next two hours of Kate's Q and A. Ultimately, her deposition gave us more than we hoped. The camera loves Kate. We all immediately recognize why she's a successful politician. Her testimony walked the line between helpful and hurtful. Kate appears to be the kind who never fails to offer a few surprises.

Ryan is next, and we plan to spend less time questioning him. We decided early on that anything we get from Ryan would probably start as exaggerations and end with lies and distortions.

"Let's take a break and do a quick reset for the afternoon," Anastasia advises our team. "Go, enjoy a good lunch. I'll give you a quick briefing before we start back at 12:30 PM. They're two hours ahead, so it'll be 2:30 PM their time. I'm sure they will be ready to call it quits by 5:00 PM."

"No problem," I say. "I could use the fresh air." I walk alone to the cafe next door. Processing time is exactly what I need. Kate seemed to know a lot about her grandmother and her childhood. I know very little about Granna's. Turns out our grandmothers loved each other and were the best of friends. Kate's words provided an image of bliss-filled days enjoyed by a family devoted to each other's happiness. If true, why has Granna never shared this story of bliss with us?

Kate's responses also confirm Granna's belief that her sister would be heartbroken to know this lawsuit was filed. I also learned that, just like me, Kate knew very little about us. When Granna married Gramps—there were no more big family Thanksgivings nor Christmases on the farm.

"Back just in time," Finola says as I return from lunch. "Your favorite person is up next."

Ryan appears ready for his first question and looks much more competent than he does in his *YouTube* video. There is no sign of the same type of joyful welcoming banter we had with Kate. Everyone is all business.

"Mr. Tillerson, you operate a bar and nightclub?" Anastasia asks.

"No, we are not a nightclub—jazz club," Ryan corrects. "We are completely upscale."

Anastasia doesn't take the bait tossed out by Ryan. She continues and gets the needed information out of him without a problem. "Mr. Tillerson—let me ask you about baking. How often would you say you bake during a normal week?"

"Zero, but that means nothing." Ryan snaps. "We outsource everything. We have the license. The Marchands cannot go out and make the same stuff and sell it under a different name."

"Have you visited the Marchand's shop or ever tasted any of their products?" she questions.

"Tell me why it's ok for someone to take your product, change the label and sell it?" Ryan continues his protest without answering the question.

"Is your answer, No?" Anastasia remarks.

He gives a thumbs down and then responds—"No," when instructed by his lawyer.

"Mr. Tillerson, I just have a few final questions," Anastasia announces less than one hour into his deposition. "When was the last time you visited the farmland sold by your family?"

"No need for me to do that," he reacts annoyed. "Why would that matter? The Marchand's business is why we are here."

"Thank you," she offers before asking her next question. "Have you compared the ingredients found in the Marchand's baked goods versus other similar baked goods currently sold in stores?"

"No—what for?" Ryan adds. "That doesn't mean that I don't know their stuff is the same as ours. I'm not a baker. My taste test doesn't matter." He continues to explain why he believes we are robbing his family and violating their family legacy. Anastasia concludes her questioning and saves us all from sitting through more of Ryan's diatribe.

We all remain seated with plastered fake smiles until the cameras turn off. "Well, that was crazy," Anastasia laughs. "I wonder if he thinks anyone is taken in by his charm. Does he really think he's charming?" No one answers. We're all too busy laughing and trying to make sense of what we just witnessed.

"Lily, sleep tonight—PLEASE!" Finola instructs. "We need you at 100%. You are too scattered when you lack sleep." I nod in approval of Finola's demand and make my way out of the conference room and away from today's spectacle. We have an earlier start tomorrow because of Luke's schedule. He's first and then me. We'll be ready. We both will bring our best to represent Granna.

---

*M*orning arrives too soon as it often does. Today, the office mood seems light. Finola has developed a talent for keeping the firm's opposing camps from crossing paths. Several partners remain offended by the amount of money they were forced to hand over. Others applaud the firm's commitment to justice and accountability. Camps remain divided, and tensions have yet to completely fade. The friendly banter going on as I make my way through the halls is encouraging.

"So very happy you decided not to dress like a librarian," Finola teases. "Dragon slayer—you've got this. Luke's here and ready."

I'm not surprised. My baby brother is much more responsible and disciplined than I've ever been. He's a machine. I'm a floating cloud. I give him a too-long and too-tight hug. He comforts me—also not surprising.

"We're ready," Anastasia announces.

"Dr. Luke Collins, thanks for coming," their lawyer says. "I promise not to keep you long."

"No problem," he responds. "I'm good for at least an hour. I left word with the hospital to call me in for help with an emergency surgery around 10:00 AM."

It takes a moment before everyone catches on to his attempt at humor, but eventually, we all join in on the laugh. Luke has a dry humor and is socially awkward like most doctors. I often remind him that he's a doctor, not a lawyer. We're definitely better at socializing and delivering jokes.

"Well, let me talk fast," their lawyer adds to the humor.

"Can you tell me about your role in your family's bakery business?" Luke is questioned. He gives me a warm glance and tilts his head before speaking. Luke's responses are delivered just as we coached, and the regurgitated facts flow with ease. I'm impressed with my little brother. His male doctor brain is capable of holding more than medical terms and football stats.

"I spent many nights every summer sweeping and mopping bakery floors," Luke explains. "Deciding to go away to college and picking a career that had nothing to do with mopping flour-covered floors was the best decision I've ever made. And, by the way, that was a decision I made when I was ten years old. By the time I was in high school, I would do everything possible to avoid the bakery. Every sports camp, science camp, and church retreat— I made sure to attend. I did whatever was necessary to not have to work mopping up *Marchand's* floors. Practicing medicine is much easier, and I think I make more money?"

Hmphhh...he just won't stop with the jokes. And he hasn't seen Granna's tax returns. She makes pretty good money. I shake my head in disapproval, but Luke ignores me and continues with his stand-up routine.

"May I ask why you are not on the board of directors," their lawyer continues. "You would definitely be considered a ranking family member along with your sister?"

"My sister loves business. I love medicine. Spending my free time reviewing financial spreadsheets or bakery marketing plans is not a commitment I am willing to make," Luke responds.

"After our mother passed, I did consider helping out, but I wasn't needed. Lily and Granna are fierce businesswomen, and our uncle is a talented baker. I would just be in their way."

Luke's performance pleased our team, and in the end, we couldn't even complain about his quirky attempts at humor.

"It's been a pleasure, Dr. Collins, and I've finished with you before the hospital's emergency call," their lawyer ends with another joke, and I must admit his delivery was much better than Luke's.

"Let's take a break before we start with Mrs. Guillory," Anastasia announces.

Luke is complimented for his flawless performance. He truly knows nothing about the business, but he is family, so they wanted him on the deposition list. Granna and Kate's mom are still pending, but because of their ages and medical issues, both sides are considering written questions. After covering family, the staff is next. Our team is dreading completing the long list of witnesses the other side wants to call. Hopefully, we can do a few more by written questions.

"Mrs. Lily Guillory, it's a pleasure," their lawyer says as we start again after a short break. "I've seen your television spot, and Kate has told me how kind you were to take her calls. I hope you know we all just want to do what's fair."

Why did he have to start with the television spot and Kate? I give a simple "thank you" and wait for him to ask an actual question. I'm not giving up anything for free.

"Well, I'm sure you understand why we are here," he states. "Let me first ask about your current role with the company?"

"I'm on the board, twenty-five percent owner, and I help manage the Los Angeles bakery," I respond. "My official title is General Counsel and Vice President of Corporate Development." I explain. "My Uncle—Elias Marchand, Jr., Is COO, and my grandmother is CEO."

Questions asked mostly cover operations and financial records. My exhibit binder was ten times the size of the others. Uncle's will probably be the same. Luke, Kate, and Ryan are not privy to bakery operations, so their questions were mostly family related.

I'm questioned for the remainder of the day with only a few breaks. I just want it over, and I don't want to come back into the office tomorrow. By 4:00 PM, I end every response with an obnoxious sigh. My last question is answered by 4:30 PM.

After a quick review of logistics for the next round of depositions, I'm free. Uncle is next week, and he is, of course, unhappy about leaving the bakery for a day. Aunt Helen will follow the next day. We say our thanks and goodbyes, and that's a wrap.

"We need to talk about your grandmother. How will she handle a deposition?" Anastasia questions.

"I don't think that's a good idea," I respond before purposefully shifting focus. "I can't imagine a scenario where Granna sitting through hours of questioning would go well? Should we go to New Orleans for Uncle and Aunt Helen's depo? I know you have someone local, but Uncle can be unkind."

"Probably, no. The budget for that would be ridiculous," she advises. "There will be hearings we need to attend in person. Let local people attend the depositions. We can still request to sit in via video and yell stop if anything goes off the rails."

We are almost out the door when Finola stops us all in order to snitch to Anastasia about Kate. "Why is Kate calling you?" Anastasia asks. "You mentioned one call, but I heard her lawyer mention calls—plural?"

"Yes, she's called the office a few times," I say. "We've spoken twice. She just wanted to let me know that this lawsuit was not her idea and that we shouldn't take the lawsuit personally."

"Why does she care what you all think?" she questions. "That's really weird, and it's even more weird that her lawyer went along with her calling?"

"I think it's probably because she's a politician and doesn't want the negative press?" I reply. "Suing your Black family may not go over well with her voters?"

"Maybe?" Finola adds. "I still think it's weird. Who lets their client call the opposing side?"

"Ummm…None that I can think of?" I say. "Don't give it any thought. I'm pretty sure I can handle Kate."

"So… no calls from Ryan?" Anastasia asks. "He doesn't appear to be one of the friendliest of people?"

"I love the French Quarter, but now I will look at the bars differently," Finola responds. "I cannot believe he owns a bar. Who would want to hang out with him?"

"What are you two not telling me?" Anastasia questions.

"There's a promo video for his bar on *YouTube*," Finola explains. "We'll send it to you. After watching, you'll see why we think he's a complete jerk, and his behavior today just further supports our opinion."

"I've never spoken to him," I say. "Seeing his video and speaking with Kate is all I need to know. She pretty much said he's a money grabber. I can't imagine the royalty payments they currently receive are anything substantial. Getting a second royalty payment from us is probably what he's hoping to gain."

"Yes, I agree. And, your grandmother only received one check when the farm sold?" Anastasia asks. "We need to review the sales documents. I've requested them, but I've been told they are having trouble locating the original documents. Unless your grandmother received a larger payment up front, the *Estate of Rosemary Cormier Romain* might owe you all money?"

"I wish…also, about the farm…," I say. "I've also learned that Granna's biological father and most of his family worked on the farm when she was growing up. I want to take a trip to Detroit and speak to his family."

"What do you hope to find?" Anastasia asks.

"Granna's against it, and that makes me more curious," I say. "I just want to know more about the farm, and more importantly, if anyone can tell me about the pecan pies and pecan butter. Think about it—what if Ada Lewis is the one who came up with the pecan pie recipe?"

"I gave some thought to pursuing that angle," she adds. "We all know who really did all the work and all the cooking back in the day."

"Exactly, Mrs. Ada may be the true creator, and then they owe us money and their brand," I add. "Wouldn't that be ironic? They came after us, and they may be the ones in the wrong?"

"Well, our list is covered today," Anastasia confirms. "Let's conference again soon and see where we are with other deliverables. How's your weekend looking?"

"I have teenagers," I remind her. "My weekends are always booked." Anastasia has eight-year-old twin girls. She'll know my pain soon enough.

CHAPTER SEVEN
Kate

Rooks move horizontally or vertically any number of squares

What can I possibly do to stop our family civil war? The Marchands are our family, even if this fact is acknowledged solely by me. Mom and Ryan—those two only consider each other family. I have no doubt that to them, I'm iffy. I try to believe they still consider me family, but my husband and kids—no. Grandma Rosey loved me. She always took time to see the true me and not just the ideal me everyone else chooses to see.

As I make the hour-long drive from my home to the capitol in Baton Rouge, I use the quiet time to gather my thoughts before tackling the day. I have an early start, and the roads are quiet. Now is the perfect time for me to take a chance.

"Lily, I'm calling to ask when you next plan to visit New Orleans?" I say. "I hope it's ok I'm calling. I'm not a lawyer so let me know if I keep breaking the law."

"Well, I gave you my cell number, so you're good as far as I'm concerned," she responds. "You may want to check again with your attorney. If he complains to us, I'll let you know."

"He's not my attorney," I reply. "I really wish none of this was happening."

"So, why are you calling?" Lily asks.

"New Orleans," I repeat. "You do visit often because of the bakery—correct?"

"I'm there often enough, but bakery talk is definitely off limits," Lily adds. "Did you need something?"

"I want you to meet my family and come to my campaign kick-off event," I explain. "It's a Sunday afternoon, after church and before the *Saints* game."

"Why would you want me to come?" she questions. "I'm sure your brother will be there, and he's not my favorite person at this point."

"No, Ryan and my mom don't usually attend," I say. "Ryan has bar stuff, and my mom can't handle the crowds. I just really want you to see that we are not all bad."

During our last call, Lily asked if I had seen Ryan's website and the videos used to promote his bar. Surprising to us both, I had not. I'd seen his original stuff, but I wasn't aware of the updates. After seeing the content, I understood why Lily may view our family negatively. I tried to get Ryan to take down his crazy drunken video, but he's stubborn, and he loves it. He thinks it makes him and the bar seem more exclusive and mysterious.

"I know you're not a bad person, Kate!" Lily offers. "Are you afraid we'll do a negative campaign ad for your Democratic opponent?

"That's not it at all," I laugh. "But you are proving my point. You think of me as a privileged, borderline racist. Or, do you think we're all just racist?"

"I don't, but why do you care what I think?" she asks. "You just learned about our family, and we've never met. Why do you care?"

"We're family and I wished we had always known each other," I admit. "I'd love to meet you in person. Please consider coming. I'll text you the info."

"Kate, you're a weird one—for sure," she laughs. "Actually, I was just in NOLA—CLE event, work-related."

"I won't feel offended that you did not reach out," I say with a giggle to avoid being offensive myself.

"Kate, still weird," she adds without a laugh. "Meeting you in person, I must admit, sounds very intriguing. And, I've never been to a Republican anything. I'll come."

"Thank you, Thank you!" I say. "You won't be disappointed—promise. Will you bring your family?"

"Too much—too soon," she replies. "Let's start with me. Besides, Uncle would never come and Granna has stopped wanting to board airplanes—too many germs— her words."

"Can I send you a campaign t-shirt to wear?" I ask. "My family will all have them on."

"No, ma'am!" she firmly states. "I'm not wearing your shirt and I am not posing for photos. I'm all for bipartisanship, but no. And, honestly—let me check out your platform. Where do you stand on the issues? Should I be concerned? Louisiana has a big jobs bill pending, and did you vote to approve the extra HBCU funding?"

"Check me out," I advise. "Maybe if I had someone like you in my ear, I would make better voting decisions?"

Naming Lilah

"I already said I'm coming," she reminds. "But, yes, influencing the Republican vote is a true bonus—still not wearing your t-shirt."

My calling Lily seemed to go well. I prayed her response would not include a few common swear words followed by a direct—"never call me again." Her actual response has been much more welcoming than I ever hoped. I need the Marchands to know I'm not some horrible person sent to destroy their world. It's important for them to know that I am sincere.

Like any good politician, I also know the importance of reaching across the aisle; I know Lily would be the perfect ally. Besides, I admire and envy Lily. She has the support I wish for myself.

I imagine how different my family would have been if Grandma Rosey had allowed us to know her sister and her family? Papaw Robert died when I was fifteen, and my dad's parents were gone by the time I was five. The family holidays I remember probably would not have included warm welcomes for the Marchand's, but I can dream.

I've been asked to coauthor a healthcare bill with Senator Wilmington, a female Democrat. She's trying to find support from at least one Republican. Why the access to quality healthcare is such a divisive topic has always confused me?

"I'm going with Senator Wilmington's team," I announce to my legislative interns. "Call her office and get a copy of her current draft. Mark key points and I'll give each of you research topics we'll need to complete before I can add content to the bill."

They all scatter in different directions because they are energetic college teens eager to please and determined to not be viewed less than the others.

Wilmington's bill also proposes changes to the foster care system and access to healthcare after age eighteen. She wants more mainstream Republican backers. That's me. My father and now my husband have held positions on the Tulane Hospital Board, and I have been in politics for over ten years. I'm rarely opposed, and many consider me a *"Golden Goose."*

Foster Children don't attract many critics or opposing groups, but I've typically avoided working on bills focused on children. I carry too many fears and too many regrets that begin with the word "child."

"We have a copy of the bill, and our notes will be on your desk after lunch," the winning intern announces. "Are you attending today's committee lunch meeting?"

"I am, and I'm late," I confirm. "But, let me see the bill. I'll mark up a few pages first." Lunch meetings start off with too much chatting about nothing and too much eating the latest Cajun big-budget buffet. Arriving late allows me to miss the worthless chit-chat while still allowing me to enjoy a decent Cajun meal.

"Anything else Senator?" they oddly speak in unison.

"Who can walk with me and jot down a few more notes?" I inquire. They all once again scatter, and the fastest intern is my shadow for the afternoon.

As I enter the dining hall, I search the room for Senator Wilmington. The room is filled with more than ten tables of legislators and staff chatting loudly and attempting to enjoy their meal.

"Senator Emory, a word," I hear before I could complete an attempted stealth move to a quiet table along the back wall. My movement up the chain of seniority has brought an unwanted spotlight to every choice I make. Even the school my children attend is now a topic for public conversation.

"Just a few," I agree with a smile. "My intern has been working all day, and I need to wrap up a few more items before the end of today. I hope you all are not concerned about your healthcare bill?"

"If you won't co-sponsor, we need you to speak out in support," one Senator responds. "You can, at the minimum, speak—can't you?"

It's a fair question, but I still try my best to look offended before agreeing to their request. I'm not sure if I'm prepared for more attention, but this year seems to be a year filled with more things unexpected and fewer things clear.

"I'm reviewing as we speak," I respond sharply. "I'll know more soon."

My ability to squash a potentially catastrophic runaway narrative has become one of my hidden talents. My morning smackdown courtesy of Lily and my afternoon Senate colleague ambush has forced me to move up my need to redirect my public image to a more inclusive stature.

The old Senator Kate spun from old money is no longer who I want to be—besides, my brother has me involved in a lawsuit that smells of greedy desperation. A critical fix is what I need.

"Senator Emory calling," I announce to the receptionist of the marketing firm I use to manage my campaign materials and website. "I need to schedule a review tomorrow with my tech rep. I want to make sure my online presence has current info."

"Yes, Senator—I'll connect you," he responds.

I'm connected to a tech rep I've worked with in the past. He's adequate—traditional ideas, but I now realize I may need to expand my circle of advisors. Lily was able to recite her issues of concern within Louisiana, and she lives in California. I realize I may not be hearing the voices of everyone in my own district.

"I'd like you to meet with me tomorrow at my offices and bring a diverse team with different ideas," I order. "I want something different. You do have the ability to show me something different—correct?"

"Certainly," he replies. "I'll bring a team, and we'll meet you tomorrow."

I scroll through my current online content, and it disappoints. Before the Marchands officially re-entered my life, I didn't give much attention to my personal perception beyond that of my voting base. I would like to think that I cared to consider differing viewpoints, but if I'm honest, I only cared to promote the side of me that would get votes.

My husband, the doctor, and I have our three children enrolled in the best private school in New Orleans. I grew up in a home overlooking *Audubon Park*. My dad was also a doctor, and my mom never worked outside our home. From a distance, my life is storied.

If ever closely examined, what I've hidden is always near the surface and not forgotten. My ability to keep things hidden has come naturally to me—I'm not sure why?

As I drive into the city, the distance in miles is small, but my world is now so far away from that of my childhood. How we became so disconnected is beginning to become more clear. I started college, met my husband, and started a new life in Metairie. I was still close to home but far enough away to disconnect from my mom and Ryan.

After dad died, we all went our separate ways to heal. Coming back together meant us dealing with our grief more closely. Being alone seemed like a much better option for us all. Ryan clung to his bar, and neither of us was really there for mom.

We are now losing her too. Ryan ignores the reality of her slipping away, and it seems cruel for me to continually remind him of the reality. I also want to ignore the inevitable, but I must make sure mom gets good medical care.

"Kate, I ordered food, but it's still not here," mom says. "Are you free? Can you come by and take me shopping?"

"I'm on my way, mom," I say. "We spoke this morning. I'll be there in thirty minutes."

It's time for us to hire extra care, but none of us wants to admit it's needed. Mom's current helpers come by in shifts during the day and nightly, but when mom is alone, things are starting to become more concerning.

I check mom's fridge and the pantry—both look well-stocked. I see the note left to remind mom that her dinner was ready and on the stove.

Mom is dressed and standing at the door, waiting for me to complete my inspection. Maybe she just simply wants to get out of the house? I found a few memory care support groups, but she refuses to consider any activity that could be described as elder care.

"Kate, please let's go," mom orders. "I don't want to be out late, and I have a long list of things I need to pick up."

"May I see your list?" I ask. "I may see a few things we should add," I, of course, see nothing missing, but I decide to check her list just in case. I also know if I hang on to her list for a few minutes, she will forget she even had a list. Is that horrible?

I check every item and put the list in my pocket. Mom is still standing by the front door, but her expression has changed. An increasingly common blank stare has begun to appear across mom's face more often than not. I hold mom with both arms and squeeze as tight as comfortable.

"Mom, I love you more than I can possibly say," I exclaim. "You are the best human I know."

"Katie Rose," she says. "Why are you being so mushy? Have you done something wrong? Whatever it is—I forgive you."

Mom has not called me Katie Rose in years. That was Grandma Rosey's name for me. I wonder why she thought of it today.

"I'm fine," I reply. "No need to worry. Are you ready to go? I wanted us to pick up fresh flowers for your back patio."

"Yes, I'd love that," she responds. "It's kind of messy back there. I've been telling the lawn guys to trim the rose bushes. We can pick out a new color for the window boxes."

"That sounds great, mom," I agree. "I'll drive, and you can pay. Do you have your credit cards?" We both laugh as mom checks her wallet.

"You are just like your brother," she jokes. "Why do you two never have money? I won't have anything to leave you in my will. You're spending it all as fast as I can save it."

Mom really could use a few fresh flowers, and we both know she needs to get out of the house more often. I will try again to convince her to join one of the memory care groups, but for now — I'll enjoy spending the afternoon with my mom and taking a little time to smell the roses.

We arrive at the garden center not far from our home. The rainbow of brightly colored rows of fragrant flowers is a welcoming escape. Mom walks ahead without me.

"Mom, should we add more color to the bunch?" I ask after looking at trays of white and yellow flowers. "How about a few Petunias?"

"I don't want a mess," she claims. "I want a clean look that I can easily transition into the next season."

I'm not sure what season she has in mind but asking too many questions is probably not a good idea. Her mood is upbeat and confident. Nursery centers have always been one of her favorite places to roam.

"Look at the Impatiens next to the Snapdragons," I say. "You haven't planted Snapdragons in forever. Let's try some. You can have your guys plant them tomorrow."

"Too busy," mom protests. "I can't keep up with too many different flowers. I want simple, Kate."

I hold mom's hand and we walk back to the area where she found the rows of Petunias and Peony blooms. We gather white Tulips and a few white Rose bushes; I may just faint in the center of this greenhouse. The flatbed I'm pushing is now overflowing.

"Let's have them plant two new Magnolia Trees," mom announces. "One on each side of the back patio. I'll name them Kate and Ryan. Have I ever told you that you both were named after my favorite soap opera characters? I never told your father."

"My name is Katherine Rose—after your mother," I respond. "What soap opera? And, when did you watch soap operas?"

"While I was home pregnant," she laughs. "What else was I going to do? We had a maid, lawn crew and night nurse when you came along. I had plenty of time to enjoy trashy television."

"Well, you learn something new every day," I join in on mom's laugh. "I never had time to watch trashy television. Where did I go wrong?"

"You wanted a career," she reminds. "You did all that class president stuff in high school, but I really thought you would let that go after you were so easily able to have babies. Most of the women in our family struggled. You spit out babies with no problem."

"Ok, that's enough," I order. "You're making me uncomfortable."

"I can't make you feel uncomfortable," she replies. "I'm your mother. You know you could have had six or seven children like those ladies with television shows about their ten children."

"Ok, I need to check your screen time," I joke. "I never realized you were a trash television junkie."

Mom allows me to add a few Geraniums to the bunch, and we both leave happy. I promise to come by tomorrow when everything's delivered to help her supervise the lawn crew. They don't need our supervision, but what else does mom have to occupy her time other than trashy television, it seems. I wonder if she watched the one where the bored housewife made out with her gardener? Is that why she has always been so obsessed with the state of her backyard garden? Humph?

CHAPTER EIGHT
Lily

Bargaining Knows Hope

The 11:00 AM downtown Houston morning sky resembles a Moonless night. Darkness is the only thing visible from twenty stories up. This is the second day the city has experienced nearly nonstop rain, and the downpour does not appear to be easing up.

During my time living in Houston, I experienced several flooding rain events, so I know getting stuck downtown is quite possible. In the past, I have been stuck on the side of the road many times for hours, waiting for the rain to stop and the water to recede. Living along the Gulf Coast brings with it an education in the power of rain and the dangerous unpredictability of flood waters.

Greg Wilson's deposition is today, weather permitting. He was our Houston pastry chef, and he now works at another area restaurant. Because of his busy work schedule, a video deposition became too complicated to arrange.

Whatever the reason this trip had to happen, I know this trip to Houston will surely be a complete waste of time and money. My efforts to persuade the litigious side of our new family to agree to drop Greg off the depo list fell flat. The more I protested, the more they pushed. They will see for themselves; we have nothing to hide.

I came up with the brilliant idea that opening a third location in Houston would be great for business. I pushed and screamed until everyone agreed. I was wrong—it failed. The bakery quickly closed. The profits earned during the mere eighteen months *Much Ado About Pecans- Houston* was opened totals less than the cost of this trip.

After all this time, it still feels weird returning to Texas. My Mother died here. I've been unable to dismiss this first thought. Moving from Houston to Los Angeles was a gift from above in the midst of my *Grief Cloud*. After mom passed, I remained in bed under my blanket for at least two weeks. Returning to work was done on autopilot. I remember very little of that first year. My thoughts were on mom, how she suffered and how unfair it was that such a kind and giving soul was taken.

I do remember the morning staff meeting when it was announced that our Los Angeles office was expanding. "I'm getting one of those spots," I accidentally blurted out in the middle of the staff presentation. It was the first time I carried around a thought other than my mom's suffering.

I prayed, fasted, and called on my Guardian Angels to help me make the move from Houston. I was done with the humidity, hurricanes, and months of 100-degree weather. I had traveled the U.S. visiting clients and longed to live in a more climate-friendly area. I considered moving to Louisiana and working in the bakery, but Los Angeles…sign me up!

As I began to allow thoughts beyond those of my mom, it felt strange but also restorative. Hanging onto my *Grief Cloud* kept mom close, but the cloud was filled with pain. Blessings received during that time were left uncelebrated because of mom's cancer. Cancer! Years later, I am still unable to grasp why such a vicious disease comes along and ruins a beautiful life?

My *Grief Cloud* remains wide, and its ends are not visible. Mom was filled with Light, and memories of her bring Love and Light to all who knew her. The cloud is not her. The cloud is me.

Winning the job in Los Angeles finally brought me to a place that felt more like home. During dad's time in the army, we lived in the San Diego area during my fourth-grade year. Southern California schools were much different from those in the Midwest— we next lived there my fifth-grade year before settling in Texas. In California, there were no hallways. We walked outside from class to class. Lunch was outside. Recess was never inside because of bad weather. There was tetherball. Who knew about tetherball?

I attended three different elementary schools in three different states. I was always a talker, so going up to strangers and starting a conversation was innate behavior. Surly, prep work for my career as an attorney.

If I picked someone too shy, too cool, too clueless, I kept searching until I found someone with my kind of weird. There's always someone for everyone. We just need patience and the willingness to keep searching.

Our family's frequent moves also helped to develop my resilience muscle earlier than most. More importantly, I also discovered early on in life how big the world is and how my current corner in life is only temporary. Possibilities are truly limitless.

"*It* was fun to catch an *Astros* game last night, but they have nothing on the *Dodgers*," Finola pokes. She came along with me to help cover the deposition for our side. "The downtown scene seems nice, but the rain—does it ever stop?"

"It's either rain or baking heat and humidity," I explain. "The weather is definitely not a reason to visit Houston. It has other things to offer."

"Yes, money, big houses, and lots of land," she says. "It took nearly two hours to drive from the airport to downtown."

"There are lots of oil money and jobs," I add. "Cost of living is low, and you can buy a mansion for less than a million dollars. In L.A., that will get you a condo. Houston has everything any other major city has to offer—you just may not want to hang around outside most of the year."

"Yeah, it seems fun," Finola agrees. "Hopefully, this depo is quick. I want to check out a few shops. A trip without new stuff for us is definitely a waste of company money."

"I've got us covered," I confirm. "Just have your credit card ready."

We grab a ride share from our hotel to a law firm located on the top floor of one of Houston's downtown high-rises. Greg is the first face we see. His salt-n-pepper hair fits him, and he hasn't lost any of his charm.

"Lily, it's been too many years," Greg says. "You haven't skipped a beat—still the same no-nonsense fire-cracker."

"Well, thanks!" I reply. "You are still the same handsome charmer that drew in all the regulars. I know your current place is doing just fine with you in charge."

"No one complains," he adds. "Houston is full of wealthy women in need of something sweet."

"Oh, now we are getting to the important stuff," Finola remarks. "I knew you were holding back."

Our fun exchange is ended when the deposition crew and Kate's team arrive. Their lawyer sent his young associate, and she is immediately sucked in by Greg's gray eyes and slanted smile. I relax and settle in to enjoy the show. The flirting back and forth is entertaining. I remember being a young attorney. I also remember being swayed by a tall, thick, handsome, witty, and talented fella. But not anymore. Well, maybe?

Greg had nothing to offer as expected, and his depo was finished by lunch. Seafood is the menu of choice, but the continued rainy downpour limits our choices. Luckily, there's a great seafood restaurant across the street from our hotel.

"Houston has decent seafood and better drinks," I inform Finola. "But we can't have too much of either if you still want to go shopping."

"We're taking a ride share," she explains. "Drinks and shopping sound like fun."

We order frozen drinks and a plate of Calamari. Gossiping was next on our agenda. Anastasia skipped this trip, so we covered her gossip first.

"She's dating a guy that talks loud and too close for comfort," Finola describes. "We've all learned to stand on the opposite side of a chair, counter, person, whatever we can find. He's the new guy, so we try to like him, but he's really just too much."

"I haven't met him yet," I say. "Is he full or cash, or does he come with other benefits? Anastasia is not easy to please."

"I think both," she concludes. "Since her divorce, she has been very selective. He's very handsome, tall, and athletic, so there's that. I'm sure he's full of energy. He's big in the criminal courts, so you know he's bringing in the money."

"Well…can't wait to meet him," I say. "Tall, rich and handsome sounds like a winner."

The rain had lightened, and the mist was refreshing as we walked off our lunch. I'm wearing my cute new raincoat with the perfect hood to protect my hair. I warned Finola about the frizzy Houston hair syndrome, so she is also prepared. It's now after 3:00 PM, and our shopping talents are ready for action.

We cover several shops and don't leave until closing. "You could really just live in Houston for the shopping," Finola proclaims. "There's everything all in one spot, and there are sales. We never have sales."

"Yeah, the shopping is pretty awesome," I agree. "But we've spent all of our money, so we need to earn a few more paychecks before we make another trip this way."

We arrive back at the hotel with too many bags for us to manage. We grab a luggage cart and secure our stash for the elevator ride up. "We'll need to figure out how to get everything home in the morning," Finola realizes as we both say goodnight.

The rolling sound of thunder greets me as I take in the view of the Houston skyline from my hotel window. It's truly a dynamic downtown landscape and the night lights bring out more of its beauty. A rainy day, warm blanket, hot cocoa, and a good movie is the perfect way to end a long day. The beach, warm sun and a margarita are others. I'll hold that thought until next weekend.

The next morning, we catch an early flight home and bid goodbye to Houston and its rain. Within minutes, we are above the clouds welcoming the Sun.

Following our trip, today is now an off day, and I've planned to spend it baking yeast rolls with Granna. But I first must get in my morning walk. Two days of hanging out eating and drinking in Houston have rendered my head and belly a fluffy mess.

I'm welcomed by a sparkling blue sky that brings with it the hope that today will be a great day. I walked an extra thirty minutes to rid myself of yesterday and to take in more of the crisp morning air before heading to Granna's.

For some unknown reason, Granna has a fully staffed commercial kitchen, but she still bakes orders at home. Her church friends can somehow tell when she doesn't personally make her signature yeast rolls. Ms. Julia is even stumped, and she's an excellent pastry chef.

"Just let Ms. Julia make the rolls next week," I protest. "We have too much going on, and I will need your help figuring out how to win this fight with your family. Stop promising to bake for your friends. Let them order from the bakery like everyone else."

"I know Julia can bake," Granna admonishes. "I found her—didn't I!"

Granna convinced our head pastry chef—Ms. Julia, to come work for her after discovering that she was the chef responsible for the chocolate chunk cookies with pecans we picked up at the *Hillside Corner Street Cafe* every Sunday after church.

"You stole someone else's chef," I remind.

Granna's wit has not slowed one bit. She runs mental circles around me with ease. And, she's correct about Ms. Julia. She's the perfect Head Pastry Chef for Granna, and Head Drill Sergeant of us youngsters, as Ms. Julia describes. She's barely ten years older than me, but I'll gladly accept the 'Youngster" title.

"How many rolls are we making?" I ask. "You know we could hang out at the Farmers Market. Didn't you say you wanted to pick up Tulip bulbs to plant along the back fence?"

I know my questions and protests are falling upon the ears of a parent who has mastered the art of ignoring the late-night tantrums of a toddler. Granna gently rubs my hand and instructs me to melt the butter and prepare her baking pans.

We've been baking together since I was two years old, and over the years, I've eaten more than my weight in raw dough. Now, tiny baking assistants are warned to not eat raw dough—another tradition from *The Good 'Olé Days* that's now a bad thing.

We have six dozen rolls finished by 5:00 PM and we're off to *Bethel* for Bible Study. Three dozen rolls are displayed in spring floral decorated baskets with our company logo. The other three dozen are given to her friends in our take-home boxes. I try to never miss an opportunity to self-promote. The yeast rolls are not under attack by Granna's family—yet. If we try to box Granna's yeast rolls for stores, who knows who may show up next claiming ownership.

Their Bible study is always well attended, and the chattered filled room does not settle down until everyone has sampled the snack table. Groups of seventy, eighty and ninety-year-old ladies should be filmed for reality television. Maybe I should produce and pitch the idea to networks? No one has a filter, and no topic is off-limits. They talk about the pastor, it's open season on leadership, and the choir director is a favorite. Also, the food never disappoints. We all know grandmothers can cook. Each member brings their specialty, and for the most part...all are amazing.

There's also Bible Bingo every third Wednesday of each month. Everyone contributes a prize; some are homemade gifts that are pretty nice—knitted potholders and even full-sized sofa blankets. I love sitting around the two big tables put together boardroom style. Most also never fail to mention how great their children are doing. It doesn't hurt to linger around and listen in on the discussions.

"Lilah, your granddaughter, just keeps getting more beautiful by the day," Mrs. Verna always offers while giving me an adoring hug. Granna gives her standard "Yes" and continues working on the buffet table. Granna is more concerned about the beauty of her pastries than she is about my pretty face.

"Who's ready for Bible Bingo?" someone yells as everyone takes a seat around the tables. I try not to win every game, but I am competitive by nature, even when competing against grandmothers. Most of the ladies are still pretty spunky, and the few that are quiet don't let on whether or not they are trying to keep control of their thoughts or just irritated by their over-the-top friends.

"Proper ladies don't explode in loud outbursts or have conversations while chewing their food," my bingo partner reminds me.

"B5, that's me," I say gently while raising one finger in acknowledgment.

"Lily, please." Pastor Davis, the newly appointed young, handsome, and single assistant pastor, quietly motions as he interrupts my Bingo mission. "May I have a moment of your time?" Granna's group gives me a concerning side glance as I smile and excuse myself from the table.

"Hello, Pastor Davis. Good to see you," I reply. "You're brave to interrupt Bible Bingo. What can I do for you? Did you receive the Grief Share books for our next class?"

"Yes, and there's one more thing," he responds. "Follow me." I have no idea what "one more thing" could possibly be about, but I'm intrigued.

"I've been leading our Church's Grief Ministry the last three years, and it's a well-oiled machine—not nearly as spirited as Granna's group, but value-added. Maybe wanting people to feel more joy after attending a grief group meeting is absurd. I've tried to make our meetings as lively as Granna's group, but I'm losing that competition. To lighten our moods, we began meeting as a group on even-numbered weeks and in small dinner party groups on odd-numbered weeks.

My first experience with a grief support group was two years after mom— I should have joined sooner. I was surprised to see how many people openly grieve. I had been hiding under my blanket or unloading days of tears in the shower. Misery may love company, but I've also learned that company helps to heal those in misery.

"Is there a report I need to update?" I ask, trying to guess why I'm being summoned.

"No, it's about a lawsuit," he answers as he hands me the subpoena sent to the church by Kate and Ryan. Well…Ok, the Cormier family. They have really overstepped this time.

"A subpoena," I complain. "Apologies, Pastor Davis. I'm not sure why this would be sent to the church? It appears this request has to do with the scholarship fund we established in honor of my Mother."

"Yes, they're requesting information on donations made by your family's business," he informs. "We didn't know you all are going through a lawsuit. Is this something we can pray with you about?"

"Thanks; I'm sure Granna would appreciate that," I say. "Please, let me give you our litigation attorney's contact number. Is Anthony Wallace still the church's counsel?"

"Yes, I haven't called him yet," he replies. "It was just delivered today, and I knew Mrs. Marchand would be here tonight for Bible Study. That was a sign for me to speak with you all first."

"Yes, I agree," I sigh as I return the document. "Have Anthony call Anastasia. They're just digging. If they want to know how much money we donate to the church, ask on— maybe it will inspire them to not be so cheap and evil."

"I'll put a few offering envelopes in with our response," he jokes.

"That's perfect," I acknowledge. "Sorry, you have to deal with this. Some people have no moral boundary when it comes to money."

"Oh, I work in ministry," he adds. "I could tell you a few stories that would blow your mind."

"Haha, I can definitely imagine," I respond.

"Here's your box of materials," he says. "I'll walk you out."

"Thanks," I reply while opening the door. "Our group is growing. We typically have at least twenty people attending each week. I like large classes. Hearing about others' experiences shows us that we are not alone. I still remember when I joined the group, and someone talked about being angry when she went out and people were laughing and eating ice cream."

"Ice cream?" he asks.

"Yes, when you're in pain, you see the world with eyes clouded by that pain," I explain. "It takes a moment for you to remember that everyone did not just experience a terrible loss and that some people are happy and want ice cream."

"Good to know, thanks!" he responds. "I'll use that in my next sermon."

Sending a subpoena to the church—Anastasia is correct. We are missing something. I skip the rest of Bible Bingo and wait for Granna in my car. I need to figure this out, and Finola can help. She has the ability to switch on the devious part of her brain and walk on the Dark Side of the street.

"I agree—this is not just about your business expanding into retail," Finola makes clear. "Why would they care about your mother's scholarship donations?"

"I'm so confused," I say. "Would they try and grab some of that money? How evil can they be—really?"

"Calm down and take your grandmother home," she replies. "I'll set up a call with Anastasia tomorrow. Hopefully, her investigator has some news that will help."

"Thanks, I really appreciate your love," I express. "This has been a crazy time for us all—I absolutely realize that, and you helping me with my family drama means a lot."

"Love you back," Finola offers in return. "Let it go for now. Think happy thoughts and enjoy your evening."

"You as well," I say before ending our call. I try to think happy thoughts, but the "why" questions refuse to release their grip.

CHAPTER NINE
Lilah

"We never know how high we are Till we are called to rise"
- Emily Dickinson

Before I became a married woman, I returned to St. Francis every Christmas. For the rest of the year, I remained in Alabama. On my second Christmas home, our family was preparing to welcome Rosey's first baby.

During our entire drive, Father could not stop gushing over the idea of adding a baby to our family. His happiness was contagious, and I'd hoped our mother would be just as excited. My leaving for school strained my mother and Rosey's relationship. She surprisingly didn't blame me. Mother found it easier to blame Rosey and Mrs. Ada.

"You're finally home," Mother gasped as I walked into the kitchen, where she and Rosey were busy making what appeared to be pies. "You know Rosey complains when I ask her to bake. I need my favorite helper. Welcome home, Lilah Grace."

Mother hugged me as if she feared I would disappear if she let go. I returned her long embrace and whispered in her ear—"I'm here until after the New Year. You have me all to yourself."

Our kitchen was filled with the perfect smells of the Holiday. Pans and flour everywhere—Rosey covered in the remains of her attempts at baking. She looked just as I had imagined—a puffy face with a grandiose belly leading her around the room, and her feet appeared too large for her house shoes.

"Why so many pies?" I asked. I was surprised Mother allowed Rosey to help with baking. "Is there a church thing this evening?"

"I'm taking two pies with us, and the other two can stay here," Rosey responded. "We'll be back tomorrow. Robert has a family dinner."

She gave me her one-armed Rosey hug, which was now more appropriate because her belly would not have allowed the use of two.

Rosey is out the door in a flash on her way to have dinner with her husband's family. He wasn't the type to allow Rosey to choose how their family would spend their time, and we would never pressure her to go against her husband's wishes. We loved her as much as we could and ignored him as much as possible.

"Come Lilah and let's eat," Mother rubbed my back as we walked towards the dining room. "We're having a church board meeting, but I know you don't want to sit through our meeting. Eat something, and then you can rest. I have lots of baking for us to start in the morning."

Our table was covered with food and was soon also surrounded by people. Having church family over was expected. We had the best pecan pies in the Parish, and Mother made pies for half the families in the area. She received all the credit, but most of the work was done by Mrs. Ada and then Adelaide.

I'm not sure how Adelaide came to work for Mother? I was mostly relieved that she had found someone to help after I left for school. Adelaide was also a recent high school graduate and newly married to a young man who worked on our farm. The Cormier's love to keep things in the family. Once we welcome one, all are welcomed.

Early the next morning, I'm greeted by the loving smell of baking bread. Those who've never enjoyed such angelic smells have my sympathy. Mother had not yet been up to share her morning tea, and Father was already out somewhere on the farm. I rushed to the kitchen to investigate in hopes of finding Adelaide.

"Adelaide, good to see you," I greeted. "How's your family?" I asked in what I hoped was not an obvious attempt to pry.

"Good," she replied. "I just had my second—a boy this time."

"Congratulations!" I offered. "You certainly have your hands full. I remember meeting your little girl last Christmas—she must have had her first birthday by now?"

"She turned one in May, and my new one was born in October," she explained.

"Amazing, who helps with the babies while you work with Mother?" I wondered.

"My mama helps," Adelaide replied. "She keeps all our little ones."

"That's a blessing," I said. "Please bring them both by for a visit before I leave, and I'll help keep an eye on them. I would love to have them over. Don't you just love the little toes and fingers?"

"Mrs. Rose has full days of pies to make every day until Christmas," she responded. "Maybe I should bring them by to visit on my day off?"

"No, that's your family time," I instructed. "I'll tell Mother that I invited you to bring them for a visit. I promise to watch them and keep them out of your way."

Adelaide and I were nearly the same age, but she seemed much older. She is married with a job and two children, so her life is older. I'm a carefree student home visiting my family for Christmas. I wonder if she considered her life fair. I felt guilty for considering my life better. Truthfully, Adelaide probably never gave my life any thought. What would be the purpose?

"It's a wonderful day for baking, ladies!" Mother proclaimed as she made her grand entrance. "I need six pies and a batch of pecan butter. In honor of my Lilah being home, let's also make an apple pie. I have vanilla ice cream we need to use."

"Your mother talks about you every day," Adelaide announced. "I know more about you than I do about your sister, and she comes by here almost every day."

We all had a surprising laugh at Adelaide's bluntness. I was pleased to know that Mother spoke of me fondly, but it was also a reminder of how my leaving was hurtful. I still hoped that my mother would come to understand that my choices were not a rejection of her or the life she created for me. I knew Mother blamed "Mrs. Ada's meddling," as she described, as the reason for my moving away.

It was no secret to Mother that Mrs. Ada would often tell me stories about her childhood and how she first learned how big the world was from reading old *National Geographic* magazines that had been given to her church. "I would dream of seeing the places from the magazines," she described as we sat in front of my dressing table mirror. Mrs. Ada braided my hair while we made up stories about the places we would one day visit. I refused to let her dream die.

The truth Mother seems unable to accept is that I learned long before hearing Mrs. Ada's stories about the vastness of our world. The poetry Mother and I read had opened my eyes and piqued my desire to one day explore our world. Mother is a true co-mastermind of my journey—not only Mrs. Ada.

Baby Emma arrived three days before Christmas and was the mirror image of Rosey—thin, wispy blonde curls and striking blue eyes.

"Lilah, come hold your niece…Emma Rose," Rosey extended her arms for me to hold her perfectly pink little girl. They both seemed perfect in every way. Rosey's a mom at only three years older than me. Will I have a child soon? As I stared into my niece's eyes, I searched for an answer to my questions. Baby Emma had just arrived from Heaven; she must have secrets to share?

"Are you crying?" Rosey laughed. "You're such a softie. You'll have your own someday, but first, you must finish school. I know I've never told you, but I'm proud of you for leaving St. Francis and seeing the world. I've only been as far as Mississippi."

"You're lucky too," I confirmed. "We are just doing things differently for now. You will have plenty of life to travel. Enjoy being a mom. This has always been your dream and Mother's too. She has not stopped gushing since Emma arrived. Every one of her church friends visited with gifts and food in hand. They sat for hours listening to Mother talk about Emma's birth and how she arrived with perfect little fingers and toes."

"Yes, Mother has received more gifts and attention than me," Rosey said. "That's nothing new. She does command attention."

We both held in our laughter as Mother gave us a sneaky grim. Her overwhelming personality allowed her to love with her entire being. When you were in her presence, she gave you her all. Sometimes we may have wanted a little less attention, but that's what most daughters believe until they have daughters of their own.

"Are you girls laughing about me?" Mother asked. She knew we were, so we fessed up. Without looking either of us in the eyes, she scooped up Baby Emma and left the room, making her way to her new rocking chair in our sitting room.

"Mother, I'll come with you so Rosey can rest for a while," I replied. "We can introduce our new addition to your favorite poet. Which *Dickinson* poem is best for a newborn's tiny ears?"

"Perfect!" she agreed. *"Hope is the thing with feathers."*

An unusually bright Winter morning sun casts a welcoming glow upon the cotton fields surrounding our family farm. This Louisiana Christmas is perfect for a large family dinner under the oaks. It's not one where a cold Winter breeze will keep us inside.

"There you are, Lil'flower," Father announced. "This weather is warm. Should we have dinner out here? We should invite your mother's group for Christmas Eve desserts."

"That's a great idea," I expressed. "It would make mother happy. You don't mind the fuss? They were just over last night. Is Mother okay? Why are you being extra nice?"

"Do you remember the day you and Rosey ran home screaming after seeing prisoners working in Henry's cotton fields?" Father recalled as he sat with eyes fixed on the fields, hoping my questions would end. "You both were excitable little kittens."

"I will never forget," I responded. "After that day, I never again walked to church with just Rosey. Mother made Mrs. Ada walk with us to choir practice when you couldn't drive us."

Workers harvesting cotton crops was not an uncommon sight but having White men working alongside Black workers was certainly not common. The cotton fields were busier that day than usual, and I immediately felt something must be wrong.

Rosey, in her customary over-the-top dramatic reaction, yells out to me, "Look, they have chains around their legs. Run!" Without even looking back to see if I was keeping up, she ran full speed towards our front gate.

"Why are they in chains?" I questioned before noticing the men on horses with guns. "Are they in jail? Prisoners?" Even as a child, I immediately knew this was not okay. I take off running as fast as my ten-year-old legs could move. Prisoners working in the fields next to our farm should not be okay with anyone. It was not okay with me.

Father's truck had reached the end of our drive as we ran towards him. "How's my Lil'flower today?" Father asked. "Where are you off to in such a hurry?"

"Did you see prisoners up the road?" I cried, exasperated as I tried to catch my breath.

"Yes, they came by and told us. Harvest is behind, so they let Henry Carpenter hire prisoners to help," he said casually.

"They have guns and chains," Rosey shouted. "What if one ran and they shot our way. I could have reached out and touched one of them. Why would you not tell me?"

"I was on my way to pick you up," he assured. "I just found out they were on the way. I didn't know they were already out here. You're safe. No need to worry."

Mother heard Rosey's yelling and began running across our yard toward us all. "Why are you making a fuss?" she yelled. "Did someone at church bother Lilah?" I never understood why she always inquired if I was being bothered until I learned why she worried someone would.

"They're fine," Father answered. "Carpenter has the prisoners out, and it caused a scare."

"I wasn't scared," Rosey declared. "I told you she's still a baby and needs to grow up. You all baby her much too much." As a thirteen-year-old, Rosey pretty much considered herself as grownup as Mother. She was wearing a bra, and her monthly "Female-time" had started. Her attitude towards me had also changed, but I didn't mind. Mrs. Ada described that "Female-time" causes a growing woman to become upset and moody because their body is changing. Rosey now had "moods," and I was still blissfully ignorant to what was going on with her or what would soon also come my way.

That evening, Mrs. Ada explained why Blacks and Whites working together outside our farm was important. "Black prisoners have been in those fields for as long as I can remember working all day without long breaks under the shade trees," she continued. "You pay attention, Lilah. Don't let anyone tell you it's not different."

At the age of ten, the only difference I noticed was the difference between families with means and those that struggled. Having parents that worked in the church exposed me to many families with less than ours. I helped prepare food boxes and rode with Father to deliver them to families and other churches. I never questioned why the families we helped were all White families.

My young mind didn't consider that poor Black families were out there somewhere. Our farm had many Black workers. I guess I thought they lived the same as I did and that the poor White families probably didn't have jobs.

Before leaving the farm, I grew to understand how our farm served as a safe haven for us all. Everyone was welcomed. Father treated his workers equally—Blacks and Whites.

The day Rosey and I witnessed how the White prisoners brought in to help with the cotton harvest were allowed to rest underneath the shade while the Black workers were made to endure the harshness of the glaring sun, we observed a different reality. I witnessed my first act of racism even though I had no idea at the time what I was witnessing.

"You don't know what you don't know" is a common phrase I wish we would take more time to consider. I'm a Black Woman who grew up in a White World. The most egregious form of racism I witnessed as a child was the disproportionate treatment of farm workers. I was never allowed to venture beyond the boundaries of my White World. I never saw the homes, churches, or communities where Mrs. Ada lived. I never gave much thought to her life beyond our farm.

After that day, my innocence began to shift, and the joyful fascination with the cotton fields surrounding our farm ended. Carefree walks along the quiet country roads we once knew were forever changed.

Rosey and I had often grabbed balls of cotton from the plants nearest to the road. Waist-high cotton bushes were the perfect height and size for our small curious hands. Rosey would grab several balls and share pieces with me. We both loved to pull them apart and imagine how this fully white ball of air was turned into the material Mother, and Mrs. Ada used to make our dresses.

At times, I would still sit on our front steps and glance at the beauty of the fields on a sunny day—little clouds of puff floating along our roads. The majesty had diminished. The harshness of truth was now forever visible.

"Why are you two looking so serious?" Rosey asked as she joined us with little Emma. "Look at this adorable face. She can solve any problem you have—give it a try. I'm convinced she arrived with ancient wisdom."

"You do seem calmer and more loving," I teased. "Did Emma tell you to be nicer to your little sister?"

"She did not," she laughed. "But she has told me to slow down and stop talking so much."

"That's a smart baby," Father added. "Give her here and let me show her around the farm. I need some advice. Production has been off." Father scoops up Emma and heads towards his office. We imagined he'd be happier with a grandson but seeing him any happier doesn't seem possible.

"Tell me more about school," Rosey requested. "You know any of these sloppy fellas around here would have married you in a second."

"Rosey, what happened to you not talking so much?" I reminded. "Emma just left. I'll go and get her so she can remind you to behave."

"Well, it's just us," she commented. "I'm surprised you have lasted as long as you have. You are pretty spoiled and soft. How are you managing without Mother and Mrs. Ada to tell you what to do?"

"Me, spoiled?" I giggled. "You have never worked a day in your life. Caring for Emma is the first thing you've ever done. When I graduate, and I will—I'm going to start my own business and hire lots of people."

"You're a woman, and who knows what kind of husband you will have— are you thinking of a Black man?" she asked. "Father wouldn't tell you, but I'm sure he would never want you to live that kind of life. I truly do not understand why you don't understand."

"I understand just fine," I confirmed. "Whomever I chose to love is my choice, and Father will be happy for me. You look at me and see one thing. I look in the mirror, and I see possibility. I am more than someone's future wife."

"It's Mother's fault that you are such a dreamer," she poked. "All that reading you did. Those are just stories. Life is not like a page in one of your books."

"Rosey, if only you knew," I said. "One day, I will take you beyond these roads and show you a world better than that found on the pages of a book."

"I hope that happens," she agreed. "At times, I envy you, but I could never imagine doing the foolish things you do. Your life was safe. Why would you change that?"

"Safe, because I was protected behind this White image?" I snapped. "Safe is not living. I want to live and not be afraid of letting people know who I am. I'm half Black, and I won't live being afraid of who I am."

"I've known you your entire life, and I don't think I will ever understand you," Rosey smirked. "Just don't forget about your sister. I want a trip to New York City."

"I promise," I replied. "I can't wait to show you the good that exists outside St. Francis."

CHAPTER TEN
Lily

Depression May Linger

Monday arrives, and Finola calls with an urgent request for me to stop by the office for a surprise that can't wait. Today is not a law office day. I've had enough of that place over the last few weeks, but I stop in to pick up my surprise.

"Lots of pictures," Finola explains as she hands me a tabbed binder sent by the other side. This is an amazing surprise. Pages with individual photo slots identified by the date and name of those shown in each photo fill a five-inch binder. Granna will be shocked to see pictures from her childhood. I'm shocked!

I, of course, immediately take my shock and the photos straight to Granna's. Will seeing photos of her family make her happy? I'm unsure. What I've learned so far has only painted a picture of an ideal life. Why would Granna move away as a teen going off to college if her life was happy? I also wonder if her family tried to convince her to stay with them and to continue living as their White daughter.

"Our house was always full of workers, church ladies, and their children," Granna whispers as her voice quivers between thoughts. "Growing up, Rosey and I were rarely the only two little ones running around."

"It is amazing that your sister kept the photos," I express. "Anastasia was told by their lawyer that your sister's daughter kept her mother's family photo albums. She sent more photos than we requested in our discovery request because she thought you would want to have them."

"I remember this day," she says as she hands me one of the photos. "Mrs. Ada made us matching Christmas outfits with hair bows. How do they have these photos? I don't remember ever seeing many of them?"

"Apparently, your sister often talked to her daughter about you," I say. "We found that she died in a nursing home—I think it was Alzheimer's? Did you know when she died?"

"We would call each other on Holidays and if something important happened," Granna replies. "When she missed a Christmas call, I called a friend from the church and was told about her moving with her daughter. She was ill and died soon after. Her daughter called after the service."

Granna tries to conceal her sadness, but we both feel the loss as we look through the remaining photos. I also feel shame for not knowing more about Granna's family. She knows every inch of me and my life. Maybe children don't make an effort to learn about their parents beyond what is seen?

"Did her daughter ever call you again?" I ask. "She had your sister's photos, and I'm sure other stuff? She never asked if you wanted any family keepsakes?"

"I never reached out to her daughter after that—I didn't want to intrude," Granna says.

"Did my mother know any of this?" I ask. "Did she ever ask about your parents and sister? Why have you never told me any of this?"

"I'm still here," she says, annoyed. "I'm telling you now. There was no need for me to have gotten your mother all worked up about my family. She had enough of her own problems, and you guys were moving back and forth all over the country. When did you all have time to meet anyone?"

"Our promo picture is how they found you," I say. "It looks similar to this page of photos. They must have been taken the same day. The house is easily recognizable—classic southern wrap-around porch and oak trees lining the yard. Wish I had known about all this sooner."

"For what reason on Earth?" she questions. "Well, now you know. What does it change? You still would have done exactly what you've done, exactly how you've done it."

Granna's always right. At her age, there's not much she hasn't experienced, and she doesn't seem to forget much. Granna has often tried to help me avoid many of life's tough lessons, but I, unfortunately, seem like the type who wants to learn things the hard way? I admit to making the same mistakes several times before the lesson is finally learned.

"Are there any pictures of Mrs. Ada?" I ask. "Doesn't look like it?"

"She's probably the one taking the pictures," Granna answers. "I don't remember her liking the idea of pictures. Not sure why?"

"Did she look like you?" I question.

"Maybe," Granna wonders. "Mother would always comment that Mrs. Ada's sons were pure Creole—whatever that means? I think she was trying to convince me I was White, but I learned who I was, and I love all of me."

"Incredible," I reply.

"I should have told you and your mother more about Mrs. Ada," Granna continues. "You should know that you are where you are today because of Mrs. Ada's hard work, prayers, and sacrifices."

"You think so?" I ask, confused. "What about your parents?"

"My parents loved me," she explains. "They made me a part of their family. I was protected and given more than I deserved, but Mrs. Ada is responsible for it all—her and God."

"Why do you think that way?" I ask, still confused.

"Mrs. Ada was the one who worked in our home and on our farm, every day from before the Sun was up until the day was gone—except Sunday," Granna describes.

"She never complained. Her work was for her family and not herself."

"She made sure you had the best life," I add. "Having you raised by the Cormier's definitely changed the lives of your children."

"Do you know what I remember most?" Granna reflects. "Mrs. Ada's knees and elbows were discolored, hard and calloused from years of literally working on her hands and knees. None of us have the same. Look at your elbows. Perfect!" Granna grabs my arm and gives it a firm kiss. "As a small child, I would sit and stare at her while she worked. She always wore dresses with an apron and hose—never pants. "I once asked her—'why do you have scabs on your knees?' that was silly."

"It just sounds like a question I would ask," I say with a chuckle. "I'm sure the work we do is nothing compared to the work Mrs. Ada did every day."

"I should have told you sooner, but now you know—Mrs. Ada is why there's a Lily sitting in her big house and working at that big law firm. She's the reason why I had the courage and the confidence to start my own bakery. Knowing the value of hard work and getting up every day, whether you're tired or frustrated, is in our blood. You are because of Mrs. Ada. We reap from what she sewed." Granna admits.

I gather the loose photos and begin putting them in an album with Granna's other family pictures. I had never noticed before today that most of the photos in Granna's family albums are photos of us, Gramps, and his family. Our family at birthday parties, holidays, and summer trips—all of us and Gramps family.

We spent the next few hours organizing photos, eating an entire pecan loaf Granna had made this morning, and sipping tea.

"Look at this picture, Lily," Granna hands me a copy of a photo I've seen before many times. I'm probably two—standing in front of Jackson Square with mom.

"Yes, I was such a cutie," I say. "Maybe I should have this photo framed?" If I frame it and put it on the buffet with all her other family photos, she'll see it more often. It's obviously one of her favorites.

"Your mother had just turned twenty-one, and we invited her to come visit for her birthday," Granna reveals. "We had no intention of sending her back, but she was insistent that she needed to 'go back to her husband' For what reason, I never understood?"

"Really, I've never heard that?" I say. "Why didn't you just make her stay?"

"She was a married adult," she responds. "We did everything we could."

I stop to imagine how my life would have been so different if my mom had stayed with Granna. It's a place I have before dreamed of as my reality. My mom may have found her cancer earlier, and she would still be here with us?

Dad refused to support mom's testing and treatment. His repeated denials that anything was wrong blocked our efforts to have mom properly treated. I know he suffered as well. The fear of loss, his anger, constant yelling, and fighting contributed to his sudden heart attack. Dying two years before mom allowed us time to better care for her, but by then, her cancer had spread. Curative measures were exhausted. Days were limited. Once again, we were prevented from enjoying time with our mother.

"Looking at this photo makes you think of how things could have been—doesn't it?" Granna drops her head and mumbles softly. "I should have tried harder. Your father was such an idiot." I'm not surprised by her words; we all know how Granna feels about my parents. She never kept it a secret. My dad was *Prince Charming* handsome with an *Archie Bunker* personality. My mother was definitely his *Edith*—beautiful inside and out.

My teenage mother and I grew up together. She married my dad at eighteen—one month after her high school graduation. I don't think Granna ever forgave either of them for interrupting my mother's college plans.

My dad had just returned from service in Germany during the Vietnam War. He was ten years mom's senior. Photos of him working as a military auto mechanic and enjoying the Summer Sun were much different from the images of the war zones shown in our history books.

When I studied the Vietnam War in school, it was not lost on me that serving in Germany probably saved my dad's life. He enlisted at seventeen, earned his high school equivalent and was trained as an auto mechanic.

We moved from army base to army base until I was eleven years old. Mom worked days and took classes at night. We were living in Texas when mom finished college and started teaching at an elementary school in Austin.

Dad left the army, and we grew up poor on a teacher's salary. Dad opened an auto repair shop that made no money. Because of my dad, Granna never helped mom financially.

Mom was always the smartest in her class, hard-working and eager to please. The patience and love she showed to everyone were truly unmatched. She continued her education and later earned her master's degree. Mom worked over twenty years in education, starting as a teacher and retiring as an Assistant Principal.

Settling in Austin brought us closer to Granna. Our car rides from Texas to Louisiana were a favorite part of my childhood.

Holidays, many long weekends, and summers were spent with grandparents and cousins.

No matter how much Granna despised my dad, he always made sure he kept his promise to mom to bring us to Louisiana for visits. We are practically Louisiana natives. Moving around so much with our parents didn't give us much time to develop an attachment to the culture of any other city we temporarily called home. Louisiana became our true home. If you add it all up, we spent more time during our childhood in Louisiana than anywhere else.

Our Louisiana home also provided a much-needed escape from our reality. Our parents' home was often shared with my dad's long-lost family, army buddies or what felt like whoever showed up in need—generous gesture for him, but not for his children who were forced to live with various questionable characters. Mom would eventually get his strays kicked out, but we never understood why he had no problem opening our home to whomever, whenever?

We both stare at the photos a little while longer and continue to dream of how things could have been, but "what if's" are such a waste of time. Aren't they? And, wanting to change the past is such a waste of energy. We, unfortunately, don't get a rewind.

"Lily, I thank God every day that you and your brother turned out so well," Granna says. "I wish your mom could have enjoyed this life we now have together."

"Here's another photo I've never seen," I say as I flip through our family photos Granna has saved. "When was this taken?"

"We were tailgating at a *Southern University* football game," she smiles. "You and your brother loved watching the marching band and the dancers. You look about twelve? You all were living in Austin by then."

Gramps was teaching at *Southern's* New Orleans campus, but they would take us to football games at the main campus in Baton Rouge whenever we were in town for the weekend. Mom would take us for visits whenever she had a long weekend. Getting away from our dad was probably her greatest motivating factor, and we loved any trip to Louisiana, no matter the reason.

"Mom looks happy," I notice. "We should have never left," I dreamt once again.

"She was happy," Granna agrees. "It's hard to explain. She had so much to feel sorry about, but she rarely complained."

"Well...I definitely didn't inherit that trait," I laugh. "I don't miss a chance to complain. If it's not right, I'll let you know with pleasure."

"Haha! I know who you are," Granna adds. "Don't say you get that from me."

"Granna, you know," I laugh. "I'm your mini-me."

The next morning, Anastasia summons me to her office to discuss an astonishing development as she described. I haven't been to her office in years. This invite has me intrigued, and it's my second surprise two days in a row. Is this a lucky sign?

Anastasia's office matches her personality—hot and spicy with warm, rich colors, eclectic artwork, and statement pieces strategically placed throughout. I now want an office remodel.

We sit at a small conference table in her office as she slides a bound report in my direction. As Anastasia and I sit staring at the pages and pages of documents and financial reports prepared by the investigator we hired to research assets involved in Granna's case, we both sit speechless for more minutes than either of us has probably sat quietly in years.

"Did you not know your grandmother is filthy rich?" Anastasia breaks the silence.

"I'm just as shocked as you, and I know you must think I'm ridiculous," I say, slowly measuring each word. "But I truly did not know. Granna has never disclosed any of this to me, and I'm sure not to any of us."

"Did you draft a will for your grandmother?" Anastasia asks. "You all don't use the same CPA firm?"

"Yes, we do," I say. "Her original CPA firm does her taxes and our corporate returns. I have never seen her personal returns. I've never thought to ask, and Granna has never offered. Well, I now see why."

"And, the Will?" Anastasia again questions.

"I know she has a Will, but she has only given us the name of her estate attorney," I reply. "She's used the same New Orleans firm since before I was born. She started with the father, then the son, and now the grandson. She considers them family and sends Christmas gifts to the entire family every year."

The need to complete an asset check was first squashed by me until Anastasia suggested it a second time after the first set of depositions. I was still on the fence but, in the end, requested it just to be safe. Safe! We're both amazing risk-taking litigators. I'm a granddaughter who proclaims to "help" my grandmother with her business affairs. Today, I see us as amateurs taken down by a shrewd centennial.

"Now, you finally know why she wanted you to stop poking around asking questions about her father's family." Anastasia continues. "Your grandmother owns most of St. Francis. She built a library for the Parish trade school and named it after Mrs. Ada-*Ada M. Lewis Library and Resource Center.*"

"I'm an idiot," I admit. "Wait until I tell Uncle and Luke. We could be as big as *Nabisco*."

"That's obviously why she hasn't told you all," Anastasia says. "She wants to spend her money her way."

"You sound just like her," I bark. "What's her way? We could have done so much more with the business. Now, we're being sued, and she still keeps quiet. Do you not see that she purchased the land her family sold? She owns the pecan farmland where she grew up. Why would she not tell us? Ryan obviously knows. Do you think Kate knows?"

"Well, she owns a lot more than that," Anastasia laughs. "She owns valuable New Orleans real estate and lots of high-dollar stock. I'm estimating your grandmother is worth around $50 million."

"Fifty...Unbelievable, this is why we're being sued," I say. "Granna now owns their family farmland. They certainly know that she owns everything except the rights to the original name and pecan products which they sold along with the estate deal."

"They most certainly know," she replies. "Most everything is owned by her trust, but it wasn't that hard for us to connect your grandmother to the trust. I'm sure their lawyer discovered this information before they agreed to file the lawsuit. This was never about pecans."

"So, Kate knows?" I again question.

"She probably does, but why would she ever imagine that you wouldn't know the same?" Anastasia adds. "I can't believe I'm defending Kate, but I don't think she was trying to pull anything over on you about your grandmother's wealth."

"Wealth?" I sigh. "Granna is wealthy."

"I'll let you sit with this for a while, but I already know how this will play out," she explains. "Your grandmother will tell you to mind your own business—'It's my money, my business and I'm a grown woman. You have no say in what I do.' Sound about right?"

"She's going to flip when she finds out I looked into her assets," I state. "If I'm in the Will, she may take me out. Why don't you talk to her?"

"No, ma'am!" Anastasia confirms. "You signed off on the asset check, and she's your grandmother. Your retainer is not big enough for this one. Muscle up and take a hit for the team."

As I gather the large pile of financial documents, my thoughts run from fear to regret, to humiliation, to betrayal. I had considered myself closer to no one more than my mother and my grandmother, and now I feel I don't know Granna at all. How is that even possible?

The courage I need to speak with Granna is currently nowhere to be found. I feel the wells of my eyes begin to fill as I hug Anastasia and head for the elevator. She says nothing and watches as the elevator doors close. I make it into my car before the hysterical sobbing begins. Next, I begin pounding the steering wheel while shouting…"WHY, Granna, Why???" Next, I admit jealousy. We have all worked hard for years to build comfortable lives. Granna could have opened the flood gates years ago. Why has she not?

I decide it's best to take my documents and tears to Noel. Speaking to Granna in any tone with a slight sense of disrespect would never be tolerated. I know better. I make the quick trip to her home and call Noel from my car. "Noel, sorry I'm outside, but let me in." Tears are still flowing.

"Come in," she says. "Don't be silly. You practically have a key. Don't you know the door code?"

She welcomes me with a concerned face and open arms. "Who did it?" Noel asks. "Is Adam ok?"

"Granna's rich, and she doesn't trust me," I blurt out. "Do you trust me? Am I a horrible person?"

"You're a crazy person, but so are we all," she laughs. "You know Granna is rich. What's the problem today?"

"She's fifty million dollars rich!" I voice between tears. Noel stares blank-faced and reaches out to hold my hand as we take a seat at her kitchen island with two bottles of wine.

"This is definitely a two-bottle conversation," she advises. "Start from the beginning."

"We're being sued because they obviously knew Granna has deep pockets," I say. "I couldn't imagine they'd spend so much money litigating for the rights to our pecan pie and pecan butter. I knew Granna was hiding something."

"I'm sorry Lily," Noel says as she pours our first glass. "Are you sure it's fifty million?"

"Here, look," I say as I give her the file of documents. "Luke and I grew up as latch key kids and had sugar sandwiches for our after-school snack. Our mom worked and went to college at night. She didn't have to work. We didn't have to eat sugar sandwiches. I knew Granna disapproved of mom marrying at eighteen and not going to college right away, but I was on the way. It was too late for her to do anything differently."

"Well, maybe she wasn't rich forty years ago," Noel tries to rationalize. "You need to calm down. Everything does not require a dramatic interpretation."

I down my first glass of wine while giving Noel my hurt puppy dog face. "I'm not dramatic—I'm just passionate," I respond in distress. "If I was sitting on millions and never told you, you would feel just as betrayed as I do."

"Yes, betrayed and also wondering why you haven't been taking us all on all-expense-paid luxury vacations," Noel laughs. "Poor little lost lamb. How will you go on?"

"Stop it," I demand. "This is serious. I am being sued because Granna is a secret multi-millionaire. She's like *Undercover Boss*"

"You are too silly," she says. "Just get it all out with me because your grandmother does not put up with your drama. She's in her nineties. Mess around, and she'll leave everything to Luke."

"He is her favorite," I agree. "As hard as I work for her, Luke will probably get everything." We both enjoy a good laugh and a second glass of wine. Noel makes pasta, and I have one of the fudge brownies she made yesterday. Her baking skills are not as good as Granna's, but her efforts are not wasted. Her pasta, on the other hand, is perfection.

Physically full after a good meal but mentally exhausted and not yet completely void of sorrow, I decide to go home and stay away from Granna's. Sleep and a clear mind are in order. I've played out in my head different versions of the conversation I must have with Granna, and so far, I haven't come up with a workable version. My current winning argument is Anastasia made me do it to help defend the lawsuit. That's basically true.

I try to stop viewing Granna's behavior as a personal attack against me. I do see how my perspective may be a little distorted. My head agrees, but my heart still aches.

CHAPTER ELEVEN
Lily

Acceptance is Wise

A blessing is once again provided when Uncle calls with instructions for me to go by Granna's and help her complete a recipe he needs — today. I don't mention the $50 Million. Speaking with Granna first seems safer.

Uncle promised one-hundred tarts for a wedding reception, and his recipe is missing Granna's secret touch. The samples he's made for the bakery have not favored well. I arrive at Granna's with documents in hand and a closed mouth.

"*L*ily, I need mom's changes to the Bourbon Pecan Tart now, not later," Uncle demands within ten minutes of my arrival. "What are you doing? If I don't get the update, we're going with what we have, and then we all look crazy."

"Granna's not finished," I say. "The first batch is in the oven, and she's mixing a different filling. Give us thirty minutes." Granna gives me a pop on my tush as she checks the oven.

"I'm not ready?" Granna objects. "Who? Not me. I didn't hear you mention that you were two hours late bringing the bourbon I needed. Ask if he's making his own *Phyllo Shells*? Store-bought ones cheapen my recipe."

I was late. I needed to stop at the wine shop and pick up more bourbon, stop by the office to drop off documents Finola requested, and pick up coffee. Overcommitting is a bad habit on my list of things I need to fix. I do "just one more thing" before moving on to the next crucial task.

Honestly, waiting causes anxiety. Rushing and being late also cause anxiety, but as I focus on completing the task at hand, the anxiety is muffled. Waiting anxiety is worse. That's why I avoid it. My goal is to arrive on time, never earlier. Sure, I'm usually late, but at least I didn't have to wait. I am ridiculous!

"Lily, check the oven." Granna instructs. "I'm sure they're ready. Set them on my cooling rack. Don't leave them on the pan. We can test them in ten minutes."

"Did you write down the changes, or should I just text them?" Granna gives me my third eye roll of the day. I know the answer to my question, but I like being an annoyance. Granna hasn't written anything down in decades. Luckily, I've gotten pretty good at dictating her words and documenting her steps.

"Roast pecans with a splash of bourbon and one cup of brown sugar over medium heat," she shouts. "He's not using enough bourbon. The flavor is burning off too quickly. He shouldn't have lost Nikki. She baked with me for years, and he obviously knows nothing. I may have to move back home."

Now I'm the one giving the eyerolls. Granna is too old to move, and she knows she's not trading this weather for humidity and hurricanes.

Within an hour, Granna has perfected the tart recipe. I send her changes to Uncle, and we all take a deep sigh of relief. I bravely ask if she has time to sit with me and enjoy her freshly baked tarts and a cup of tea. With tea in hand, she walks toward her back patio without saying a word. I leave the documents in the kitchen and only bring the platter of tarts.

"Granna, something has happened, and I'm not sure how to discuss this with you," I say.

"Discuss?" she questions. "Are you ill?"

"No, sorry," I continue. "Nothing like that. We're all fine. It's lawsuit stuff." Granna looks relieved and then disinterested in listening to me discuss the lawsuit.

"What is it, Lily?" she says. "And, don't ask me again about going to Detroit or St. Francis. I'm not interested in traveling, and I'm not sending you out to bother good, hardworking people for no good reason. Let this be. Nothing needs your help."

"Well... Not quite!" I object. We both pause with opposing looks of surprise. I immediately adjust my tone and let out a small cough in an attempt to mask my irritation.

"Warm my tea and bring the pot," she orders. "You seem to need attention, and I'll need more tea." I follow orders and return with Granna's tea as quickly as possible.

"I now understand why you are concerned about me asking family questions and why you would accuse me of spying on you." My voice must have risen a bit because she gives me a strong disapproving look. "Sorry, Granna."

"Lily, just get it out," she demands. "You don't have to tip toe around your words."

"I know about the library you named after Mrs. Ada; I know you now own your family farmland, and I know you have millions of dollars," I blurt out in one long string of confessions. "I don't know why you have kept all of this a secret. The other side obviously knows. That's why they are suing us."

"None of that is a secret," Granna proudly proclaims. "The people who need to know— know. Why do you think you need to know my every move? I'm your grandmother, not your husband… Not your child. You are my child. Do your children know what you do with your time and money? No, they don't."

"Not the same," I reply. "I didn't get them sued."

"I didn't get you sued! You are the reason we are being sued," she defends. "If you had just let things be, we'd be fine."

"I'm trying to grow the business for us all, but this entire time you knew I didn't need to try and make more money," I say. "You have made plenty of money."

"Yes, me—not you all," she adds. "You all need to work and make your own money. My money is my money. I have given you all plenty."

"What will Uncle think when he finds out?" I ask.

"He'll probably think the same as you," she admits.

Knowing Uncle also has no idea of Granna's fortune provides boorish comfort. I would have been unbearably broken if Uncle also knew, and they both were keeping this a secret from me.

"Uncle works hard at the bakery," I say. "He could hire more staff and travel."

"I gave him my house and part of my bakery," Granna replies. "Why should I give him more. He's a man. He needs to work. I've also paid for everyone's education and new cars at graduation. Did you think I was emptying my bank account on you all? I always say to everyone that's listening—I'm here to help more than just my spoiled children. Look at you—SPOILED!"

Granna is much less surprised and less bothered than I anticipated. She actually has a sneaky grin plastered across her face.

"Uncle needs to know because of the lawsuit," I explain. "Can we talk to him together?"

"Talk about what?" she asks with a laugh. "You snooping into my personal business."

"No, you being rich and being sued because you are worth millions," I explain. "They are after your money, not our pecan products."

"Let's call him now," she agrees. "You two can know all you want. I'm not going to change one thing."

"I didn't think you would—don't worry," I say. "I may want a new Mercedes, but I know you are not going to buy me one."

"You are right about that, my dear Lily," Granna grabs my hand to shake in agreement.

Uncle's last batch of tarts is baking, and because he's thankful for Granna's help, he doesn't complain when we tell him we need to have a family conference.

"Do you want to lecture me about my new pastry chef?" he asks. "I'll keep looking for more help."

"No," Granna interrupts. "Lily has news about the lawsuit and my money."

I begin to explain to Uncle why we looked into Granna's finances, and I hit the highlights of her investments and estimated worth. Uncle is surprised, but he doesn't seem offended. He begins to discuss with Granna that he knew she received money after Gramps died, but he never imagined that she would have been able to grow her money into tens of millions.

"I learned to hang around smart people, and I learned their tricks," Granna explains. "I made lots of good investments early on."

"Well, why didn't you teach us?" I complain.

"I teach you some, but you two are know-it-alls," she replies. "Learn to listen and pay attention. You're both still young. I can help you grow. Maybe I'll give you the list I share with my ladies."

"What ladies?" I ask, confused. "Are you talking about that secret Bible study group you meet with once a month—the one we are never invited to join?"

Granna hands me a report with the title *"Rich Nana's"* highlighted across the top of a document filled with stock tips and quarterly earnings reports. "Who put this together?" I question. "And, *Rich Nana's*? Is everyone rich? Why have I not been invited?"

"You know—no children allowed," Granna confirms. "I started this group in 2006. We work with a few different financial advisors. When I started, I had a few million. Today, I have more."

"Yes, ten times more," I announce. "I'm thinking you are meeting with church ladies having Bible study and talking about your grandkids. You are sharing stock tips and making investments. What is happening in this world?"

"My money has grown more than I ever imagined," Granna says with another huge grin. "Mostly because of the property I purchased in New Orleans and some from good stock buys. You all may get one million each and some stock. The rest is going to your mother's scholarship fund, the women's business grant program I'm starting with the church, and St. Francis. Grow your own money. I started with one dollar. Make me proud and do the same."

The news of Granna's wealth is still a bit raw, but I decide that doing a little more investigating of my own will help calm my discomfort. Finola finds a Federal Trial Court Practice CLE being held in New Orleans, and we quickly sign up. Our firm will pay for the trip, and while we are there—in my 'free' time, I will check out Granna's properties. I'll also do a little real work and check on Uncle at the bakery and visit the Federal Courthouse to look in on the judge assigned to our case.

After arriving in New Orleans the night before, we finish our first morning session and then take the afternoon off to run an errand for Granna. It's a beautiful day, and a long scenic drive will do us both a lot of good.

Fractured treetops covered with moss line most of the ride across the *Atchafalaya Basin Bridge*. Rushing to make it to the bright lights of the big city and to break free of the seething summer heat and humidity led me to take for granted the beauty of my family home.

"Thanks for riding with me to Lafayette," I say. "Granna loves these specific macarons in Lafayette. She often has them shipped, but she called the owner and asked her to make a special box for me to pick up."

"I'm loving it," Finola replies. "I've been to New Orleans many times for conferences, but I've always taken a flight into the city. I've never been outside of New Orleans."

"Well, that's good to know because I have a double motive," I laugh.

"When don't you?" Finola joins in. "Is this a spying trip? How far is St. Francis?"

"St. Francis is on my list, but not this trip," I say. "My hope is that this gesture will soften Granna's mood, and she'll stop accusing me of snooping. I'm just protective—truly."

"Yeah, ok," she smirks. "I'm thankful for the excursion and especially for the food!"

Finola is a true Midwest girl awed by the undeniable allure of the Louisiana landscape. I suppose I should understand her delight. I'm awed by the bright red, orange and yellow tree-lined streets and hills found in the Midwest during the Fall. The four seasons don't make traditional visits to Louisiana or to California.

Our drive from New Orleans to Lafayette turns into an unexpected memorable experience for us both. Finola's first outburst of amazed admiration happens as we travel across the *Bonnet Carre Spillway*. It took her a moment to realize we were traveling across a bridge surrounded by water as far as the eye could see.

"This is amazing—look," she instructs. "The water is such a beautiful shade of blue, and it goes on forever."

"Yes, it's over the spillway," I say with an "as if" tone. "Water flows from the *Mississippi River* to the *Gulf of Mexico*. It's supposed to help prevent flooding, but not always. This bridge is one of the largest in the world. We will actually drive over another bridge just as long before we make it to Lafayette."

"Why have you never showed me this?" she questions. "Louisiana is amazing."

Her second words of admiration come as we cross the *Mississippi River Bridge* in Baton Rouge.

"Wow— This bridge runs high," Finola proclaims. "Is it because of the ships? Look at the ships. Amazing."

This bridge is really not that high. I tell myself. The bridge leaving Lake Charles terrifies even me—Finola would probably pass out during that ride?

"That's the *Mississippi River*," I inform. "Look to the right, and you can see downtown Baton Rouge and the State Capital Building. Fun fact—for years, no building could be built taller than the State Capital. Isn't that crazy?"

As we cross the *Atchafalaya*, her next words of admiration spill out.

"Please open the sunroof," she demands. "This is so beautiful. Don't you want to just take it all in? I bet we can feel the breeze coming off the water?"

"The Bayou, you mean—what's beautiful?" I ask. Crossing the *Atchafalaya* between Baton Rouge and Lafayette has become an eyeopener for us both. I've, of course, crossed this bridge more times than I can honestly count, and never have I paused to take in its beauty.

"Is this a real bayou?" she asks.

I'm thinking—NOT to the sunroof and WHAT—to the "real bayou" question.

"There are hundreds of smelly trucks on this bridge," I reply as I open the sunroof. "Let me try to see what all the excitement is about."

"We are taking that Swamp Tour I saw," she announces. "Please tell me you've tried one?"

"No, ma'am—I have not," I say. "I spent my summers exploring the woods and swimming in rivers with my brother and cousins. I don't need to take a swamp tour. I've lived the swamp life."

"You're lucky," Finola discerns. "I see why your uncle refuses to move."

"Yes, Louisiana is one of a kind special," I agree. "We are lucky."

Finola's adoration inspires me to pause and to make more of an effort to take in the moment—just to look around and appreciate God's Work. There's pure beauty everywhere. Now is a good time to notice.

Arriving in Lafayette, Finola offers an equal amount of praise. The city is full of rich history and plenty of old town charm. We sit for a while outside the macaron shop and people watch while taking in the Sun.

The shop's euphoric aroma is a perfect blend of coffee and baked cookies. Granna's macaron order has been securely placed in a freeze pack, so we also order plenty of extra macarons to enjoy during our ride back to New Orleans. Each colorful flavor is delicately adorned with either strings of sugar or drizzles of caramel and chocolate—the most beautifully delicious box of goodies.

"Ok, we're crossing the same stuff on the ride back," I announce to Finola. "We could travel off the main highway, but that will take a lot longer. Have you had enough sightseeing for this trip? Maybe on our next trip, I'll let Uncle take you South of New Orleans. Now…That will really blow your mind."

"I'll be ready," she announces. "Louisiana is now my favorite State."

"Well…welcome to the family," I say. "You know that also means you are now a *Saints* Fan—no more of that "*Cowboys* are American's team stuff."

"Oh…well…you know I love me some *Cowboys!*" she laughs. "I can just be the crazy *Black Sheep* of the family."

Our hotel is on *Canal Street,* so we'll have a short walk to the bakery and the *French Quarter.* I've also decided that *French Quarter* shopping will be on our agenda. I "need" to buy a few more pieces of authentic New Orleans art. "I'm due for a splurge," I say out loud to myself.

"Our flight is not until tomorrow at 7:00 PM, so we can hang out tonight and stop by the bakery tomorrow," I say. "What do you have in mind? Shopping?"

"Let's catch some music," Finola says. "I know a great place."

"You do know the fun spots," I admit. "Maybe you'll get another celebrity selfie. It's amazing that you have met more celebrities in New Orleans than you have in L.A."

"I have been here a lot — conferences, meetings, any reason I can find especially if it's a business write-off," she adds. "Our last group of associates was much more fun and livelier than our current stuffy litigation group. You should have joined us last summer — never-mind, I know you are way too conservative for most of my shenanigans. Forget I said anything."

"Not politically," I joke. "Just socially. I used to get a little wild, but then I went to law school and started judging reckless behavior. Visiting State Prisons scared me straight."

"We don't go around committing felonies," Finola laughs. "I think you don't trust yourself. Letting down your guard frightens you, and after Daniel, you've pulled back even more."

"Don't!" I yell. "Don't say that I'm different because of what he did," I'm immediately disappointed in myself for the words I've just spoken. Why do I think such things? I know I've changed — we've all changed.

"You're ridiculous!" Finola snaps. "You need more therapy. When was your last session?"

"Aargh!" I growl. "I want this to be over. I don't want this to be my identity. I will never again allow myself to become so vulnerable."

"That's a horrible way to live," Finola admonishes me as she grabs my hands. "Trusting yourself and trusting the people who love you is never wrong. Being vulnerable and allowing people to love you is never wrong. You trusted Daniel—we all did. He is super smart, super handsome, and very charismatic. He is also evil, selfish, and an abuser. He used his power for evil. Don't allow his evil to dim your light. You are powerful beyond measure."

"Really, you're quoting *Marianne Williamson*." We both laugh at the reference. A poster of *"Our Deepest Fear"* graces the wall of our new managing partner. I think she put it up to frighten the remaining male partners and to remind them to walk a straight line.

"So… can we also enjoy a little weed?" Finola asks.

"Way too far! I have no desire to completely let my guard dogs have the night off," I inform. "One day, I may run for Senate or President or secure a Supreme Court Nomination. I don't need photos of me dancing on tabletops going viral."

"Yeah, you just might," she mocks. "I'll take you to a nice family-friendly jazz place."

Finola, of course, is correct about me and my fears—I am afraid to let loose. I let my guard down and allowed a fox to destroy the hen house I was in charge of managing. Letting loose in law school landed me in an inappropriate relationship with my civil law professor. Letting loose in college—I woke up the next morning on the couch of someone I barely knew. I drove my best friend home after a party, and she threw up on the floor of my brand-new car. I know too well how to let loose and enjoy myself. I now also know that I can only manage a one drink maximum. By drink two, losing my shirt is a high probability. I had enough excitement and mischief before I became an attorney, wife, and mother. Now, I just want to avoid excitement and save the world.

Our night out was calm and uneventful— just as I had hoped. I'm up early so that I can drive by Granna's properties without Finola. I don't need the extra judgment.

Granna has several rental units by the colleges, and all seem fully occupied. I could have probably negotiated better rental rates, but who's asking me? "No one," I say to no one.

I make it back to the hotel and grab a spot in the cafe minutes before Finola appears.

"I really enjoyed the nice quiet jazz place," I offer with plenty of sarcasm as I enjoy a warm croissant and cup of chicory coffee for breakfast. "And, you know I cannot stomach those hurricanes. You are nothing but trouble when you escape from home. What would your children think?"

"My children?" she asks with confusion. "I'm the mother. They need to impress me. I feed them. It's not the other way around."

"Ok, don't end up going viral. I've warned you," I say. "Cameras are everywhere."

"Make sure you mention paranoia during your next therapy session," she advises. "Too much education is not good for you—know less, think less, worry less. Please."

"We are here for a CLE," I remind. "Today's session is about human behavior and jury selection. I'm sure to discover many more reasons to be paranoid."

"Well, maybe you should skip it and go visit your uncle," she suggests. "Work in the bakery today and eat sugar. Geez, your family is in the bakery business. Why are you not more fun? Who works in a bakery and ends the day unhappy?"

"Law school—remember?" I laugh. "I barely worked in the bakery. I grew up in Texas with a schoolteacher mother and military father. I have issues."

"Let's have another croissant, and maybe we can figure out the meaning of life? Can you handle the truth—about life?"

We both enjoy a laugh as Finola gives her best *Nicholson* performance. I think every attorney has practiced the trial scene from *A Few Good Men* in their bathroom mirror.

"Come on, woman," I order. "You are just a quote a minute. Let me hear all about this truth you think you know."

After a morning of lectures, we are free to enjoy the afternoon before heading to the airport. Uncle packaged Finola a box of her favorite pecan clusters. She's such a charmer, and she makes best friends wherever we go. My Uncle has made sure Finola has a take-home box, and he gives me nothing.

"Now I can fly back to L.A. in peace," Finola states. "You are the best uncle ever. I'll take Lily's place—just say the word."

"They're stuck with me," I reply. "You have your own family."

"I've put together the financial documents you need to take back," Uncle says. "Nothing too out of the ordinary. They are really fishing for dirt that doesn't exist. I wish they would all just go away."

"We all agree," Finola confirms. "This is a money grab and a money drain. Both sides are wasting time and money fighting in court. At least you all get discounted legal services. The other side may go broke when they get their final legal bill."

"It's their own fault," I say. "This case should have never been filed. I've spoken to Anastasia about the settlement. Hopefully, they will go away and leave us alone."

"Wouldn't that be great?" Uncle agrees. "I also want my time back. Every time I have to look for a file or copy a document, I'm wasting my time and losing money."

"Soon!" I say. "This must end soon—for us all."

We have time for a quick meal at the creole soul food place next to the bakery. Granna is our only source of real Louisiana cuisine in Los Angeles, so one last good meal before leaving Louisiana cannot be missed.

"It's good to just sit for a minute and enjoy the river," Finola exclaims. "I pushed for us to take this trip and attend this CLE because we were both nearing the edge."

"I hate to complain because my ambition has once again caused trouble," I say. "It was my idea to go national, my idea to expand, my idea to pitch to big box stores, my idea to go on television."

"Was it also your idea to keep the world spinning on its axis." Finola laughs. "You must get yourself off the Pity Train."

"I really do try to let things go, but I check my to-do list and—then stress, guilt!" I add. "Stopping my mind at the end of the day is getting harder, but this trip helped. I forgot about my problems at least twice. That's something. Thank you very much!"

"I'll take it," she laughs. "Should we have the crab cake balls?"

"They're awesome—absolutely perfect," I say. "And, the coconut shrimp, let's order those…yummy, yummy, help me!"

We have two boxes of treats to carry-on: Granna's box of macarons and Finola's box of pecan clusters. TSA rules list foods as permitted carry-on items, but they have the right of refusal. We should not have a problem unless a hungry agent decides that our treats look threatening. I'm sure many try to bring home a little bit of Louisiana's best. I just hope our boxes will fit in the overhead.

"We get in late," Finola reminds. "Did you clear your weekend, or do you have teenage stuff?"

"I think I'm good, but I've been forgetting to add stuff to my calendar," I laugh. "Seeing a mark on each day of my calendar was too much-added stress."

"Once again—the world knows how to spin on its axis," she says. "Take a break. I'm ordering you to nap and not read any papers. Try to enjoy your weekend. Stay in your PJs all day and eat ice cream."

"Adam threw away my ice cream—he's a jerk!" I proclaim. "Remember he's on a no added sugar kick," I hear Finola's advice, and I would love to relax the entire weekend, but even the thought of such an extravagant gesture frightens me. I have a long list of worries to examine.

"Oh, my," she adds sarcastically "Your life is really hard. You're an educated, experienced attorney. Find a hiding place and buy more ice cream. If he finds your stash, threaten him. No one will blame you if you tell them he keeps throwing away your ice cream."

We both nod in agreement because her assessment is true.

Our flight is not crowded, and our treats fit perfectly overhead. Our bellies are full, and our minds need a break— we both enjoy a good long nap.

"*I* have a thought," Finola says as we leave the airport. "Ice cream, sugar, carbs—they get such a bad rap. It's now better to eat bacon and red meat. How is that possible?"

Finola is not in the mood to follow Adam's rules, so we stop for ice cream on our way home and don't check the label for added sugar content. Life is Good.

CHAPTER TWELVE
Lily

Too much information should not be a bad thing?

"*I*'m home family—if anyone cares," I shout. "Nothing? Are you all pretending to be asleep?"

"We're here mom," Josh yells from his favorite spot in front of the den television. "Dad's already asleep. He only made it ten minutes before the snoring started."

"Let him sleep," I say. "I brought you ice cream, and he doesn't get any. Where's your sister?"

"Dad let her sleep over Aunt Noel's," he says. "They have some kinda all-day theater thing tomorrow, and Aunt Noel said you need the day off because you are yelling at people again. Is it true?" Noel and Grant have obviously been talking to Adam.

"I think so—there may have been some yelling?" I reply. "It's been a rough few weeks. That's why we need ice cream."

As the papers in my bag begin calling me, I do my best to ignore them. I know that I should resist. I'm curious to see what Uncle put together and allow my legal wheels to turn, but my brain is tired.

"Done!" Josh says as he swallows his last spoon of ice cream. Adam continues to snore across from us as we finish the movie he and Josh had been watching.

"Let's take a ride to Granna's to deliver her macarons," I offer. We may need to wake her, but this way, I really can sleep in tomorrow. I know she'll call bright and early in search of her delivery.

"Let me drive," Josh requests. "I can do it."

"Ok, but you must listen and pay attention," I instruct. "If you question me, you're out of the driver's seat."

"Deal!" Josh agrees as he runs full speed for the garage.

"Let's take your dad's car," I say. "He's asleep. We'll be back before he wakes up."

Josh is actually a pretty good driver for his age. Adam taught them both when Lydia received her permit. I must really be tired to have agreed to let Josh drive me around at night.

"Did you bring Granna's key?" Josh asks. "You know she's not getting up to answer the door. Call her first. You know about her gun?"

"Did she let you handle her gun again?" I question. "I told her no. Does anyone listen to me?"

"Don't fuss at her tonight, please," he says. "No yelling. And, please stop with the questions. I'm trying to concentrate." I let Josh concentrate, and we both focus on the road.

Granna's home sparkles like Christmas all year round. Surrounding homes are equally adorned. We let ourselves in, and Granna immediately calls out to us.

She's tucked in for the night with a book of her favorite poetry opened in one hand. "My macarons, please," she pauses before continuing her reading. Her voice warms the room, and Josh cannot resist cuddling up next to her. Granna reaches out for us both and plants gentle kisses on our foreheads. Impromptu poetry reading with macarons and love are all family favorites. Life is really good.

Josh and I have now had ice cream and macarons. I'm having a sugar meltdown, and Josh is having a sugar rush. He insists on driving, and I'm too depleted to protest. We say our goodnights and begin our journey home.

I struggle to keep my eyes open and try to count the blocks we are away from our home. Suddenly, there's a *thump, clump, plop...* and I'm shaken by Josh's screams. I'm unsure whether or not I am dreaming. I couldn't have fallen asleep that quickly, but now my eyes are wide open.

"Mom, I tried to miss it," Josh proclaims. "Somebody left something in the road."

That something was a broken tree branch that hit the tire perfectly. We have a flat— in Adam's car. I hope he's still sleeping.

"You picked Dad's car," Josh reminds.

"Fine, blame me," I say. "I'm innocent. I was sleeping."

"That makes it worse," he replies. "You're supposed to be watching me."

I call roadside assistance, and we wait. This could be a teachable moment for us both, but I'm in no condition to try and teach my son how to change a flat car tire.

"When we make it home, let's go in quietly and avoid your dad," I say. "We'll keep quiet for now. I really do want to have a restful Saturday."

"Sure, mom!" Josh acknowledges. "I'm not saying a word. He'll try and take my phone because of you. We should have taken your car."

"No, we shouldn't have," I laugh. "My car is new. I don't need teenage driver damage to my vehicle. I just need to order your dad another spare and we're good. I'll take care of that Monday."

"Good plan," he says. "Let's hope he doesn't get another flat tire before Monday."

"Why would you say such a thing?" I complain. "You know I worry. Now I'll have to check on it tomorrow."

"Just tell him to drive your car," Josh suggests. "Don't you need a detail or something?"

"Son, you're a genius just like your mother," I announce. "My Saturday in PJs is back on!"

Monday arrives and I spend it at the bakery. Tomorrow is a law office day that I will use to take a flight to Detroit. Discovering more about Granna's family should help to fill in more of the missing pieces we need to win this stupid lawsuit. No one will notice I'm gone—I'm certain.

Michigan in late spring, after the days with snow has ended, can be just as alluring as a West Coast Day. The sky shares a familiar shade of turquoise blue, and the air is crisp in the morning and mild in the evening.

Detroit offers a complex mosaic formed from the shells of once-thriving middle-class neighborhoods. Tudor and Dutch home designs with tree-lined sidewalks created communities where, even after White Flight, Black Americans thrived. The automotive factory jobs eventually dwindled, and many families left soon thereafter, but the giant factory conveyor systems and manufacturing framework still remain. The abandoned systems loom over parts of the city like dinosaurs escaped from a museum.

The SUV I rented has a sunroof with a panoramic view. I love sitting up high and taking in the view. I don't understand the appeal of cramped sports cars. Driving a car feels like sitting on the ground and moving in slow motion.

Granna's biological father had five brothers. Four lived with him in the Detroit area. All have long passed away, but I did my research and found plenty of nieces and nephews. Gail Lewis, the daughter of Franklin's oldest brother, was born in St. Francis, and she remembers the farm.

This trip may be a complete waste of time, but I have a gut feeling that won't go away. If Mrs. Ada's family knows anything about the Cormier farm, I need to know. Anything will help at this point. Our newly found family is out for blood, and I'm in search of an ally.

I turn onto a long tree lined street with about six well-kept homes and more vacant lots. I park along the street in front of Ms. Gail's home. During our call, she asked that I stop calling her Ms.

Lewis. "Thanks for having me, Ms. Gail. I'm Lily— we spoke on the telephone," I remind. "My grandmother is Lilah Cormier from St. Francis. I called about stopping by today?"

"Yes, come in," she gestures. "You look a lot like your grandmother. It was all the talk when she married Black."

"I've learned," I say. "All these years, I never questioned why I didn't know much about my grandmother's family."

"Well, your grandmother is hard to forget," she explains. "She was the Cormier's favorite child—always doing something in the town and at school."

"Favorite? Why do you say that?"

"She was the cute one and super smart," Ms. Gail says. "She was always getting an award for something. Her going away to college was the talk, and then she married and never returned. She was many years older than me, but I remember her. My daddy worked on their pecan farm. Your grandmother was always hanging around and talking to us friendly."

"Thanks, Ms. Gail; I appreciate you talking to me," I say. "Do you remember that your grandmother, Mrs. Ada, also worked for the Cormier's?"

"Why are you thanking me?" she questions. "I'm happy to tell you all about St. Francis and Ma'Dear—my grandmother, Ada Mae. She kept a close eye on the Cormier girls. She didn't want none of her people getting any ideas. Back then, slipping up with the wrong girl led to your death. That's why so many of us moved to Detroit. The jobs were better here, and leaving the South saved my daddy and his brothers."

"Saved them—how?" I question.

"Two brothers left St. Francis early on," she says. "One of them got caught with the wrong girl, and all anyone knew was that it was one of those boys kin to Ma'Dear."

"I'm sorry," I express.

"Why are you sorry?' she adds. "They shouldn't have been ignorant. Plenty of girls in St. Francis tried to get with the boys in our family. Ma'Dear was mixed with something. The men in our family were all handsome. My daddy and the next oldest were married, so they left them alone. Most of us soon followed and left St. Francis. Now, here we all are—living up North."

"When did you leave St. Francis?" I ask, trying to discreetly understand how she and Granna are related. It doesn't appear from our talks that she knows Granna is Franklin's daughter. No one in this family seems to know, and I'm not the one to deliver this news over ninety years later.

"My daddy let me move here after high school. I stayed with the middle brother and his wife. I helped with the kids and went to Beauty College. I was the best hairdresser in Detroit until my hands started acting up."

"I'm sure you know your stuff," I offer with a soft approving smile.

"Yes, I do," she admits. "Stop putting so much heat on your hair. It'll curl up naturally."

"Thanks, I'll try," I say.

"Ms. Gail, did your family continue to visit St. Francis often or talk about your life there?"

"What's to talk about?" she responds. "We knew everyone left for a better life. No other questions were needed. It's not like today. You all ask questions, get in the streets and protest—

during my day, we kept quiet more than we should have. Things changed in the Sixties, but by then, we had all left the South."

"Ms. Gail, you mentioned having papers you'd like to show me?" I ask, hoping she will have something to help support our case. She hands me a file folder with two large envelopes. One has tax records, and the other photo identifications and stacks of family photos. "Thanks for letting me take a look at your family photos and documents."

"It's just paperwork we kept of daddy's—nothing special," she explains. "This is the only file I found with his name. Your family may be in one of those photos? I'm not sure, but this is what the farm looked like back in the day."

She hands me a photo with a familiar shot of the barn.

"Which one is your dad?" I ask. "Are these his brothers?" I hand her a photo of three young men standing next to a lady I'm hoping is Mrs. Ada.

"Yes, my daddy, his brothers, and this is Ma'Dear." Ms. Gail returns the photo to me. "You know Ma'Dear pretty much ran that farm. All our family worked there at one time or another. After Ma'Dear passed, the farm went down. The family started moving away— some to Chicago, but most right here to Detroit."

"This is your father, and who are the other two?" I hold the photo with one outstretched hand and circle the faces in the photo with my other hand.

"My daddy's brothers—Franklin and Joseph," she replies.

I try to contain my excitement when it's confirmed that I am holding a photo of my great-grandfather. I think of Granna and whether or not she'll be happy to see her father's photo?

"Ms. Gail, I would love to copy the photos if you don't mind?" I ask. "I'll take you with me, and we can have dinner — anywhere you want. I'll treat."

"Can we bring my great-grandbaby?" she asks with a smile. "She'll be home on the bus in ten minutes."

"Of course," I offer. "How old is she? She won't mind hanging out with us?"

"She's ten." Ms. Gail says. "Going out to eat will make her little day."

I gather the photos I'd like to copy and return everything else to the folder. The photos were the only items from St. Francis. She had lots of old personal employment identifications and paperwork but nothing about the farm.

"Now, Ms. Lily?" Ms. Gail reaches out for an embrace. "Are you going to tell me which one of my no-good family members is your father? I know you didn't come to Detroit to ask about a farm that shut down years ago. Which one is it?"

"Ms. Gail, no!" I respond with a slight chuckle. "I know both my parents. That's not why I'm here — really. But l will say that the rumors about Mrs. Ada's boys hooking up with the wrong girls are definitely true, but I'm sure most of your family already knows that rumor?"

"Rumors, truth, proof…have you done one of those DNA test things?" she asks. "I had to stop my kids from signing up. Too many side children, aunts, uncles, and cousins started popping up all over the place. It's ridiculous. Too bad no one's rich. The one dollar we all have won't help a soul."

Ms. Gail's great-granddaughter, Joelle, arrives, and she is just as excited about dinner as Ms. Gail predicted. Joelle is the perfect ten-year-old— energetic, confident, and curious. She is polite and respectful but full of intelligent and confident questions. I told her more about me in five minutes than Ms. Gail, and I had discussed in over one hour.

"I want to go to *Disneyland* one day," Joelle announces. "Have you been?"

"Many times," I reply. "I'm pretty much an expert. When you make it to California, I'll be more than happy to be your personal tour guide. I know all the tricks to get in as many good rides as possible. Do you like rollercoasters?"

"I think so, but I've never been on a really big one like the kind at *Disneyland*," she says.

We decided to have dinner at a nearby *Main Lobster*. It was the one restaurant we all agreed upon. I haven't had their buttered lobster tails in ages, and my dinner dates also felt in the mood for warm biscuits. I ask about famous restaurants in Detroit, but they weren't interested, so *Main Lobster* wins.

Ms. Gail taking care of her great-grandchild after school wasn't something I gave a second thought, but Joelle made sure I knew the full story. Joelle's exuberance is refreshing. I miss having similar conversations with my two. Teenagers definitely use fewer words.

"My dad's in jail," Joelle announces. "He killed my mother when I was three—Domestic Violence situation. My other grandmother is not stable. Grammy is the only responsible person in our family. I hope she's around until I finish high school."

"Why is that something you just blurt out to a complete stranger?" Ms. Gail scolds. "Do you tell this to everyone you meet?"

"Depends?" she states. "I like her, and I also want her to know that if we're coming to California, she has to help. We're living on Social Security."

"That's enough," Ms. Gail orders. "No more talking until I have something to eat."

Our dinner is pleasant. Joelle entertains and never lets a silent moment linger too long. I haven't yet asked Ms. Gail about Mrs. Ada's baking. The dessert menu provides the perfect opportunity for me to inquire about her family's baking traditions.

"My grandmother has a bakery business—I think I mentioned?" I say while we all review the menu.

"You may have?" Ms. Gail responds. "What looks good on the menu to you?"

"My favorite is her pecan tarts," I add. "She makes pecan pies, pecan butter, pecan bits, and pecan croissants. Those are her most popular."

"Pecan butter?" she questions. "I haven't had that stuff since I left Louisiana. You'll have to send me some. I bet it's good."

"It is good," I say. "My kids love it. I will send you some."

"So, your family is still in the pecan business?" she asks.

"Kind of," I respond. "We have a bakery in New Orleans that specializes in all kinds of pecan goodies. We don't have a pecan farm— we buy from different farms in Louisiana and Georgia."

"That's nice," she says. "I was the only business owner in this family. Everyone else worked for Ford or GM."

"I think I'll have the brownie with ice cream?" I reply. "It has nuts. What about you both?"

Joelle announces her selection—the ice cream trio. Ms. Gail orders cheesecake.

"I wish I knew how to make Louisiana food?" Ms. Gail remarks. "I moved away before I learned how to cook."

"Really, what about your parents and grandmother?" I ask.

"My mama passed before I left Louisiana," she explains. "My daddy, uncles, and plenty of other family was already here."

"Sorry, you've had a lot of loss in your family," I say. "Life gets lonely without our loved ones."

"I'm eighty-eight," she announces. "When you're around as long as I am, you have to learn to keep moving. It's hard, but death comes for us all. Don't waste your living mourning too much. Your time will come soon enough."

"You see," Joelle exclaims. "I told her we need a Will. I've been thinking of who I can live with next, and the rest of our family is not looking good. My friend Olivia's mom said I can live with them whenever I need, but I should stop worrying about that right now and focus on the fifth grade."

"I think that's excellent advice," I say. "You know I'm an attorney. I can help with the Will, and if you ever need my services, just call. Everyone from St. Francs is in some way related. I'm certain we are long-lost family." I know we are long-lost family, and I'm also certain Ms. Gail knows the same. Granna's father and Ms. Gail's father are brothers. That makes them first cousins. I think that makes Joelle my fifth cousin. I think?

"I've enjoyed meeting you," Ms. Gail says. "I hope you find what you are looking for even though I'm not sure exactly what it is?"

"We're being sued by the Cormier family," I finally admit. They are accusing my grandmother of stealing their ideas and recipes."

"What Cormier family?" she questions. "Your grandmother is a Cormier."

"Yes, but her sister—Rosemary's children inherited the Pecan Farm and everything along with it. My grandmother was given half of the money when the farm was sold, but her sister held on to the rights to make and sell their pecan products."

"Pecan pies are made every day, and anyone can make one if they tried," she adds. "We used to have all kinds of pecans and other stuff around the house when someone brought leftovers home from the farm, but we never baked much. We sometimes used the pecans to make pies, and we ate plenty right out the bag."

"That's what I may need to prove?" I explain. "Anyone can make a pecan pie, and the way my grandmother makes her baked goods are unique to her and not a company secret she's stolen."

"What did your grandmother tell you about coming up here to ask about Ma'Dear?" she asks. "You think Ma'Dear taught her how to bake? If she did, she didn't teach any of us anything other than pie baking. We never made any of that special stuff you are talking about."

"She told me not to bother you all," I say. "Mrs. Ada was very important to my grandmother. I'm sure you can understand why?"

"I have an idea," she asserts. "Maybe we'll come out to California, and I'll get to visit your grandmother?"

Joelle lights up at the mention of the idea. Her excitement makes us all want to bring the idea to reality.

"When school is out for the summer, I can make it happen," I offer. "We would be honored to have you both visit, and I want you to bring Olivia if it's ok with her mom. You'll need a ride buddy for all the roller coasters."

CHAPTER THIRTEEN
Lily

Knowing the Truth does not make it Real

"*T*rust More— Worry Less!" I repeat these words of prayer on a loop during my morning drive to the office. The other side wants to depose our staff, but our staff having to spend their day sitting in a law office is not going over well.

Depositions have been requested for basically everyone— even our office professional. He answers the telephone, takes customer orders, and orders supplies. He's probably never picked up a mixing spoon in his life.

After our fifty-million-dollar reveal, Anastasia decided it was best for her to travel to New Orleans for Uncle and his staff's depositions. No big reveals were made by either side. Granna and Kate's mom have both been allowed to submit answers to written deposition questions. Hopefully, our staff will be the last round of depositions.

We have a 10:00 AM start time, so we were able to go into the bakery this morning and at least complete our daily prep work. Ms. Julia is up first this morning, and then her two baking assistants, along with our admin, Nathan, in the afternoon.

Anastasia gives each her standard procedural review and pep talk, and we all get ready for another long day.

"Ms. Walker," their lawyer announces as he begins his interrogation of Ms. Julia. She doesn't try to hide her displeasure, and her attempts to escape his inquiry are comical and impossible for any of us to ignore.

"How many more questions?" Ms. Julia asks. She has only answered about four questions of the twenty he will most likely ask.

"I just have a few more important questions," he announces. "Is it ok if I keep you another hour or so?"

"An hour longer?" she objects. "What could I possibly talk about for that long?"

"Let's talk about the recipes you were given," he says. "Do you and your staff use printed recipes?"

"We have them, but Mrs. Marchand and I baked together in the beginning, and I learned by sight," she answers. "The staff follows my lead. They know a lot of stuff by memory, but we all switch things up a lot."

"Are recipes kept in a binder or stored electronically?" he questions.

"We all have *iPads* we use to keep track of our baking schedule and ingredient lists," she responds.

"Is your answer 'yes,' you use printed recipes whether essentially printed on paper or electronically captured?" he asks.

"Sometimes—yes," she replies. "Most times, we use our brains. When you do something every day, you don't need a reminder of what goes next."

"Are you aware whether or not recipes are stored in a secure area like a vault or locked in a safe?" He continues.

"No, never," Ms. Julia answers. "Why would we do that?"

"Great, I understand," their lawyer says.

"Recipes are saved on the computer," she adds. "If there are printed copies, I don't keep track of them. I send changes to Mrs. Marchand and the staff via email."

"Thank you," he says. "Let me ask you a few questions about the pecan pies, and then I'm done. Are you the person who makes pies for the bakery?"

"No, none of us in L.A.," she confirms. "The pecan pies and pecan butter are made and shipped out of the New Orleans location."

"Have you ever visited the New Orleans location?" he questions.

"Yes, I've been," she says. "I have been out to train with their staff."

"Did you observe their baking processes?" he asks.

"I saw the equipment and the packaging they use for the gift baskets, but that's it," she responds. "I don't know anything about how the machines work or anything about the ingredients."

"Ms. Walker, how long have you known Mrs. Marchand?"

After a long stare and head rocking, she blurts out, "fifteen years or so?"

"Has she ever given you a handwritten recipe or a notebook of recipes?" he continues.

"In fifteen years, I'm sure. We write stuff out all the time. We write recipes. We speak them out while baking. We pull them out of the air. We're bakers. That's what we do," she answers.

"Do you recall how many recipes that may have been?" he says.

"In fifteen years, no. Like I said, we bake using lots of recipes, and most are made up as we go and not written down." Ms. Julia repeats.

"Thanks for that," he replies. "One last question. The pecans you use each day, how are they delivered."

Anastasia and I give each other a confused look. We are not sure why he would ask such a question. Why would our pecan supply matter?

"We receive mostly shelled pecans, but sometimes they come in cracked shells," Ms. Julia responds. "We like to have both on hand and use different ones for different recipes."

"Well… that's all I have for you," he concludes. "Thank you again for your patience."

Their lawyer keeps his promise, and Ms. Julia is released within the hour. The other three are in and out by 4:00 PM. As with our other depositions, no one offered differing information, and nothing spoken was harmful to our case. Anastasia gives us all a thumbs up, and everyone except me is out the door without pause.

"We need to review your grandmother's deposition responses," Anastasia directs. "Tell me about the name changes."

"Yes, *Much Ado about Pecans World Famous Pecan Pie* has been our best seller for over a decade," I admit. "Granna's pecan butter also sells very well and is sold out as soon as it's put on the self. When *Marchand's* was open, it was called *Marchand's Famous Pecan Butter*. We've kept an eye on our competition, but no other pecan butter brand ever gave us reason to pause. Our pecan butter was a local favorite, and we were more than satisfied with that success. Pecan pies is obviously a more competitive market."

"Ok, when the farm was sold, the rights to *Cormier Farms* pecan pie and pecan butter recipe was sold separately to *Cajun Made Foods*?" Anastasia asks. "They still sell it locally in grocery stores—mostly in North Louisiana, Monroe, and the Shreveport area."

"Granna agreed that her sister and her sister's husband took care of the sale," I add. "Their lawyer sent paperwork for her to sign, and she did. A week later, she received a check in the mail."

"Your grandmother is a shrewd businesswoman," Anastasia continues. "Did you ask why she didn't involve herself more with the sale?"

"She had her attorney—the same firm who currently handles her estate, review the paperwork," I inform. "I think she felt guilty about abandoning her family."

"Well…she did an amazing job multiplying her fortune," Anastasia remarks.

"Granna's sister and her family had moved to Lafayette," I continue. "Her husband was some kind of plant operator."

"The money paid for the house and farm was split 50/50," Anastasia reads. "It doesn't look like your grandmother was included in the sale of the rights to pecan products."

"That is a question we need answered, but who knows the answer?" I contemplate. "Kate's mother's memory has faded. The sale documents don't show much. Do you think *Cajun Made Foods* may willingly answer? Should we subpoena them or send one of your Louisiana guys for an office visit?"

"Definitely start with a Louisiana guy," she replies. "Let me see if we have anyone that grew up in North Louisiana. A local may get more info."

"Granna said her sister made sure she received half for the sale," I answer. "Her sister knew that's what their parents would have wanted. Maybe because the pecan product deal was a separate royalty, she didn't think it would amount to much?"

"Discovery is pretty much done!" Anastasia confirms. "I don't see that they have anything to support their claims. Our Motion for Summary Judgment is almost ready. If they have anything we are missing, they need to reveal their cards or fold. Do you think they will try to discuss settlement?"

"We need this over," I say. "Granna owes them nothing. I don't think she would agree to give them anything—she shouldn't. Let's file the motion and see what counter they provide. I also see nothing."

"When is your trip to St. Francis?" she asks.

"Next week," I say. "I've invited Granna, but so far, she refuses to travel. I'm meeting Kate in New Orleans. She's driving and showing me around. I promise not to talk about the case."

"Why are you going with Kate?" Anastasia asks, annoyed. "How did this collaboration come about?"

"She asked about my next trip, and it came up," I admit. "I told her the trip was market research for our commercial rollout."

"You're really keeping me on my toes with this case," she laughs. "No talking about the case. We'll work on our summary judgment motion when you return."

"Yes, I promise," I say with conviction. "Don't worry."

"*I*'m rolling out all the dough today," Ms. Julia blurts out as she walks in and grabs her apron. After we all endured yesterday's depositions, no one questioned her bad mood. We're all a bit more sluggish this morning. The kitchen has a normal stream of classical tunes playing, but *Beyonce's Freedom or Bruno Mars's Uptown Funk* are pipped in if we need a quick pick-me-up. I switch over to our Dance it Out playlist, and everyone takes five to join in and let loose.

"Okay, now I'm better," Ms. Julia announces. "Coffee and cardio have my blood flowing."

"Whew, yes, we all needed that," I say. "I really appreciate you all supporting our company and each other. I hope you all also know how much you each mean to Granna."

"I said we were better—stop trying to make things all mushy," Ms. Julia insists. "We have too much work to catch up. Someone come over here and help me with this dough."

We are behind on our weekly orders because we spent yesterday answering deposition questions. Today is our pecan cluster day. We package them in six-ounce resealable bags. Our frozen pastries and frozen yeast rolls go out in orders of twenty-five units each per store. We currently supply 30 stores. Our goal is two hundred units per day. We are behind, which may mean late nights—*Heaven* forbid.

"I don't smell another pot of fresh coffee!" Ms. Julia drops her rolling pin and makes it to the coffee system before anyone else registers the request. "I made the first pot this morning. What are the rest of you all doing?"

Nathan keeps our daily coffee supply fresh, but he's out sick—sick of depositions. It's an unwritten rule that when Nathan is out, whoever arrives first makes the coffee for the day. No one fesses up, so Ms. Julia covers the task, but we all know that before we leave for the day, she'll have more words to share about her covering coffee duty.

My apron is on, and I'm moving products in and out of the ovens as quickly as possible. Cooling takes about an hour, and then we pack. We hit one hundred units by Noon and take a break for lunch. One hundred more to go. We should make our today's 4:00 PM pickup schedule.

Back at the bakery for a second day in a row, and it still doesn't feel like another workday. Days here feel like a cheat day. The smell of baking bread provides an unmatched comforting aroma. Maybe I work here just for the smells? Also, sharing space with others who work in a space surrounded by joy has helped me maintain the same level of joy when I return to the law firm. If Granna had not taught me to bake, I might never have experienced the reality of working in a place where everyone does work they love.

Practicing law has been a dream since childhood because I talked a lot and never walked away from an argument. I loved to read and could easily retain huge amounts of information. Law School was a good fit for my talents. The practice of law is an enjoyable challenge, but the office and courts are filled with people who hate it all. I still don't hate it. I'm grateful for the opportunity to help those in need. Gratitude is fulfilling, but Joy is power.

Our shipments for the week are back on track. Joy of work increases productivity. The rest of the day is spent experimenting with new recipes—another one of my favorite times to work at the bakery! The staff is working on a tart with key lime filling.

"How's the filling?" I grab a spoonful, give it a try and let out a big YUM as Ms. Julia smiles in agreement. They rarely miss the mark and often create winning recipes. Key lime tarts will be perfect for a summer rollout.

"How's tomorrow's dough coming along?" I ask, but somehow Ms. Julia immediately knows that I need something. While the staff was experimenting, I decided to give our marketing materials another look.

"I'm done," she answers. "What do you need?"

"I'm trying to pick new packaging designs, and I'm down to ten photos and four fonts—way too many," I say. "Please Help! I'm trying to come up with a change just in case we need to after the lawsuit is concluded."

I've tried over one-hundred variations. I know perfection is not a real thing but attempts to achieve the nearly impossible is a challenge I often seek. Thoughts of shoppers walking by our pastries on shelves and stopping to gaze at the intriguing photos on the packaging or the inspiring wording and vibrant coloring are images that run on a loop in my daydreams.

"Let's see," Ms. Julia motions as she grabs her next set of ingredients. "You need help with your picture boards? You've been at that desk staring at the same stuff for weeks. Maybe if you eat something, your brain will work better."

Ms. Julia always tells me I need to eat. I'm fit— not skinny by any definition, and I don't look like I need an extra pound. If she saw my late-night snacking, she would understand why I'm never hungry during the day.

"I'm trying that intermittent fasting," I inform Ms. Julia. "It's supposed to help with cellular health, digestion, and weight loss— maybe? You do realize we work in a bakery— too many temptations to sit around and eat all day. And, I'm too short to carry extra weight. Just please come and look at what I've done with our new marketing stuff and give me your honest thoughts."

Picking my favorite photo is turning into torture. Asking for help is also torture. What if she picks a picture I don't like—then what? Can I narrow it down to my three favorites then I will be happy no matter which one is chosen? Maybe I can narrow it down to five?

Granna with a basket of pecans under a huge oak tree is my favorite, but her on the front porch in a rocking chair is enchanting. The shots of the farm and factory are good too,

Arrgh...okay, I'll trust Ms. Julia. She seems to be giving each photo a good look, and the look she just gave me is her standard— "Stop overthinking and make a decision" command.

"You know my thoughts are nothing but honest," she replies. "The one with the basket of pecans is the best." Ms. Julia picks up the photo and hands it to me after taking less than ten seconds to scan the other photos.

"That one is perfect," I agree. "What about this store endcap design? Which one should I use for the main backdrop?"

"Pecan Trees and the barn," she says while sorting through the photos to find the best one. "Here, this one. You can see the pecans on the tress and all over the ground. The barn showing in the background highlights everything you need."

"This one is perfect," I again agree. "I love the hint of light covering the yard. It will add authenticity to the print."

I imagine Granna as a young girl sitting under a tree, her mind filled with a sense of wonder, igniting her desire to see what existed beyond her small Louisiana town. I imagine her admiring the majesty of the trees reaching upwards towards the clouds inspiring her to believe that she also could achieve such heights.

"These pictures will give the packaging a sense of home," Ms. Julia offers.

"Thank you so much," I say. "Why didn't you come in here last week and help me sooner?"

"I have my own work to do," she laughs. "Come out here and help me fold the croissants."

"Nope, can't get flour all over the photos," I laugh. "Catch me next time."

"That's exactly why I should have let you suffer," she jokes. "Let me call and tell Mrs. M you are not helping."

We all do our best to make Granna proud and to keep her happy. Growing our business and winning this lawsuit are equally urgent. If I screw things up, I will have to change my name and relocate.

*P*ackaging pecan clusters for grocery store shelves was an idea sent to me as a gift from above. Our Houston bakery was not a complete waste of time and money because it's there that I connected with a *Big Box Store Buyer*, Whitney Chambers.

"More locations are a way to go but getting your products on store shelves is often a better growth model," Whitney advised during our first meeting.

She was a recent New Orleans transplant living in Houston and was familiar with Granna's bakery. Whitney had visited both the original bakery and French Market location. She worked as a retail big-box store buyer and encouraged me to pitch our products. Selling in stores was a wild idea, I thought, but as I learned more about the process, I grew more eager to commit.

"I'll introduce you to a great sub-packer in Louisiana," Whitney offered. "You will probably also need an industrial kitchen," she instructed while jotting down the first major to-do's I would need to complete.

"How will I ever thank you?" I asked. "This is really something I never considered."

"It's an extension of my job and my pleasure," she replied. "I get paid to help businesses grow. Retail customers expect us to have a unique variety of products. They come shopping at our stores looking for new brands."

"That's amazing," I added. "And, refreshing too. So many companies fight against change and don't welcome new ideas."

"Competition and change are both negatively viewed by too many," Whitney said. "We wouldn't have *iPhones* if we had settled for the flip phone. Why did we need 4K flat-screen televisions? The big-screen monsters of the 90's worked well. What's done can often be done better. And besides, discounting someone's dream often makes them more determined to prove you wrong. At least, that has been my M.O. Helping small businesses take on the big guys is so rewarding."

I think of Whitney's advice as I work on our branding. We had lots of promotions in mind for the Holiday Season. The rollout of our pecan pie and our three most popular variety of pecan clusters was planned first. Pitching Granna's pecan croissants and yeast rolls confused suppliers, so I backed off for now. I'll get them in stores next. I'm still working on a good tie-in.

By 4:00 PM, equipment is shut down, and we are out the door with boxes of leftover croissant dough. Leaving without something to bring home is not allowed. What's the point of working in a bakery if you don't make extra for us all to bring home? Our families send us back if we don't bring home a box filled with goodies.

I arrive home to an empty house. Lydia has after-school theatre practice, and Josh has football practice. I'll have the house to myself until 6:00 PM. I'm showered, in my comfy sweats, settled in on my favorite spot on our sofa, under my blanket, enjoying warm croissants by 5:00 PM. I order tacos because I missed dinner yesterday. I realize I don't know what they had for dinner yesterday—hope it wasn't tacos from *Fuzzy's*? Oh well, round two of *Fuzzy's* may be on the way.

Left over cookie dough is also put in the oven and will be ready when the food arrives. I've done all I can to make up for an extra busy day. For now, I'm succeeding.

CHAPTER FOURTEEN
Lilah

"I never ran my train off the track, and I never lost a passenger."

Harriet Tubman

After our Honeymoon trip to Detroit, Elias and I returned to Louisiana, but for the first time, I did not return to my parents. My home would no longer exist within the protected roads of St. Francis.

As we drove South, I thought of Mrs. Ada and how her home probably resembled Elias's family home. His parents lived about thirty miles outside of Baton Rouge.

The roads leading off the main highway were narrow, with deep drainage ditches on either side. The houses sat near the road and looked identical in size and shape. It was the end of a hot summer day, and many were outside gathered on their front porches enjoying the slight evening breeze.

My new in-laws greeted us as our car pulled into their front yard. There was a slight driveway, but too narrow to leave room for cars to come and go. As we made our way with luggage in hand, Elias showed me around his family home. There were two bedrooms and one bathroom. Elias' youngest brother was still living at home and attending high school. I apologized for taking his bedroom.

This would be our first home together until we moved into graduate student housing. Elias would be working towards his graduate degree in math, and my degree in English would be put to good use as a teacher at the university campus elementary school.

"*Southern University* sits on the *Mississippi River*," Elias explained. "We can sit and watch the ships pass and enjoy the evening sunset. There are general stores and lots of good food spots around the campus. We will have everything we need."

"I'm nervous but mostly excited," I said. "Your family has given us everything we need for our apartment. They went all out for our wedding. I think this entire town showed up and gave us a gift. All I have to do is unpack. I am not sure why I'm so anxious?"

"It's a new town and a new school," he continued. "Baton Rouge is not as welcoming as New Orleans, but it's not as bad as upriver. Well, for me anyway."

"Not funny!" I objected. "You should really stop trying to make me out to be some kind of porcelain doll. I know pain, and I have worked hard to have this life. You did not earn my college degree. I earned that all on my own, Mr. Marchand."

Ellis tried to ease my anger with his sultry smile and soft kisses, but I have never been able to let go of my anger easily.

"Don't get yourself all worked up, Doll face," he laughed. "Everyone will welcome you just like they did at *Tuskegee*."

"Don't start calling me that," I ordered. "You sound like a hoodlum."

"We can check in at 9:00 AM," he announced, ignoring my criticism. "Let's leave at seven. I want to be the first to arrive. We want the best apartment they have. Let the late birds get the one with the broken refrigerator."

"I hope the campus and the people are as nice as *Tuskegee*," I hoped.

My mother-in-law, who had obviously been listening to our conversation, comes to her son's defense. "Don't be so paranoid, Lilah!" she advised. "If you're nice to people, they will be nice to you. Just don't show up acting like you are better than anyone else. Speak to people. Everybody expects everybody else to look you in the eye and say hello."

"Mama, she knows," Elias corrected. "She just spent the last four years in Alabama."

"I'm just reminding her to not show up acting all shy and special," she adds. "You either, Elias. I'm not letting either of you move back home with me. You both better make something of yourselves. No one in our family has your education. It's important what you are going to Baton Rouge to learn. Make me proud, son."

"Yes, Mama," he agreed. "We both will."

I remained silent. Continuing the conversation was something I was smart enough to know would not turn out well for me.

The day before we were to leave for Baton Rouge, my attempts to remain excited about starting my new life were beginning to exhaust me. Four years ago, I had never ventured far from St. Francis. Trips to the beach in Biloxi were as far as I had traveled.

By the time I graduated college, I had visited Washington D.C., Chicago, and New York City. Most wonderfully, I was no longer a young White Louisiana girl. I was now a married Black Louisiana Lady who would be teaching young Black children. My childhood dreams would never have believed this day.

"Why the sad face?" Elias wondered. "You don't want to leave mama's house?"

"That's not it," I smirked. "I'm a wife now—not just a student. I guess I'm just now realizing that my dreams may have to change."

"What dreams need changing?" he asked. "Your dreams are my dreams. We are not just moving for me. I want you to also find something for yourself. Now that your dream of becoming my wife has come true—what is your next dream?"

We both laughed at his arrogance. Elias may have intended his words as a joke, but we both knew he believed his words, and I must admit I believed them as well.

"Elias, stop patting yourself on the back long enough to help me pack this last box," I ordered. "What time tomorrow are we leaving?"

Focusing on Elias's dreams first was time well spent. Our tomorrow was for my dreams. I would often quietly ask my dreams which one wanted my attention first? Elias showed me that I needed to add goals to my dreams. I set a goal to leave Louisiana for college, and I did. My degree is evidence of that. I was a cheerleader for Elias and became surrounded by the bounty from his dreams. My bounty was next, and it did not disappoint.

It took only two weeks for Elias and me to know we were home. Our new home was perfect. I introduced first graders to poetry and started a poet of the week board that my little ones decorated each week. Love and learning were everywhere, and I could no longer imagine any version of my life that could have been better.

My evenings were devoted to my love of baking. I made pecan pies and pecan butter for all the teachers. I would bring treats before our Thanksgiving and Christmas breaks and make batches at school whenever Mother sent me a box of fresh pecans. It was surprising for me to find so many people who had never tried pecan butter. Growing up on a pecan farm may have made me slightly biased, but peanut butter is too bland. Pecan Butter brings a much heartier and tastier bite.

"Elias, I'm going to plan to one day start baking full-time," I announced. "We are settled, and I think it's time for everyone to try my pecan butter and pecan croissants. I also need to visit with my parents this weekend and pick up more pecans."

"Visit St. Francis?" he inquired. "I can drive you."

"No, you have a class to prepare," I said in an attempt to justify my not inviting Elias. "My mother wants me to visit, and she's sending my father to pick me up."

"Are you afraid to ride with me to St. Francis?" he questioned. "I've never been to the place where you grew up. What harm would it cause? Does no one know about you marrying a Black man? Does anyone even know you are not your parents' White daughter?"

"This is not a conversation I can have today," I demanded in another attempt to again avoid Elias's questions about my family. "My parents came down to visit us, and they stocked our refrigerator when we moved in. You've met my parents and my sister. There is nothing else in St. Francis for you to see."

"I need to see St. Francis," he replied. "And the more you avoid me taking you, the more I know I need to visit. Why are you hiding who you are? You don't owe anyone anything. Who are you protecting? Is it your parents?"

"I'm protecting you," I yelled. "I don't want any harm to come to you. Please don't push me yet. We will visit soon. Now, I'm not ready— please just accept how I feel."

"I grew up in Louisiana," he argued. "I'm not some clueless Northerner."

"You grew up in South Louisiana," I reminded. "It's not the same as growing up in St. Francis. My family lives upriver, and I grew up on a farm where people that look like you worked for my family. They ate at our kitchen table, not our dining room table."

"You think your parents would not welcome me into your home?" he pondered. "Have you asked them? And, if you think they wouldn't welcome me, why would you go? You are my wife. Do you understand what that means? Will you visit without our children?"

"Please," I begged. "Let's talk about this later. I will sit down and talk to my parents this weekend. I've never asked them about us visiting. I know that sounds horrible and insensitive, but it's the truth. I've done my best to avoid causing either of you pain, and now I'm only causing everyone pain. My parents want me to visit, and my husband wants me to stay."

"How do you look at yourself in the mirror?" he said confusingly. "Do you see who you are? Do you see my wife, or do you see a little White girl from upriver?"

I didn't answer his questions that day, and it was years later before I even tried.

When I look into the mirror today, I still see Father's Lil'flower. I see the stress of my years, but my eyes still hold all my beauty.

"Granna, why are you sitting in the dark?" Lily asks. "You haven't opened your curtains? Are you having a migraine?"

I do my best to not let Lily see how much the pictures of my sister she was given has upset me. I miss Rosey every day. We fought like sisters should, but she was always the best friend I ever had. Rosey seemed happy with her married life, but like Mother, she had a hard time carrying a child. After Emma Rose, there were two miscarriages before I finished college. Rosey was the mother we all had longed and prayed for her to become, but the pain of loss touched her early. I pray she knew how much I loved and missed her.

"I'm just moving slow today," I say. "Why are you up and out so early? Did you go for a run?"

"Granna, what is it?" Lily asks. "Let me see."

I hand her the photo I have been staring at since last night. It's the last photo I remember taking with Rosey. It's the two of us with her daughter. I was home for my last visit before my college graduation and wedding that followed two weeks later.

"After that day, I returned to school, graduated, and married," I explain. "I didn't visit St. Francis much after this day. I regret not giving them the chance to know you all. Maybe they would have welcomed Elias? I never gave them a chance."

"You were afraid. I'm sure they understood," Lily consoles.

"Yes, but my mother loved me so..." I explain. "I should never have stayed away as much as I did. Fear is really no excuse for abandoning your family. Could you even imagine walking away and never seeing me again?"

"That's not what you did, Granna," she reminds. "I hate that you feel this way because of a stupid lawsuit. I'm so very sorry."

My parents always welcomed anyone...no matter their race—Black, White, Asian, anyone. Why did I never give them the chance to know Elias and my children? It would have shocked the town for me to show up with Elias, but my parents would never have let harm come to me. I guess I just didn't want to burden them with any difficulties caused by my choices.

"Your biological mother died when you were a little girl. Do you know when your biological father died?" she asks.

"Not exactly?" I say. "I learned eventually, and I don't really remember how? I think his wife called and spoke to Elias? And, please stop calling them that. Just say, Daisy and Franklin. You know their names."

"Yes, sorry," she responds. "We've received details about your family from the other side, but you haven't told me much. The stuff I know is your sister's side of the story. What's your side?"

"It's my life, Lily," I protest. "It's not a story to tell. I swear Rosey is probably on her way down from Heaven to set her children straight. And our parents—none of this is going over well with any of them."

"I'm sure you're right, Granna," she agrees. "Can you tell me what you know about Franklin?"

"The day after our wedding, we drove to Detroit to meet him—Franklin...Franklin Lewis," I explain. "He was married and had children. His wife didn't make a fuss about me visiting. She knew why Franklin fled Louisiana for safer grounds."

"You drove to Detroit?" I ask. "You both had just graduated from *Tuskegee* and had a wedding. Was an airplane not considered?"

"Your grandfather was a poor Black man with a brand-new shiny college degree, a hand-me-down car, and no money," she laughs. "Don't be silly. We were lucky his parents gave us their old car. Driving his new bride to Detroit was a wedding gift from his family. They wanted me to know about my family. Family meant everything to them."

"That was generous and considerate of them," Lily says. "How was the drive—back in the day?"

"It's a twenty-hour drive from Louisiana to Michigan," I say. "Elias' family arranged ahead and reserved hotel rooms at welcoming locations ten hours out each way. Remember, *The Green Book*? You only know about it because of the movie."

"Not true!" Lily defends. "Maybe Lydia and Josh don't know, but I know my history."

"Your grandfather was not afraid to travel," I explain. "He was used to traveling all over. He didn't think twice about taking the trip."

"How did you even know how to find your father?" Lily questions.

"Mother had told me his name," I say. "Back then, that's all you needed to call the operator and get someone's telephone number."

It was our Honeymoon, and we were both grateful to start our new life without secrets. As with all family secrets, the truth battles to break into the light. Elias wanted us to both know Franklin. Telling our children that we know nothing about him would never have sat well with either of us. Elias had a huge close-knit family, and I only had me — by choice. I still don't know where I found the courage to live this life.

"Did you call and ask to visit?" Lily questions. "That seems like an impossible thing to do? 'Hello, I'm your daughter, and I'm on my way to your house.' What did you say?"

"We called, and Elias told him we were married," I explain. "He told Franklin they needed to meet — face-to-face, man-to-man."

"Amazing!" Lily expresses. "Why have you never told me this story? And, don't say I never asked. Why would I ask such questions?"

"You talk too much, Lily," I laugh. "Most times, there is no reason to talk at all. You suck all the air out of the room."

"Fine, tell me what happened — please!" she asks. "I'll keep my mouth shut."

"We were greeted warmly and allowed to ask all of my long-held questions," I say. "He didn't answer many, but at least I know I asked. He told us about the 'trouble' he caused. I reminded him that he was talking about me. I was the trouble."

"I'm sure he didn't mean it that way?" she offers.

"Franklin told us about staying alive as a young Black man growing up in the South," I say. "Mrs. Ada and her family put together money and sent him North. He talked openly about being grateful to leave St. Francis and how he knew they saved his life."

"Do you think something bad would have happened to him?" she questions. "I don't even want to imagine."

"He also questioned how I found him?" I say. "That was such a crazy question. He thought Mrs. Ada led me to him. She had died many years earlier, but even if she hadn't, I don't think she would have told me about Franklin? She never told me she was my grandmother."

"Was Franklin surprised that Mrs. Ada never told you?" she asks. "Maybe he was always expecting you to show up asking questions?"

"I also didn't understand why Franklin never looked for me," I say. "I refuse to call him my father. He's Franklin—that's it."

"Well, did he explain why?" she asks.

"He talked about having a large Louisiana family," I say. "That explains why my mother was concerned about your grandfather's lineage. When I told Mother I met a Black man from Louisiana, she was not happy. I think she imagined Elias being my cousin or half-brother."

I laugh when Lily looks at me the same way my mother did when I told her about Elias. I was never worried. Mrs. Ada had told me enough about her family, and Elias' family was from the

Baton Rouge and New Orleans area. St. Francis people left for the North—not South Louisiana. Elias and his mother also made sure Ada Lewis was not in their family line.

"Granna, none of this is funny," Lily responds. "Were you never worried?"

"I was angry—not worried," I say. "Mrs. Ada had six sons and a large family. Franklin knew about me and never told anyone. Mrs. Ada never told anyone. I'm not a Lewis, but either way, Elias's mother made sure they were not related to anyone with the last name Lewis."

"They were also trying to protect you," she says as we both laugh together. "You don't think Mrs. Ada was ashamed of you—do you?"

"No, not at all. Why would she be?" I say. "Franklin made excuses and asked me if I expected Mrs. Ada to sit me down and say 'Hello, I'm your grandmother child'. I didn't!"

"Did he seem happy to finally meet you?" Lily questions. "Maybe he was embarrassed?"

"His wife seemed more interested in meeting me," I respond. "He was polite, but I can see how he may have been embarrassed. I was his mistake. I know that."

I also didn't ask about my half-siblings, and Franklin didn't seem willing to talk about his children. We gave each other kind hugs, and he told Elias to take good care of me. He didn't need to say that. Elias knew more than Franklin about taking care of me. I left Detroit as I had arrived—the daughter of Rose and William Cormier.

"My parents and Rosey came to visit us the year after our wedding," I say as I begin to open up more to Lily. "Elias started graduate school and had a teaching job at *Southern University* in Baton Rouge. My family would come and visit our campus apartment. No one gave them a second look. Elias visiting the farm would have been different. There were plenty of Creoles in Baton Rouge. My family fit right in."

"I know you were happy when they would visit," Lily says. "You did your best, Granna. They certainly knew how much you loved them and you know how much they loved you."

"Did you know that Elias's father walked me down the aisle," I explain. "Another regret! I only thought of my pain and protecting my new family—horrible!"

"Granna, stop," Lily begs. "Don't let the enemy win. Your Faith is too strong for you to live with any regret. You know who you are."

"Yes!" I say. "Thank you, my sweet grandbaby. I did something right. My children are a treasure—all of you."

"Speaking of treasure... I do need to ask you one more question about your portfolio?" Lily continues with a slight hesitation in her voice.

"Absolutely not!" I firmly answer. "Today is not the day for you to ask me questions about money. I'm still not sure how I feel about being investigated."

"You were not investigated," Lily tries to explain. "It was trial prep."

"Explain it how you must, but I know what you have done and I'm not playing along," I firmly state. "Go enjoy your Saturday and stop trying to count my money."

I take the photos I've been crying over all morning and place them in the back of my Bible. The best thing I could think to do was to surrender the pain of my regrets to Jesus. The memory of the first time Elias met my father was then sent to comfort me.

The first Christmas break after we began dating, Elias walked me to the edge of campus, where I met my father for pickup. Their meeting was warm and cordial, unlike anything I had imagined. Elias also called and spoke to my father before our wedding. He asked for permission to marry me, but I didn't ask my father to walk me down the aisle. I honestly didn't even invite them.

CHAPTER FIFTEEN
Lily

Love often gives us our meaning and our rest

The ability to identify the joy that exists each day is a talent difficult to master. Today, I find joy watching two fluffy caramel-colored puppies tussling on the sidewalk with no thoughts of continuing the walk their human companion had planned.

As typical, Josh is last to exit the field house, but today I don't mind. I open my sunroof and enjoy the mild evening breeze. The spring football game is next week. Spring, Football, and Summer Vacation make the top of my list of the best gifts we receive each year.

"Anastasia, what's up? You're calling late," I ask, surprised to see her name on my caller ID. Before she can answer, at least twenty scenarios of disaster race through my mind like a room full of toddlers trying to grab a ball.

"I finally received the estate documents your grandmother signed," she says with a hint of joy that she tries to conceal. "I just pushed send. You should have them."

"Arrghh... Finally!" I scream before forgetting that I am sitting in a parking lot filled with parents and teens. "You wouldn't just send me bad news without prep, so I know it's good news. Please just tell me. I beg of you. My hands are shaking, and I'm too nervous to read."

"We're in the clear," Anastasia boasts. "She didn't sign anything giving away her rights to start a competing business or create similar products. I would even say she's free to use recipes or packaging ideas she learned while working on the farm."

"Hallelujah! Thank You, Jesus," I shout, then look around to see if anyone noticed. If I wasn't at my kids' school, I wouldn't care, but if one of their friends reports that "I saw your mom acting weird," I won't be allowed back on campus for a month.

"It just popped up, and I knew you have been stressing," she explains. "You'll have to repent for all the worry you allowed over the last few weeks. Worry time is wasted time."

"At long last, now I can sleep," I confess. "I think all my worrying may just have miraculously transformed the language on a sixty-year-old document to make it say what we needed. Especially since we found out Granna is rich. She could've lost millions."

"Haha! Ok, well, can you change the numbers on my last bank balance and add a few zeros?" She adds. "If that works—that would be worry well spent."

"Let me see what I can do," I chuckle. "This may be a super-secret gift we can use during other trials."

"Sure thing, darling! Now let's get to work on our Motion for Summary Judgment," Anastasia advises. "This piece of evidence should wrap everything up nicely."

"The thought of a trial was always such a waste," I add. "An MSJ should be granted. Let's meet in the morning. I'm ready to shut this case down. Do you think we should ask for fees and expenses, or would that be too much? I'm trying to get this behind us, and I don't want to be bothered with collecting money from my new family in perpetuity. I'm not sure what kind of money they really have. They're not poor for sure, but they may be paper poor. Political campaigns and French Quarter bars are expensive."

"Are you sure he owns the bar, or does he just drink there?" she asks about Ryan.

"He owns it or most of it, but it also looks like he drinks most of the profits himself," I explain with a not-so-subtle jab. Ryan is the relative you develop a plan to avoid during Thanksgiving Dinner. "Am I required to continue speaking to any of them after we win?"

"Please, I don't speak to most of my relatives." Anastasia laughs. "Lose their numbers!"

Josh finally makes his way toward my car. Lydia has a late theater practice, so he's stuck with me. Having a high school Junior and Freshman still makes me pause whenever I'm reminded that my kids will soon be off to college. I was blessed to have the flexibility to spend time taking them to school every morning and volunteering when needed. I don't know how I will fill my days once I no longer have homework helper duties and teens with overloaded schedules.

"How was practice?" I ask, knowing all I will get is the standard "fine."

"Fine...can we get food?" He asks. "I really just want pizza, something quick and easy."

"We can stop by *Moody's* and get singles," I offer. "Do you know what kind your dad likes?"

"Yeah, I can order his too," Josh replies. "Thanks!"

"Excuse me?" I say in shock. "Are you showing gratitude without being asked?"

"Funny, mom," he reacts. "I say thank you. Love you, Mother. Now, let's get food."

With our pizzas quickly acquired, we're home in time to enjoy the warm slices all covered with extra cheese.

"Adam are you home," I call out. "I have great news. The contract and estate documents are just as we had hoped. All's good."

"That's great," he responds. "I hope you can now start sleeping through the night. You've been sleeping like a newborn infant. Have you been eating every time you get out of bed?"

"Why can't you just be supportive?" I scold. "Stop at 'That's Great' and leave my midnight snacks out of it."

Food never lasts long with teenagers. Josh managed to finish all of his slices before Adam and I finished one.

"Parents," Josh says. "I need to start the drivers' class this summer, and I have a question. Am I getting a car, and I don't want Lyddie's? She can take that car to college. I want my own car…a *Mustang*.

"Ha, no way Dude," I inform. "How about a *Ford Escape*?"

"Nerd car," he jokes. "Dad! *Mustang*?"

"Let's talk about that after we see your grades," Adam promises. "Straight A's gets you a vote. If not, no driving class this summer, and your mom's picking your vehicle."

"One B," he requests. "The calculus teacher is impossible. I think she has it out for me."

Watching Josh challenge us the same way I did with my parents has me screaming KARMA. I knew I wasn't the best, but now I realize I was just plain aggravating. My dad eventually started telling me to "just shut up," It didn't work, but at least he tried.

"I'm sure your teacher doesn't have it out for you personally," I reply. "I can email her and go over your test?"

"That's ok. I'm working on it," Josh says.

"Yeah, that's what I thought," I add. "Let me know if you need help." I offer to help because I know it's what Josh is seeking, but I also know he's not one to let an unfairness go unaddressed.

In sixth grade, he alone organized a fundraiser to help raise money for an opponent's school football field after playing the team. Josh's team lost, but he came away with admiration for his opponents and no sorrow for his team's loss. "They win games with a worn-out field and missing benches in the stands, and we have the best of everything and lose," Josh reasoned. "They deserve better, and we need to appreciate our gifts and work harder." He and Granna are always the first to remind us to give back.

Naming Lilah

"Don't worry about my calculus grade," he replies. "I got it."

"Ok, son," I say. "I'm excited to see you get it done."

Our pizzas are eaten, and I immediately remember the additional cookie dough I brought home a few days ago. I have a win to celebrate and cookies in need of baking. I also need to call and share the news of our win with Granna and Uncle. Calling them is next on the agenda after I bake cookies.

Granna and Uncle were relieved to hear of our estate document discovery and shared our optimism. The sunshine is beginning to edge its way over the massive mountain range we have been attempting to climb. Our Rebellious Spring is moving towards a Victorious Summer.

Our Motion for Summary Judgment was filed, and we are patiently waiting for the judge's ruling. The court's staff has hinted that the judge may want to hear arguments and that he has also questioned our mediation attempts. We trust that the facts are aligned in our favor but we agree to talk. Anastasia plans a trip to New Orleans for in-person mediation discussions.

My duties have now shifted to cleanup. Anastasia has ordered me to finalize Granna's settlement proposal by the end of the week. We don't plan to concede much, but I'll try to put together something resembling an offer.

Granna is sitting at her kitchen table with a magnifying glass in one hand and a flashlight in the other. Two photo albums are opened, and photos are spread across the table.

"What's all this?" I ask. "Did you find more photos?"

"Yes, look!" she excitedly answers. "Some of these look just like the ones you got from Rosey's children."

"Oh, wow!" I say. "You're right. Where did you find these? We may need to show them to Anastasia. Looks like a few may have been previously sent with our discovery response?"

"I was looking for one of my summer hats, and I thought it was in the set of boxes at the back of my closet," Granna explains. "I don't remember this storage box—anyway, I dragged it out, and these were inside."

"Whose handwriting is this?" I ask. "The album has notes written on the side of each photo."

"Rosey gave me these albums the last time I visited her in Lafayette," she recalls. "I don't remember bringing them to California. Maybe EJ packed them up, and I never knew they were there. This entire time, I've had these photos."

"That is amazing," I say. "We'll do Spring Cleaning and check the back of all your closets. Who knows what else we may find? Do you have any hidden art or diamond jewelry tucked away?"

Granna gives me her standard eye roll and head shake of disapproval. I was just asking. She may in fact have a famous painting or five-carat diamond she also forgot about.

"This is a photo of my mother and her sister," Granna says. "My real…you know, not real?"

"Biological mother," I respond.

"Yes, that sounds so weird to say," Granna shakes her head with disgust. "Did you give any photos to their lawyer?"

"Yes, I may also need to send this one as well?" I say while flipping through the sticky pages of photos. "Let's see what else you have found."

We organize the loose photos first and then begin removing photos from the two photo albums—most of which are permanently stuck to the pages.

"This is Rosey and me," Granna states happily. "I'm probably ten, and she's thirteen. I'm nearly as tall as she is—Rosey definitely took after our father's side of the family, round and chunky with bright blonde hair."

"Yes, you do look like your mother," I add. "This photo of your mother and 'mother/Daisy' does resemble you. They really look like twins in this photo. How many years were they apart?"

"I think four?" Granna replies. "Mother was married with Rosey when I was born, so Daisy was probably twenty and Mother was twenty-four by the time I came along."

"Did you find a photo of Mrs. Ada?" I ask, hoping the answer would be yes.

"That's why I took out the magnifying glass," she reveals. "I think this is her standing on the front porch watching after Rosey and me?"

"I see her, Granna!" I excitedly express. "Just perfect. Ms. Gail would love to see this photo."

"Why do you think that?" she asks. "Would you want a photo of me watching after someone's White children playing in the front yard of their big fancy house?"

"Why not?" I ask. "It's the truth. There's nothing shameful about that. Look what Mrs. Ada's children were able to achieve because of her sacrifices and hard work. Look at you. Look at me."

"Well, her children don't see it that way," she proclaims. "They see themselves as mistreated workers of White people."

"Why would you say that?" I question. "Is that how you felt they were treated? Is that why you left the farm?"

"They weren't treated like equals," Granna continues. "Mrs. Ada worked on her hands and knees scrubbing our floors. I never saw my mother on her knees cleaning anything. My only chore was putting away my clothes after Mrs. Ada washed and pressed them."

"How was your father with the farm workers?" I ask. "You said he and Rosey were always working together."

"She was out there ordering the workers around just like our father," she says. "Her work was standing behind our father giving orders to men twice her age. She was like a little parrot. Mother and I would sit on the porch and have a good laugh watching her perform."

We've been piecing together Granna's family history for months, and I now realize there is still so much I have yet to understand about Granna's life. There is true Joy covering Granna's face in the photos we are holding and, on her face, staring back at me today—an endearing Joy I see for the first time.

"Lily, I want to plant another Magnolia Tree in the front yard," Granna announces for no apparent reason? "Alice has two trees in her backyard, and I love looking over at them. They look like a friendly couple chatting. My tree up front also needs a friend to chat with."

"Sure, I'll order one," I say as I lean in for a hug just because I know we both need one. I'm overwhelmed by the experience of viewing Granna's family photos. I cannot imagine what she is feeling.

"Elena and Elias, Jr.—God blessed me with the two most wonderful children," Granna boasts as her thoughts, not surprisingly, shift towards mom. "I just don't know why He took my baby girl so soon. We sure do need her still."

It's been many years since we lost mom to cancer and the hurt still lives with us every day. We have grown better at trying to replace the feelings of anger and loss with memories of times spent laughing and loving mom. I think we all now accept that the pain will remain, but Joy can begin to move in and remind us to focus on the Love.

The first Christmas without Mom, Granna gave each of us two handmade painted wooden bookmarks with familiar sayings accompanied by graceful flowers and colorful designs.

"Cherish the Love, not the Loss"

"Remember how they lived and not how they died"

I began repeating those words several times throughout the day and still repeat them at times when Mom whispers to me. "I see you, Mom, and your Love helps me stand and face each day." The words spill out before I realize I'm speaking.

"Well, why are we such crybabies today?" Granna asks. "Let's just go over to *Garden Emporium* and look for a tree. We need to get out in this sunshine and make ourselves useful. Oh, and my flowers. Did I tell you Mr. Norman retired, and his son took over his gardening business? That child has no idea what he is doing."

"Sure," I grabbed my keys and headed for the door before I remembered the real reason for my visit. "Have we even talked about why I came over?" I laugh nervously. "We need to discuss the case."

"After shopping and lunch," she says. "I have a new box of seasoning I want to try."

"Yes, Uncle said he sent a box, and half of it's for me," I comment even though I know she has no intention of sharing.

"I don't know why he tells you such things?" Granna declares as she closes the door behind us. "I'll use everything he sent. Order your own."

I'm enjoying my favorite spot on the floor of my closet as the remains of yesterday peak from behind the rows of clothing trying to protect me. I wrap both arms around my shoulders and squeeze extra hard as I repeat in the loudest voice I can tolerate, "I am safe. I am well. I am Loved!" My go-to anti-anxiety mantra never fails. I'm hidden from the world, and I am safe.

The settlement terms I've been tasked to compile are overdue, but I am still too wound up to do real work. A low-fat mocha frosted beverage will provide the perfect sugar/caffeine boost, so I decide to drive along the coast and let the sun filled sky lead me to the perfect stopping point.

It's another beautiful Southern California day. The cost of living may be much higher than in other areas, but it's worth every dollar.

A familiar walking trail catches my eye first, and I'm dressed for the challenge. My closet leads me towards my pink Nike's for a good reason. I start out without earbuds. Taking in the sounds of the day seemed more appealing. I almost choose to leave my cellphone, but then my *Tummy Alarm* reminds me it's a workday.

The trail is busy but not too much to annoy. After sprinting up the first hill, I appreciate getting in a little cardio for the day. The path is level and worn in areas because of the steady foot traffic. The top of the path has great views and lots of sitting areas that provide rest and the needed inspiration to continue walking along the trail.

The moms' groups are out today doing yoga. It's peaceful to watch, but I don't know why I always decline opportunities to try outdoor yoga. Maybe it's *Downward Dog* in full view of the world that discourages me? Also, I can't hold *Tree Pose* as gracefully as most.

The ideal flat top rock is unclaimed, and I sit with raised arms to hug the Sun. *"Today is a Day the Lord has made...I'm grateful for it all."* I sing with no one close enough to hear. Just then, my *Tummy Alarm* again tries to get my attention, probably to make me feel guilty for taking time out for myself. I immediately tell it to shut up, but then I'm annoyed that I still have such thoughts.

The vicious circle begins. Guilt, shame, regret, blame...just make it stop! I give myself a hug and remind myself that I am loved and that I deserve to show myself compassion.

CHAPTER SIXTEEN
Lily

My time was never truly owned

𝒟ays are still stopped more often than I ever imagined possible. Since mom, I have grown conscious of the need to live each day to its fullest, but worry, regret and fear of the unknown future continue to steal an unacceptable amount of my time.

"Daniel's wife called," Finola informs. "Heart attack last night. He died." We both sit silently in her office for over a minute before I finally respond with a question.

"Why did Caroline call you?" I question without considering whether or not my reaction is insensitive. Finola and I had both spent time socially with Daniel's wife. Maybe she views me as the enemy?

I was the lead attorney on the Japan case. Daniel was one of my mentors. I'd been to his home for dinner with his family. I didn't speak with him first. I supported the claims of our staff without listening to his side. What I experienced and what I witnessed with my own eyes were the only facts I provided. That was enough.

"She asked about you." Finola continues. "I told her I'd let you know and check-in with her later to see if she needed anything. Caroline wants us to attend his service. Do you think he drank himself to death?"

"Did she specifically ask for us both to attend?" I say without answering her question. "Don't you think that's weird?"

"I don't think she knows specifics about Daniel and the firm?" she replies. "He was in his sixties. He probably just told Caroline he was retiring. Unless one of the other partner's wives spoke to her, I doubt she knows anything. And, you know most of their wives fall in line with their husbands and with firm mandates."

"Then, why wouldn't she call me?" I ask. "It's just weird. Should we go to the service?"

"Yes, it's in two days," she confirms. "No one around here has mentioned it yet, but I'm sure they know or will soon know. I'll call you when everyone starts talking."

"Ok, and I think he could have drank himself to death," I say. "He loved the firm, the power, the attention, the prestige. Losing it all, I'm sure, was difficult for him. They have grandchildren. This will be hard for them all. We should go to the service."

I return to the office the day before Daniel's service. My walk from the reception area to Finola's office was long and stoic. I offer a simple "Good Morning" to anyone I pass. I'm not willing to discuss Daniel within these walls.

"Ready?" I ask as I place the food and fruit baskets ordered by the firm on a rolling cart I snagged from the mailroom. Finola and I have been *"voluntold"* to deliver firm condolences—pasta, fruit, salads, sandwiches, cookies, chips, wine and several sympathy cards.

"I'll never be ready for this, but let's go," Finola responds. "This place has been unbearable. We've been divided for a while, but now the verbal attacks are flying unhinged."

"Did someone say something to you?" I question as I ready myself to charge down the hall towards whoever dared to direct their anger towards Daniel's victims.

"Let's go before you make things worse," she orders.

Caroline greets us both with strong hugs and smiles. I'm relieved but still not convinced we are welcomed. "Come sit for a while," she says as she walks down a long hallway to a sunroom filled with flowers and trays of food. "Here, set your baskets in this spot."

"Certainly," Finola replies while squeezing my hand.

I'd visited their home many times before, and the perfectly placed furniture guarding each room is still in its same perfectly placed spot. The black and white photos of their four children still rest along the entrance wall of their foyer. I now know that perfect surroundings do not make perfect people.

"Here, you two—let's move these things to the kitchen." Caroline motions us to follow. "I think I need to sit for a moment. I've been moving all day. But I'm so happy the firm sent you two. Daniel loved you both. When he was forced to retire, he trusted you both to continue the good work he was doing at that firm."

Finola and I nod in agreement, saying nothing.

The 2020 year-end financial losses were used to cloak the bad behavior of the "retiring" partners. Daniel was the first identified, but his reveal led to the uncloaking of three other senior partners. Without the courage of a twenty-five-year-old, we would all still be circling the same foul-smelling animals in the center of the road.

After an hour of chatting without Finola and I confirming or denying any comments about Daniel, we are saved. Caroline was needed elsewhere, and we were politely excused.

"That was torture," I complain when we are safe inside my car. "How are we going to make it through the service? Did you hear Caroline say, 'Daniel loved you both.' Why would she say that?"

"Either you or I worked on every big case he had," Finola says. "He made it a point to mentor and promote women. We considered him an ally. The thought of Daniel crossing the line was one neither of us wanted to entertain."

"Stop...I can't," I say while trying to catch my breath. "I'm so sorry." Once again, unexpected tears begin to appear. Daniel's dead, and even after his death, his massive presence still looms large in my life. He was the first partner to give me a real chance at the big cases. I noticed that he flirted with everyone a little too much. We were even warned by a few of our senior support staffers on day one. Giving Daniel a compliment about his new tailored suit or the new fitted polo shirt he wore on casual Fridays would get you an invite to after-work happy hour. We all knew how to pull his strings, but that was often followed by enduring his sloppy drinking antics.

"Always look for ways to better your team." Daniel would remind. "When your team is the best, you are the best." His wanting to create good teams by surrounding himself with teams of talented women seemed sincere. Asking me to bring my newly hired junior associate on an international trip should have given me more pause, but I was only focused on my own advancement. I blindly followed his lead and refused to acknowledge the roadkill left behind.

"Lily, you need to tell Adam," Finola demands. "Maybe telling him will help you let go of the pain. You are keeping a big secret from your husband. Have you even told Noel?"

"I've only told you and the firm's internal investigators," I snap. "I could never tell Adam or Noel. They both would not understand why I continued working for Daniel for years. Adam would not understand why I didn't immediately tell him. We are trained to meet with colleagues in the hotel lounge, never let anyone into your room, and never go into anyone's room. That's what we are advised to do. We all received the training."

"The training is sometimes lost when you're in the heat of battle," Finola reminds. "Daniel would stand behind me and reach across the table to pick up a pen. He'd brush against my breasts, and I'd catch him looking down my blouse. I'd ignore him, take my promotion, and warn the next associate to avoid showing cleavage around Daniel. We all put up with too much for too long. We all now admit we should have spoken up sooner."

"I stopped meeting with him in his office early on for those same reasons. I wish we had spoken up sooner," I reply solemnly. "After the Japan trip, I knew something was off. He apologized for "acting weird" and said he was emotional because he had just found out Caroline had a cancer scare. I believed him and told him I understood. Why did I do that?"

"You trusted him," she replies. "He always praised you and promoted your achievements."

"Yes, after that trip, he assigned me another big case and never treated me differently," I recall. "It's just all so impossible to understand."

"Tell Adam," she again says.

"Let's talk about it later," I request. "We're just emotional because of the funeral. I want to move on. I don't want Adam looking at me and wondering about Daniel. We have traveled together for years. We've worked on tons of cases together."

"Listen to what you are saying," Finola pressures. "You don't trust your own husband to believe you. How can we expect women to speak up when victimized by men like Daniel if you can't even tell your own husband?"

A response is unnecessary, but my increased bevy of tears says it all. Besides, anything clever I come up with will just be a sad excuse. I don't know why I think Adam wouldn't believe me. It's the same reason I made excuses for Daniel's behavior and accepted his lies. I wanted to remain safe behind the familiar faces. I didn't want to face the unknown. I didn't want to destroy what I believed to be true. I wanted Daniel to be the champion he portrayed. I wanted to be the smart, strong woman I portrayed. I didn't want to be a victim.

The day begins early because sleep decided to fight back. The black power suit I've chosen to wear was a replacement for the black laced dress I selected yesterday. Today, I'm feeling less gentle.

"Please come on Mother," Lydia yells as she stomps towards the garage. "I want to get an early start to work on my project," she's sixteen, and her choices are driven by her need to create new content for her next social media post. I don't believe she's rushing this morning in order to work on a project. It's either a boy or social media driven.

Both teens are in my car and ordering me to "go" before I can gather my thoughts in protest. We're warned that moody teenagers are more difficult to parent than toddlers, but until you experience the eye rolls and the dismissive looks given by the same children who once ran with excitement to greet you every time you entered a room, you think such remarks are nonsense.

"Why are you dressed up on a Friday?" Josh questions.

"Her old boss died, and she's going to his funeral." Lydia answers. "Keep up."

"Pray for the family," I say as I pull into the drop-off line, "He has grandchildren your age."

They both provide agreeing hugs accompanied by a quick, "Have a good day, Mother" then they're out of my car and on their way.

The past few days have been difficult, so I decide on a chocolate smoothie for breakfast. I add protein powder to help make me feel less terrible about my choices. Chocolate and prayer will help me make it through this morning.

It's a relief to see Anastasia with Finola. With Anastasia here, Finola won't badger me about Adam. And we're at a funeral, so my tears will fit in just fine.

"All the big guys are here," Finola says. "Let's find a good seat."

The service starts, and our chief equity partner has been tasked to give the eulogy. Daniel is portrayed as a hero. His family is comforted. His colleagues are satisfied. We are inconsequential.

Our Saturday was not overscheduled, and I was thankful to enjoy a quiet morning alone. To my surprise, the evening soon arrived without me noticing, but I kept quiet so as to not cause movement by others.

"Are you changing out of your pajamas anytime soon?" Adam asks, disturbing my solitude. "You're giving your children the idea that sulking around all day is acceptable."

"Well, that's a ridiculous thing to say," I bark before continuing with more profanity-laced remarks I'm not even sure why I'm making? "If showing emotion and caring for myself is a bad look then let it be a bad look. Your opinion is just that—your opinion. It's Saturday, and you are not my father, and you cannot tell me what to do."

Funerals still put me in a funk I'm unable to easily shake off. I just want to sit with my feelings and see if today is the day I figure out the meaning of Life.

"My parents had us up every Saturday morning doing chores before we were allowed to take the rest of the day off for fun," Adam continues. He's one of those adults that still has both parents—just simply clueless. "Discipline is a skill taught and developed with practice." He continues to ramble on, trying to make his point heard.

"Adam, go away," I order. "Why did you even come in here talking to me?"

"I'm checking on you," he says. "It's 5:00 PM. Your children want to go visit friends. Did they ask you?"

"Yep, let them go," I answer. "You should drop them off. I know the parents. It's fine."

"And, you are going to do what?" he asks. "Ride with me, or they're not going."

"Why is it always on me?" I complain. "You have nothing to do, and I am busy solving many world problems."

"Is that what you are calling it?" he laughs. "Get dressed, and you can figure it out in the car," I moan and drag myself off the sofa and away from him.

Thirty minutes later, I emerge. "I have clothes, happy?" I say.

"Perfect." Adam answers. "We're dropping off the kids and taking food to Grant's so we can watch the game. Their kids are also going to the Parker's. It's some kind of backyard movie party.

Noel said she spoke to the parents, and they all have a ride home."

"I know! I said the mother called," I respond. "I've already told you that. Does Noel know you are bringing food to their house? Did you even ask what they wanted?"

"I'll just take wings," he says. "Why, is that not good?"

"I'll order something, and no—wings are not good," I reply with the appropriate disapproving hand gestures.

"Fun! I need more fun," I say to Adam as we drive to meet Grant and Noel. "Let's go somewhere fun. We can put on real clothes and have a proper meal." Adam agrees, and we call to share our new dinner plans. Why is it always easier to help others than it is to help ourselves?

The streets are busy, but not unusually so. The night skyline offers a burst of welcomed energy, and we decide to dine on the restaurant's rooftop to better enjoy the view.

"Lily, what drink?" Adam is, of course, ready with a drink in hand.

The fellas stand up to greet each other while Noel and I get lost in a dancing bear hug.

"I've missed you terribly. Let's order lots of calamari and wine," I request before releasing our hug. This is the fun I sought.

My mind is beginning to allow room for thoughts other than lawsuits and loss and sadness. Noel is always up on the latest, and she doesn't mind taking the lead on delivering all things steamy.

"Josie's moved out and has a new boy-toy hanging around. He's around the same age as her oldest son that's graduating college. Her doorman keeps getting the two confused. Who has time for someone that needs to show ID when ordering?" Noel updates me on the new divorcee at our kids' school.

"She's probably impressed with his lack of baggage, no mortgage payments, parent-teacher conferences, and aging parent concerns," I say. "And, I'm sure his endless stamina is another BIG plus." There's a benefit in hanging out with the youth, but my energy is better served outside the bedroom.

"Let's shake off the day. This music should help get you out of that chair." Noel's not wrong. A few people have been dancing most of the night, and it looks like they need company. We grab the fellas and take over the floor.

"Thanks for agreeing to go out. We needed a moment to escape even if it's just a few hours." Adam pulls me close, dips, and adds a gentle kiss to the left side of my neck. Body kisses are much more arousing than a simple peck on the lips. Sex has been off lately...has it been months?

Josie's boy-toy probably shows up ready within a moment's notice, ready to serve. No need for planning or romance. Parenthood also moves romance down the list, but have we moved it off the list?

Adam's eyes still show the same strong, funny, handsome, and admiring man I've known most of my life. Love and respect are romantic...paying my mortgage is romantic. Who needs hours of unlimited stamina?

Salsa is up next, and I never miss a chance to show off my moves. Maybe I'll remember to also show off my best bedroom moves when we make it home?

CHAPTER SEVENTEEN

Lily

Our time was never truly seen

Adam is today's luncheon keynote speaker for a national corporate diversity conference being held this week at the Los Angeles Convention Center. I'm here with our teenagers because we wanted them to see their dad in action. School is out for the summer, but they both have a busy summer camp schedule lined up. Spending a summer day with their parents was not a part of either of their agendas.

Adam's a dynamic speaker, and this will be their first opportunity to watch him deliver a message before a large audience. I'm excited to witness their reactions. The banquet hall is filled from one end to the next with tables of ten. We're seated at a table with Adam's co-workers, most of whom we've hosted at our home for dinner. They all also have children, so any event with a "bring the kids" option is always a big hit.

After our salad plates are removed, Josh reaches for the cheesecake before our lunch entree makes its way to the table. Lydia grabs his hand without even looking his way, and Josh yells out, "Snitch!" I give them both "the look," and they immediately turn their attentions back to the video introductory presentation playing before Adam's speech.

"Today, we are honored to have with us Adam Guillory, Vice President of Diversity and Inclusion for the Lokeridge Corporation a Fortune 50 Industrial Manufacturer..."

"Thank you for that amazing introduction. I didn't know I had done all of that?" Adam begins with an attempt at humor. His delivery seems effortless, and the full, rich tone of his voice has hooked me since the moment I first heard him speak. *Toastmasters* training paid off big for us both. I joined *Toastmasters* to better my trial skills, and I walked away with a husband. I admire my husband, but I often look at him as a man who can't be trusted to see me as I am.

Adam grew up in an undramatic middle-class family. He had supportive parents and many caring mentors. To my disappointment, he has grown into one of those people who believes his success is a result of his hard work. In my eyes, he is worse than the privileged. He's where he is because he had a mother, father, and grandparents who made sacrifices for their family, prayed for him, and overly praised his every act.

As Adam's message nears its ending, the room appears to have followed his every word. Even our teenage children seemed to have been listening. Current racial tensions have been as high as they were during the 60s Civil Rights Movement. Adam focuses more on the current racial climate of the U.S. and less on corporate hiring. The idea that people in power do not make efforts to expand their circle of influence beyond the select groups that look similar to them has been the message Adam most often promotes.

"Religion, politics, gun violence, race relations, and COVID are topics no one wants to discuss," Adam presents. *"The Greatest Generation* endured a World War and Economic Depression. How will our generation be viewed in fifty years? Are we getting anything right? Are we coming together to heal our country and world?"

Adam knows that luncheon audiences want a quick message given between their meal and dessert. His closing line is delivered with a passionate and dynamic tone that earns him a standing ovation.

"Dad did a great job!" Lydia announces to the table. Josh nods in approval before taking another bite of cheesecake.

"I'm happy you both enjoyed the experience, especially since you were forced to spend a day with your parents," I offer.

"Yeah, mom. It wasn't so bad. Maybe I'll come to another one of these things." The table laughs as Josh grabs my slice of cheesecake and continues eating between breaths. Hopefully, he'll come back for the intriguing conversations and not just because of the food.

After giving Adam our high-fives and words of admiration, I'm off with the kids to Granna's. She wants our help picking out forget-me-nots for her garden. Someone encouraged her to start the tradition of planting fresh flowers on Gramps' birthday and on their anniversary, so twice each year, we are now tasked with helping her replant her backyard flower boxes. The kids love helping Granna with chores, and they never complain mostly because she always slides them cash when I'm not looking. My grumpy teenagers also seem happier when she's around. I've accepted that they no longer have the same reaction when I walk into a room, but it's nice to see that Granna can still inspire a joyful response from her grandchildren.

"How're my favorite people," Granna boasts as she greets us on the landing outside of her front door. "I have a surprise."
"We love surprises," I say. "What's up?"

Before Granna could answer, Joelle bolts out from Granna's front door revealing the biggest smile I'm sure I have ever witnessed.
"I'm here," she screams as she grabs hold of me for a tight hug. "I wanted to surprise you." My teenagers look on in shock. I imagine they are thinking, 'who is this strange child who thinks our mom is worthy of such an over-the-top welcome?'
Joelle is followed by Ms. Gail and a similar-looking pre-teen girl who I assume is her best friend, Olivia. When I gave Granna the copies of photos Ms. Gail allowed me to copy, Granna asked for Ms. Gail's telephone number to thank her. I never imagined that they would continue to talk or that Granna would bring them here for a visit.

"This is unbelievable," I exclaim while returning Joelle's big hug. "You're here—in California."

"Your grandmother is amazing," Ms. Gail says. "It's our loss for never knowing her."

"Well, she definitely got me this time," I laugh. "You being here is nothing I ever would have guessed possible. So…I assume you both know you're related?" Granna and Ms. Gail both nod in agreement. "Thanks for letting me know," I add sarcastically.

My teens remain puzzled by Joelle's enthusiastic greeting. I remind them that I am awesome, and once upon a time, they also greeted me with similar reactions.

"I had Julia rent a party bus," Granna reveals. "We are taking our guests on a tour, shopping, and all the other stuff young people like to do."

I'm not sure why Granna is acting so giddy, nor do I understand how Ms. Julia got involved, and no one said a word to me?

"What about *Disney*?" I ask. "Joelle's never been. We have to give her the Guillory Tour."

"They just arrived this morning," Granna says. "You all can take them to *Disney* tomorrow. That's your thing. You know I can no longer handle all that walking."

"Can we also bring a friend?" Lydia asks. "I'll start planning our ride schedule."

The bus was a hit with both the teens and the pre-teens. We stop for photos on *Hollywood Boulevard*. Joelle and Olivia try to snap pics of the hundred-foot palm trees that line the streets around Beverly Hills.

"Mrs. Granna," Joelle says. "Thank you for allowing us to visit. I love it here so much. Can I come back again?"

"You just got here, girl!" Ms. Gail responds. "Enjoy this trip and stop begging for more. Show some gratitude."

We all get a good laugh watching the different wide-eyed facial expressions Joelle makes when she discovers any new thing. Losing her mother does not seem to have dampened her Light. Maybe it's because she hasn't' finished puberty?

"That Joelle is a real firecracker," Granna remarks. "She's almost another Lily—too smart and annoyed that the rest of us don't catch on as fast as she can. I think Joelle will grow up and give Lily a run for her money."

"Fine with me," I joke. "The more people like me, the better."

The food truck plaza is open, so we stop and pick up a few treats from our favorites. Granna also likes to try out the competition whenever she has the opportunity.

"They should be tired?" Ms. Gail admits. "We traveled all day, and they hardly slept last night. When I told them we were taking a morning flight to Los Angeles, I don't think they have been able to sleep much since."

"I'll see if I can get rooms at the park," I offer. "Moving from park to park will work out better if we are staying close by, and it's Joelle's first trip. Let's just go all out." Why not? I ask myself. Also, Granna has only one guest room. I'm not sure where she planned to host our guests? A hotel will be a welcomed treat for us all.

The party bus returns us to Granna's, and I drive our guests to check into their hotel. Granna thanks me for my quick thinking and save. She has lived alone forever and rarely has overnight guests. I'm not sure why Granna imagined she could host three guests?

I requested a *Disney Princess* themed room, and it was, of course, another big hit. The loud squealing excitement did not go unnoticed by anyone within one hundred yards. Hanging around this bunch of energy has given us all a renewed sense of adventure. I think everyone should want to see more things through Joelle's pre-teen eyes.

The next day was filled with as much joy as we could carry. *Disneyland* seldom disappoints. We arrived as the gates opened and stayed until the closing fireworks.

"We want to take Mrs. Granna a thank you gift," Joelle requests as we enjoy breakfast the next morning. "Would she like a *Mickey* Hat?"

"She'll like anything you give her," I reply. "I think we should give her a picture of us in our Mickey hats. She would love to look at our beautiful faces every day." We take a group photo in the hotel after breakfast and prepare for our next adventure.

We spend the rest of our morning enjoying the beach. The Sun is high, and the waves are smooth. None of us is unimpressed. The breeze flowing off the water, the meditative sounds, and the unmatched scents help make an oceanside visit incomparable.

After we all take too many selfies and are completely covered in sand, a shower and nap are in order. Granna and Ms. Julia are hosting dinner.

Ms. Gail and Granna share a grandmother—Mrs. Ada. They are first cousins meeting for the first-time decades after they both left their family hometown. It's a remarkable chain of events created by the nightmare started by the Cormier's Lawsuit.

"Did Gail tell you about the other pictures of Franklin she found?" Granna asks. "Let's put them with the pictures of Daisy."

"Yes! Let's put them together and see who you look like," I joke. Granna did not join in on the laugh. "I'm just kidding— take a joke, why don't you."

"Gail, if you ever need an extra grandchild, Lily is available," Granna laughs. "I'll keep my two great-grandchildren, and you can take Lily back with you."

Joelle and Olivia are still in awe of our day spent at *Disneyland*. Most of their evening was filled with giggles and gazing at the picture gallery on their cellphones. Granna and Ms. Gail shared memories of Mrs. Ada and St. Francis. I enjoyed moving between the two conversations and basking in the joy of this moment.

"Joelle, my Granna wants to trade me to Ms. Gail for you," I shout from across the room.

She turns and runs towards me at full speed. Out of nowhere, we both create our best superhero stance and defend our positions. Olivia is not far behind. She barrels into us both, and the three of us fall to the ground in laughter.

After we all eat more than we should have, Granna packs up the remaining deserts for Joelle and Olivia's trip home. I return our guests to their hotel and give an extended goodbye. They'll take an early morning ride share to the airport and arrive back in Detroit before dinner. Joelle assures us all that she is now more than capable of taking care of both her grandmother and Olivia. Her first airplane ride was all she needed to become a learned seasoned traveler.

Now that Granna and Ms. Gail have connected, the time I spent tracing Mrs. Ada's family history and their contributions to the Cormier Farm was worth my efforts. I found nothing to help with the lawsuit, but I found family. The dark cloud brought in by the lawsuit is beginning to fade under the optimistic glow of love.

"Ms. Gail and crew are back in Detroit safe and sound," I say. "So, will you now please tell me how and why you pulled off their visit."

"Why must you know everything?" Granna responds. "We've been talking since your trip to Detroit. Gail is a good person— she helps me feel connected to Mrs. Ada."

"I'm so happy you reached out to Ms. Gail," I add. "She is a good person, and I just love her granddaughter. Joelle's personality has stuck with me, and now they all are a part of the Cormier-Marchand Family."

"They are," Granna agrees. "I thought we needed a fun surprise.

"It was a perfect surprise, thank you," I say. "You pulled off the unimaginable."

"Well, thank Joelle," Granna adds. "Every time I spoke to Gail, Joelle jumped in and asked about you. I knew bringing her here would put a much-needed smile on both your faces."

Naming Lilah

𝓘 return to Granna's bright and early the next morning. The time spent with Ms. Gail, Joelle, and Olivia was an unexpected and welcomed surprise, but I'm still unconvinced this was an innocent social visit.

"Granna, I know there's more to Ms. Gail's visit," I announce. "Why did you really invite her here?"

"Lily, stop with your constant worry and just accept the good time you had with new friends," Granna advises. "Lydia and Josh will probably keep in touch with Joelle for life. That's a good thing. Our family has had so many more advantages than most. You should welcome the opportunity to expand your family circle."

"Well, now—that's a shocker," I remind. "You don't feel the same about Kate and her mother. You have not once asked to meet with them, or do you even ask anything about them."

"I know Rosey's family," she quips. "My sister and I grew up in the same home. I know all I need to know about them."

"You can't believe that?" I question. "You haven't seen Kate's mom since she was a child. You've only spoken to her over the telephone about Rosey a few times before Rosey died."

"Don't be so disrespectful," Granna objects. "You make it sound like I've done something wrong. Is that what you think? Am I wrong for whatever reason you may think?"

The questions shock me. It was not my intention to judge Granna, but her bias is becoming more obvious, and I've found no reason for her to treat the two sides of her family so differently. She has never uttered a negative word about her parents or her sister. It's hard to imagine how Granna was able to leave her loving family and start a new life without them.

"If I invited Kate to town for the weekend, how would you react?" I question.

"Are you angry about Ms. Gail?" she asks, confused. "I thought you would love seeing them. You seemed happy. Was I wrong to invite them?"

"No, that's not what I'm saying," I respond. "I loved every moment of their visit. Inviting them was a very pleasant surprise. That is not what I'm trying to get you to understand."

"Just say what you are upset about," Granna orders.

"It's not that I'm upset. I never want you to think you upset me," I say. "I just want to understand why this is happening. Why is your sister's family suing us, and why do you not seem to care anything about them?"

My questions anger Granna as I had feared. I truly did not want to upset her or make her feel attacked by my actions.

"I will never understand you," she responds exasperated. "Why can't you just accept what you're told for once. Everything went well with their visit. There is no reason for you to try to make it into anything else."

"You can't make up for the pain Mrs. Ada and her children endured, and it's not Rosey and her children's fault," I try to offer. "It is not our fault for any of this. Why are you acting like all of this is your fault?"

"It was Mother's idea to start making pecan butter, but hers was too bitter," Granna explains. "Mrs. Ada fixed her recipe, and that's when we started selling it to everyone in the town. But, the pies were always Mother's recipe. We all followed it exactly as she had taught us."

"When, Granna?" I ask. "When did the recipe change?"

"I don't remember the exact day, but it wasn't long after we started selling it in batches. We started when I was still young—maybe eight or nine."

"You were so young, and that was over eighty years ago," I say. "What do you actually remember?"

Granna searches for the memory, but we both understand that the details could not possibly be very clear. While I trust what Granna is saying, I still don't understand why she hasn't mentioned this before today, and I also don't understand why she wanted Ms. Gail to visit?

"I want you to take care of Joelle," Granna announces. "If you do this for me, I will know I've made amends. Make sure you provide for her through college."

"What are you talking about?" I say in a too dismissive tone.

"It's my money, Lily!" Granna asserts. "You went to college and law school with my money. You moved to Los Angeles and got married with my money."

"My job moved me to Los Angeles, but the rest you did," I correct. "What's your point?"

"You know my point," she argues. "You didn't get here alone, and I need you to see better than I did. I acted like I made this rich life all by myself. I didn't, and I will no longer ignore what I've done."

"What have you done?" I ask, confused. "What?"

"Rosey was not the only sister I had," she whispers. "Franklin had another daughter. His wife told her about me, and she came to New Orleans to find me. I turned her away."

"Turned her away how?" I ask.

"After all Mrs. Ada had done for my parents and me— all she sacrificed," Granna continues. "I turned her away, and I did nothing."

"Still confused," I say. "What did she want? Was she trying to get to know you?"

"No, Franklin was sick, and they needed money," Granna replied. "I was rude. I let her know that Franklin turned me away like I was nothing. I had no intention of helping him. I could have helped. The bakery was doing great, and we had plenty of money. I let my anger guide me in the wrong direction."

"Still feeling guilty at your age," I ask. "Well, it's never too late to make amends, but I am surprised that you still feel guilty."

"You listen to nothing," she responds angrily. "If it wasn't for Mrs. Ada, the pecan butter would not have been improved. It would never have sold. I would not know how to bake as well as I do. I would not have lived the wealthy life I did, and I refused to help her son."

"That was decades ago, and you were angry," I offer. "So, you grew to hate both sides of your family? I don't get why, and maybe I will never understand why?"

"I never hated anyone," Granna corrects. "I just wanted to be free of St. Francis."

CHAPTER EIGHTEEN
Lily

We dance and frolic until hope is shown

Simply knowing you did nothing wrong can often yield enough power to fuel the hope needed to withstand an unjust attack. Anyone can sue anyone for anything. It's an unfair part of our justice system.

A lawsuit can be filed, and your only option may be to respond and request reimbursement of fees spent. If you're lucky, your unjust losses are recovered. More often, unfair disputes are simply tossed out of court, and both sides are left with a tremendous amount of unfair legal fees.

After months of discovery and trial prep, Aunt Rosey's Estate has cost us all a huge waste of time and money for what appears to be a pointless endeavor. Our team of three attorneys and two paralegals pack up months of trial prep and try to look on the bright side.

The judge has ordered us to appear in person for our MSJ Hearing, but the day before, we must meet with a mediator. We're going to New Orleans—that's something.

"That was a long flight, and I'm more than hungry," Finola announces. "I would love a drink and plenty of good Creole food."

"Let's check into our hotel, and I promise to not disappoint—as far as dinner is concerned," I laugh. "The rest of the night, you have to figure out on your own." We all have a good laugh and promise to huddle as fast as possible after arrival back down to the hotel lobby for dinner.

As soon as we land, as promised, we waste no time catching our hotel shuttle and making our way into the city. A long dinner is just what we need to relax our minds and fill our tummies. Also, a team dinner gives Anastasia time to rally our team and cover the highlights before tomorrow.

"One drink—ok, two drinks maximum, people," Anastasia demands. "I don't need slurring, red-eyed people in the morning. Give me your best foot forward, everyone. We can drink all night tomorrow. Promise!"

"Meeting in the lobby at 8:00 AM," I remind. "Quick breakfast then on our shuttle by eight-thirty. Bring a book, snacks, and a sweater. It'll be a long day."

Everyone agrees, and we are all well fed and tucked in by 10:00 PM sharp.

The morning is clear and welcoming. We all manage to gather early in the lobby before our ride shows up.

"Let's take a walk and get our juices flowing," I suggest. "We are so very close to the finish line. A few more hours, and this nightmare should be over."

"I agree," Anastasia offers. She seems much less on edge. Seeing her more relaxed also lets me know she's confident about our chances.

"Let's go," Finola joins in. "I spotted a coffee shop we need to try."

The smells from the coffee shop greet us as we near the corner, and they lead us to the most quintessential cafe. The handwritten menu along the shop's back wall appears to change each day. Several enticing coffee blends are shown, and we all find a favorite. With coffee in hand, we catch our shuttle to claim our victory.

The mediator bills each side $1,000.00 per hour, and his office accommodations almost make you less annoyed by the hefty price—well, almost. Each side is provided with its own suite of offices with a conference room, lounge area, workstations, and even restrooms. There's a menu for on-call meal service to go along with the fully stocked fruit, pastry, and snack table. I grab a chocolate beignet and enjoy the expansive view of the *Mississippi River*.

Anastasia is not distracted by all the fancy accommodations. She's started both paralegals to work reviewing and organizing the documents provided by the other side. Finola and I are perched in front of the floor-to-ceiling windows watching the ferry boats on the *Mississippi* like it's 1925.

"We need to get a good settlement for your family," Finola proclaims. "What your grandmother has accomplished should be protected."

"Counselors!" Anastasia shouts. "Battle time. Review your notes, and work on your wish list. We're having a joint session first, and then we're back in our separate areas until— until. We're getting this case settled."

"Absolutely!" I agree. "I'm done with this. We're all wasting money and time. It's just pointless."

"We all agree with you," Finola adds. "But, for today, try and keep an open mind."

"My mind is free," I say. "I'm looking forward to receiving their opening demand."

Our mediator, Edward Donaldson, is a former federal bankruptcy court judge. He's been a highly sought-after and respected mediator since leaving the bench five years ago. He's probably quadrupled his salary.

"Thank you all for trusting me to help you navigate through the issues," he says. "You each have an outline of our schedule and estimated time commitments. We'll do our best to follow this standard. If we're successful, by 6:00 PM, you'll all leave feeling you have been treated fairly, and a just conclusion was reached. Lastly, please, everyone, call me Ed."

Naming Lilah

It's now 10:00 AM, and Ed starts with the other side. He'll hear our opening at 11:30 AM. First offers are planned after lunch. Our suites are designed to keep us within its walls until a settlement is reached.

We order po'boys for lunch— shrimp, catfish, and oyster. Salads are also ordered to help balance out all the fried food and sugar we've eaten.

"I have the first offer," Ed announces as he hands us all an outline of terms.

> *Fifty of the one-hundred acres of land in St. Francis currently owned by Mrs. Marchand.*
> *Fifty-percent royalty from the future sale proceeds of pecan pies and pecan butter.*
> *Five million for lost revenue, damages, and attorney fees.*

REJECTED!

"Offer rejected!" is our immediate response.

We work for the next hour to draft a counter within the parameters set by Granna—absolutely no cash. *"No cash"* was underlined and circled.

"Do they think we are the *Apple Corporation*?" I snap. "Our first offer is $25,000 to purchase the rights to the pecan butter recipe they sold and a one-percent royalty from Marchand's pecan pies and pecan butter."

"Let's send it over," Anastasia agrees.

Ninety minutes later, an offer similar to their first was returned. We sent back our original offer, unchanged.

By 6:00 PM, no additional progress was made, and our mediator agreed to report our efforts to the court. We were excused.

The next morning, we all arrive in court early and prepared. Our argument easily withstands their attacks, and the judge advises that he'll make his ruling soon. We all leave the courthouse before Noon.

We all deserve a little fun, and what's more fun than winning money?
"Casino, anyone?" I ask. "Today seems lucky. We should ride this wave until at least tomorrow. Are we all in? We can play a few hours and catch a late flight."
No one objects, so…casino here we come.

"What's your game?" Anastasia asks. "I think I'll start with *Roulette*. I am feeling extra lucky, and I love shouting 'always bet on Black' and 'let it ride' while holding a glass of their best free alcoholic beverage."
"I'll join you," I reply. "I usually start with the slots, but today is a lucky day—*Roulette* it is."
"Ok, but don't jinx me," she jokes. "Your grandmother always reminds me that your luck seems to run high and low. Some days you cannot catch a break."

"Stop talking to Granna about me," I order. "I have enough issues. I don't need you joining in on the *'Fix Lily'* chorus."

"Oh no, I would never try to fix you," she confirms. "But, she did complain to me about all the money you spent on a kitchen renovation."

"Why would she even tell you about that? Goodness!" I laugh. "No one is spending her money. The bakery makes enough to cover its own expenses. Granna needs to stop spreading falsehoods."

"We should schedule a celebration dinner next week," Anastasia suggests confidently. "It would be great to have a glass of wine with your grandmother."

"Great idea, but only if you agree to not ask about me," I say. "The stories she tells are not true. You both need to focus on something else and stop trying to analyze me."

After arriving back in L.A., we all try to continue our normal routine while we await the judge's ruling.

"We will win on summary judgment, and a full-blown trial will not happen," I repeat these words daily until I am convinced they may actually be true. We always trusted that the law was on our side. Food cases are tough and usually get nowhere. We all lost money, but I try to look on the bright side—we gained a new family. How could that be bad?

𝒜t last, the judge rules. "Just received the calls," Anastasia shouts. "Judge ruled in our favor, and the plaintiff has decided not to appeal. It's officially over."

"Hallelujah!" I also begin to shout. "Thank You, Jesus. This fight had to end. It was draining us all—emotionally and financially."

"Yes, I'll send my bill with the standard sisterly discount," she says. "I'll also look out for the new set of pearls you promised. I need a longer strand for this new power suit I just picked up."

"You got it," I agree. "Another win for the books. Do you even remember the last time you lost a case?"

"Uh, no—but again, don't jinx me," she orders. "I may need your help on a trial I have coming up next month. Talk to Finola. I've already begged her for help."

My next call is to Granna, and we join in with Uncle. We all agree that a big celebration is in order, and until then, we toast each other from afar. The staff will get the news in the morning—maybe I'll bring balloons and gift baskets from Noel's shop? Surely, she won't mind putting together four little baskets by 9:00 AM?

𝒩oel is excited to hear about our victory but not excited about my early morning celebration basket request.

"I will have them ready by Noon," she relents. "Why do you think you can call me at the last minute? My shop doesn't open until 10:00 AM. Who's making baskets at nine?"

"I'll come help and bring you breakfast—cranky," I offer. "You can go in early. What else do you have to do? We won the lawsuit. I need balloons."

"You're impossible, and I don't know why I love you." she replies.

"I give you free legal advice, and I own a bakery—you eat for free," I add. "What's not to love? And I also practically helped you raise your three children. None of them will make it into college if I don't help them write their essays."

"Ok, smarty pants," she laughs. "I'll meet you at nine. Don't call me in the morning and try to get me up earlier—just meet me at the shop at 9:00 AM. And, don't come without pastries and coffee. You should go and pick up some of those kolaches Finola likes so much."

"Anything for you, my darling bestie," I agree. "See you at nine."

I'm waiting at Noel's shop with goodies in hand before 9:00 AM. She arrives timely, and we put together the most perfect balloon bouquets.

The drive to the bakery is problematic because I cannot see out any of my rear windows. I manage to arrive in one piece and carry my celebratory gesture without losing one balloon.

The staff can read the excitement on my face, and the balloons are, of course, an immediate giveaway. We all have a big screaming group hug and give thanks for the end of this collective nightmare.

"Good thing this mess is over." Ms. Julia announces. "*MajorMart* called. They want to see you next week."

---

*W*ith *MajorMart* on my mind and a victory in my pocket, I've decided to start the day by making a morning stop at Granna's. I'm ready to continue working towards a major Big-Box store deal. I also bring an excessively wrapped, with too much sparkly tissue paper inside a large gold box, an artist-painted serving tray I picked up when I was in New Orleans. I've been holding on to it, waiting for a moment like this. Granna loves original New Orleans art.

"Lily, you look much prettier today wearing that great big smile," Granna says as she grabs my cheeks. "I've missed seeing this face. That old grumpy, meddling, nosey, busy-body face overstayed its welcome."

"Granna, I love you too," I offer with a slightly disapproving nod. "I wanted to catch you before your walk and bring you a celebration gift I've been holding."

"That's very thoughtful," she adds with a hint of mischief. "I also have a gift for you."

A legal-sized envelope with the name of her New Orleans estate law firm is on her favorite reading side table next to her favorite chair. She typically only allows poetry books and cups of tea on her side table.

"What's this?" I ask as she hands me the envelope. She takes my gold box and rests it on her lap as she peaks inside.

"Oh, Lily! This is lovely. You know I have other dishes from this artist," Granna announces. "I will take this to our next Bible Study. Now, open your gift."

I slide her ottoman a few steps away so I can sit across from her as I open her gift. Is it a new will, and she's removed me? Am I getting more? Am I the executor? What could it be? As I hesitate and my mind continues speculating, Granna blurts out, "Will you just open it, please?"

> *"Please allow Mrs. Marchand's granddaughter,*
> *attorney Lily Guillory, to assist with the*
> *Tillerson Family acquisition negotiations."*

As I read the letter Granna's estate attorney has prepared, I look to Granna for answers before continuing. The stack of documents includes instructions for a due diligence review and proposed terms for the purchase of the rights to package and distribute the pecan butter sold by *Cajun Made Foods*.

There's also a letter to Kate's family attorney requesting they meet to discuss the *Cajun Made Foods* purchase and the continuation of their royalty rights—payable going forward by *Much Ado*.

"Why are you doing this now," I ask gently. "This is the last thing I would ever have imagined. After all these years, you want to involve your family in our lives. Have you told uncle?"

"Not yet, I wanted you to review the documents first, and if it happens, we will tell Uncle," Granna explains. "It's nowhere near a signing point."

"Amazing!" I cannot think of the next proper words to say.

"I want you to start working with my attorneys—slowly," Granna informs. "You will have access to this matter first, and if it goes well, maybe more. You are not to order anyone around, and you are not to ask questions about any other investment. Follow my rules, Lily, and we'll see if I can trust you with more."

"Trust me," I say angrily. "I know you don't trust me. I knew that for sure when I found out about your investments, but I'm still hurt by your words. You don't trust your only granddaughter."

"This is exactly why," she adds. "Everything is so full of emotion. You think too much with your heart. You are a good attorney, but you are horrible with money. I've always seen that. If you can't admit your own shortcomings, why should I trust you to make money decisions for me?"

"Fine, I will prove you wrong," I state. "I am a good attorney, and I will show you I've learned to be a good businesswoman. I will work on this purchase and outperform all your so-called good, trusted money guys."

My comments seem to have been delivered with confidence, and Granna looks impressed. I am a good litigator, and I know how to bluff and convince a jury, but I have no idea how to close this deal. Maybe Anastasia can coach me?

CHAPTER NINETEEN
Lily

Our Love becomes ignored routine

There is not a time that I have found when the pain of grief completely fades. Grief may show its face daily—especially in the moments that carry a memory of those we love. Our Mother is with us in every moment my brother and I spend together, and every time I have a question about parenting or about aging. Who is available to answer my questions? My Mother is a part of who I am. As long as there is a me, I've found that my Mother is with me in every part of everyday life.

Mother is with me today as I plan another trip to Louisiana. I wish Granna would come along, but I realize that she will most likely give me a "No." Mother, Granna, and Louisiana begin all of my favorite childhood memories.

Today, I'm taking another trip to Louisiana— more trips in six months than I typically take in six years. This trip to Louisiana was due to take place earlier but was postponed because of the judge's mediation order and MSJ Hearing. It's back on my agenda because of the *MajorMart* presentation and Granna's deal with *Cajun Made Foods*

"Granna, do you think you're up for a flight to Louisiana?" I ask. "You haven't been in years, and Uncle would like to show you the expansion."

"I see everything just fine on my tablet," she replies. "It's just as good as face-to-face."

"You know it's not," I say. "I don't understand why you and Uncle refuse to travel. Granna, you used to love to travel."

"That's when my knees were in much better shape," she laughs. "I really did love to travel."

"You know you'll have wheelchair gate service," I explain.

"You also know I don't like being wheeled around the airport—disgusting," she answers.

"What if I take you to your favorite macarons shop?" I suggest.

"Maybe if you get a non-stop first-class flight? Granna says. "Why do you need me? We'll also need a handicapped hotel room. I need the railings in the bathroom. It's too much trouble. There's nothing there I need to see and no one to see who can't come and visit me. I'm staying here!"

"Fine!" I relent. "I understand. No pressure—really. I just thought it would be nice for us to visit together. I'm going to visit the library you named after Mrs. Ada."

"Don't go bragging about yourself or me," she orders. "That place is for St. Francis—not you. Mind your manners, Lily."

"I won't embarrass you. Promise!" I reply. "Stop worrying. You could join me and make sure I follow your rules."

"If you do anything improper, I will hear about it right away," she adds. "Mind your manners, and don't upset anyone with your questions and meddling."

"I will video chat with you and take lots of pictures," I propose as a compromise.

"I visit St. Francis often," Granna explains. "If I close my eyes now, I'm there. My mother is singing at the piano, Mrs. Ada is braiding my hair, I can see my father in the yard, and my sister is annoying us all. I'm never far from home. Home is with me always, just as you are, and I also see their faces almost every day. Well…I see your face every day whether I like it or not."

"Thanks, don't sound so happy to see me," I laugh. "You know you love seeing my face every day."

"All this family stuff is hard, I know," Granna remarks. "I also miss my daughter and Louisiana. I still miss my Mother every day. You can't run or hide from loss. There's no need. It will always find you."

I've scanned the photos Granna has and hope to find the same scenes when I arrive in St. Francis. Kate's driving with me from New Orleans to St. Francis. This time I welcomed her company. She's visited the area often and may in fact help me find the spots shown in Granna's photos.

None of this is anything I think will help finalize our negotiations, but maybe if I learn more about Mrs. Ada and her family, I will also learn more about the Cormier's and the farm. Granna still knows so little about the Lewis side of her family while they were in St. Francis, and I think that's a mistake. I don't think Granna would welcome my snooping around St. Francis asking questions so I'm keeping my snooping plans a secret.

"Granna, do you think anyone in St. Francis remembers you?" I ask.

"Such a silly thing to think about," Granna answers. "The people I knew are probably all dead. What 90-year-old is still walking around St. Francis thinking about me? I moved away at eighteen— too many years ago to count."

"Do you remember anyone from high school?" I say.

"I hope you are not going to St. Francis because of me?" she questions. "You are wasting time, Lily. Life is happening today. Focus on that and stop looking for something that doesn't exist."

A call from Uncle saves me. Granna is occupied while I finish scanning the remaining photos I need for my trip.

I give Granna a kiss and say my goodbyes. Visiting much longer risked me slipping up and saying the wrong thing. I need to protect my position as Granna's favorite.

A long goodnight's rest was essential before my flight. Traveling with Kate will be a chore, but she will help me navigate the Louisiana countryside. The numerous holidays and summers spent with Granna in New Orleans never included a trip to St. Francis.

I stop at the hotel gift shop for snacks before heading to my room. I also consider downloading a few podcasts, but I know

Kate will not shut up the entire trip, so instead, I add Tylenol to my travel supply.

"Lily, I'm five minutes away. Are you ready?" Kate eagerly says. "Do you want to stop for food? They have a great spot on the way."

"I'll be ready," I say while entering my hotel room. I quickly began to arrange my treats in the backpack I purchased for our trip. "I'll meet you out front, and no, to food. I just want to get there and see what we can see. We can eat on the way back. I have snacks for the road."

"Fine," she agrees. "Can we at least get coffee?"

"Whatever, Kate" I say. "I don't know why I agreed to let you drive me anywhere."

"You're stuck with me for two days, and don't forget you said you'd meet my mother." Kate reminds.

I must have been on my second glass of wine when I consented to that request. Kate's determined to create this new *Big Happy Family*, and I'm sure my meeting her mother is a part of her master plan. Because of her mom's condition and her brother's… whatever his problem may really be…her need to add to the family is not that surprising.

Granna was actually the reason I asked Kate if she'd visited her grandparents' home. I had been bombarding Granna with 20-questions every other day, and I think she had enough of my busy mind. She had reached the end of her daily allotment of patience when she also suggested that I ask Kate.? Finding answers for myself is the simplest and less stressful option for us both, and visiting St. Francis is sure to help answer many of my questions.

Kate arrives punctually and surprisingly drives a trendy luxury SUV. I had pictured her in a minivan.

In no time, we are on our way. Kate acquires her coffee, and we are out of the city and crossing the *Bonnet Carre*—it never disappoints. There is always something new to discover, and the endless waterways leave me intrigued. How long did it take to construct the hundreds of miles of bridges covering South Louisiana from Lafayette to the tip of the state far south of New Orleans? How were the concert pillars placed in the spillway? Let me Google it.

"Now, when you visit NOLA, we can hang out. I want to show you my favorite spots. You know Ryan owns one of the best bars in the Quarter. I'll find out which band is there tonight. He has the best. You'll love it."

"No way!" I assert. "I am not going to Ryan's bar. I will in no way give him the idea that he is forgiven for what he did and all the lies he stirred up. Even if he picks up the telephone—which I never expect him to do and apologizes, I'm still not going to his bar."

"Don't be so hard on him," she defends. "Ryan was spoiled by mom and dad. He's used to getting his way and having things handed to him. That's why he can't maintain a relationship."

"NO, Ryan," I maintain. "And, stop trying to schedule every minute of my trip."

Kate trying to control the agenda is not surprising, and my resisting is only expending precious energy needed to make it through the next two days.

"Well, what time can we go by my mom's?" she asks.

"Tomorrow morning, I plan to meet Uncle at the bakery," I say. "We can meet your mother for lunch."

"I'll pick you up," she asserts. "I haven't been formally introduced to your uncle. We should definitely meet. It's weird that we live in the same area, and he's never met any of us. Tell me about his wife and children."

"We have work stuff and should be done by Noon. You can meet him when you pick me up for lunch. His wife works with him. She'll be there. They have one son. He's in Med School at *Howard University* in D.C."

Uncle is a typical dude that will not entertain Kate's "Ra-Ra-Ra we're family" cheers. I hope she doesn't think he'll come over for Thanksgiving. He barely visits his own mother.

"Ok, Noon will work," she responds. "Should I pick up my mom first?"

"Uncle wouldn't mind," I say. "Is your mom up for that much excitement?"

Kate's been more than open about her mother's struggle with dementia. Meeting too many Black family members in one day may be a bit much for her to handle.

"We should probably pick her up on the way to *Monarch's*," Kate states. "I hope she's having a good day."

Lunch at *Monarch's Palace* will be a treat. I loved going there with mom and Granna. It's like stepping back in time. Well, an alternate time where we all were welcomed to dine. Its historic colonial designs, formal dining settings and tuxedoed wait staff offer a glimpse into a time long gone. I imagine the romance of it all without adding the reality of the evils of the South.

"Thirty miles to St. Francis," I announce after checking my phone's *GPS*. I've been keeping track just in case Kate misses a turn. She's a very intelligent person, but she's also too easily distracted and excitable. Today, I'm the victim of Kate's endless random tangents, started by a song on the radio. Again, why did I agree to this drive?

"Yes, you'll love it," she proclaims. "It's just like the photos. My mom took us to the house and farm when we were kids. We visited the church our family started and our great-grandparents' grave sites. Your great-grandparents too."

"Yes, I'm sure they will be surprised to see me visit their graves," I joke. "We don't want any uprisings."

"You are so silly— stop joking around about the dead," she warns. "You're in Louisiana. I'm sure your grandmother has warned you about Spirits."

"Granna, not so much, but my grandfather's family—always," I confirm. "I remember visiting Gramps' older sister. She lived in the "Country," I'm not sure where exactly, but she made us kids stay outside all day. She put a canister of *Kool-Aid* on the porch in case we wanted a drink. There was no running back-and-forth inside the house. The air conditioner would not survive."

"Haha...You don't seem like the type of child who would have followed that rule." Kate adds. "Did you cause a revolt?"

"No, at first, I enjoyed running around the yard, climbing trees, and building forts," I explain. "When we were older, I started refusing to go to the 'Country.' Luke still liked going, but I was done with the dirt and long days in the Sun—besides, she didn't let us play music. She would yell at me to stop playing the devil's music. I guess the Louisiana Spirits didn't like 90's R&B?"

"No—especially on Sunday." Kate laughs. "My grandma didn't let us listen to music either. I think that's another reason Ryan is such a wild child. He's making up for growing up with Southern Baptist on one side and strict Catholics on the other."

"St. Francis has kept its charm," I say as we drive down the town's Main Street. "It's nice to see stores open and people out and about."

"Yes, it's a cute town," Kate agrees. "The high school is at the end of the street. I think both our grandmothers graduated from St. Francis High School. We should take a picture out front. That would be so cool."

I'm not opposed to the idea. Granna would more than appreciate and enjoy seeing photos of her old home and maybe we could use a few—without Kate—on our website.

"That actually sounds great," I say. "Let's get a few shots of Main Street and then the high school. We can also take a few selfies or see if we can find someone around to take a photo?"

We both have our phones, and I brought along a camera with a good lens. I've had it since the kids were small, and I was one of those *Insta Moms*. That ended when they realized why I was always taking their photo. Teenagers...argh!

The high school has maintained much of its historic charm, but the outside of the main entrance has definitely been renovated. We take photos in front of one of the older brick buildings along the side of the school near the football field.

"I'd like to get one more photo of the football field," Kate says. "I think my grandma was a cheerleader. Do you know about yours?"

"I don't think so, but with my grandmother—you never know?" I reply. "I'll ask."

After photos, we take off down the same road until we reach a narrow road surrounded by cotton fields. I've experienced this view many times before. Gramps' family home was across the street from a large corn field, and cotton was grown along the road coming into the town.

"There's the house." Kate brings her SUV to a stop at the edge of the driveway. "I'm not sure who lives here now?"

"I'll take a few quick photos," I announce. "If someone comes out, we can claim we are with the tax office."

Anastasia found that Granna had previously rented the home, but she could not confirm if there's a current tenant. I share none of this information with Kate.

"Ok, that sounds good." Kate chuckles. "The processing facility was over there behind the barn. I think it was torn down before the farm was sold?"

"I see the tree in Granna's photo," I say while snapping another photo. "It's just amazing to see in person. Life—this is where it all started for our family." The house still looks well maintained and still holds its beauty.

"Our appointment with the church secretary is at 2:00 PM," Kate reminds. "She said they have birth, baptism, and death records we can view. Did you ask your grandmother about the Black church? My mom didn't know. I thought about asking the lady at *St. Francis Baptist*, but I felt she might think I was crazy?"

"Why would you think that—silly," we both laugh. "I asked Granna, but she wasn't sure which one Mrs. Ada attended. I honestly think she pretended not to know because she didn't want me snooping around asking about her father's family."

Our focus is shifted back to the Cormier's, and we stop to visit our great-grandparents' grave sites. We leave flowers Kate remembered to bring. The thought never occurred to me.

The cemetery is accompanied by a large tan brick church which looms high over the street corner it occupies. We enter the church and are greeted by the most appropriate looking Baptist Church secretary.

"Pleasure meeting you both," she greets us before guiding us to her office near the back of the church. "I have everything ready for you young ladies. The Cormier family is one of our founding families. I also found a few photos."

Kate and I are both awed by the number of documents and photos found. Holding Granna's baptism record visibly moved me. A photo of our great grandparents taken with the church elders even made Kate tear up. Granna will be so happy to have another picture of her parents. I think she only has one or two that I have seen.

We snapped copies of the photos with our phones and were allowed to photocopy as much as we liked. Kate and I both made sure to leave the church large donations for Sunday's collection box.

"I'm so happy we did this together," Kate expresses. "I hope you can one day think of us as family. I know it's too soon—especially for Ryan."

We both laugh and take in the remaining views as we head back to the main highway. It's now after 4:00 PM, and I must admit, my day with Kate was not that awful.

The next morning, Uncle and Aunt Helen are already working at full speed by the time I make it to the bakery. They both give me a quick hello hug and instruct me to begin helping fill orders. After eating two freshly baked croissants, I'm ready to work.

"Kate's picking me up at 11:30 AM," I announce. "I'm going to lunch with her and her mother at *Monarch's*. She wants to meet you both. Is that okay?"

"Meet us—why?" Aunt Helen asks. "We are not interested in handing out any more family discounts."

"We surely are not." Uncle jokes. "I don't mind meeting her, but this will not be a regular thing. If you want to know them, that's fine, but we are not interested."

"No, I understand," I say. "Just meet her this one time, and hopefully, she won't start showing up here asking for food," I joke without disclosing that Kate has a problem with boundaries. I can't be sure that she won't just start showing up unannounced.

Kate arrives at 11:30 AM sharp and surprisingly seems nervous to speak. This is new and definitely something I've never previously experienced.

"Thanks for meeting me," she strongly says as she extends her hand.

"I'm Helen." My aunt says as she reaches in and gives Kate a big hug. "This is my husband, Lily's Uncle, Elias."

"It's such a pleasure to meet you both," Kate says. "I've had your pecans well before this whole mess ever started. You're pretty popular in the city."

"Thanks for saying that," Uncle responds. "We work hard to keep our family legacy alive. My parents worked hard to create this business for us. I don't want to mess things up. Lily, on the other hand...?"

"Okay, let's not start talking about me," I express before Uncle can say another word. "Kate, let's go. We'll be late."

Kate is unusually quiet on the ride to her mother's. I don't dare speak. The quietness is a nice, unexpected treat.

"This is my mom's," Kate announces as we pull into her driveway. She has a stately home near *Audubon Park* that looks like it's been around for decades but is well maintained like it was built in this decade.

"Is this the house where you grew up?" I ask. "It's really nice. This is a great area—so close to the park."

"Yes, we grew up here," she states. "Now, you see another reason why Ryan is such a spoiled brat."

"I really didn't need any additional proof." We both laugh and try to hide our giggles as Kate opens her mom's front door.

"Mom, it's Kate and Lily," she announces. "Are you ready for lunch?"

Kate's mother is dressed in her Sunday finest with the perfect handbag. From appearances, she looks completely normal.

"Pleasure to finally met you, Lily," she responds softly, unlike that of her boisterous children. "You really do look like your grandmother. Kate warned me I would think so, and she was correct."

"Thank you for having me and taking time for lunch," I respond. "I'm enjoying getting to know Kate. She's actually quite refreshing and very funny most times."

"Oh, yes," she smiles. "Kate's a people person. She's been the same way since birth—she never stops talking. She was class president in high school. I wasn't surprised when she decided to get into Louisiana politics. Lord knows we could use a smart woman who is not afraid to speak her mind."

"Yes, that perfectly describes Kate," I agree.

Lunch at *Monarch's Palace* is just as I remembered. The piano music playing in the background softens the mood and helps make the food taste better. Kate's mom has an innocent elegant demeanor reminiscent of a nineteen-fifties housewife. Granna would have loved to know her, and Kate is lucky to have her mom, even though I know it's hard for her to view this time with any amount of Joy.

"Lily, how was your fish?" Kate asks. "How was your steak, Mother?"

We both expressed our pleasure and greeted the dessert tray without hesitation. After dessert and coffee, we are all ready for a well-deserved afternoon nap.

Kate drops me off at the bakery first so that she can make sure her mom is settled in safely at home. Our lunch was much more pleasant than I had imagined. I thank them both and make a quick exit back to my life.

CHAPTER TWENTY
Lily

What matters most is both given and received

The black-and-white prints of the photos we took in St. Francis were transformed flawlessly to resemble painted images. I can practically see Granna running through her front yard and rolling through the grass. Her cheeks would have a slight hint of pink from the Sun, and her hair would flow with the wind.

Because of Granna and mom, I also try to never miss the beauty that surrounds me. Whether driving in a car, walking through my neighborhood, or planting flowers with Granna in her garden, I now notice the beauty.

Noticing a bird as it swoops through the trees, smelling the welcoming scent of a bushel of flowers, feeling the warmth of the Noon Sun..."There's always something beautiful to witness, Lily. Look up and tell me what you see," Granna often says.

My meeting with *MajorMart* should be finalized soon, so I hope to complete our promotion package by the end of this week.

"Good morning Granna. I'm about to video conference with Uncle and go over the final proposal for *MajorMart*," I call to offer my standard invite even though I know she no longer likes joining in on most of our company calls. "Do you want to join?"

"Too early for me to work, but I'm putting on my shoes to go out with our walking group—it's Tuesday," she reminds. "You two talk and fill me in later."

"Sounds good- enjoy," I reply. "I'll come by on my way home and bring you the leftover dough. Are you baking for tomorrow's Bible Study?"

"Don't I always?" she answers. "Go make your call and let me put my shoes on."

Aunt Helen put me on Uncle's morning schedule, but I can tell he's really not interested in chatting. Keeping our call short so he can get back to his morning baking routine is his obvious goal.

"Any ideas? Look at what I have so far," I try to pan my camera over the posters covering my desk. "Remember the thought I had— many people also know the Marchand name. What do you honestly think?"

"I think you have more than enough," he states definitively. "Keep everything with the *Much Ado* name and send the proposal."

I agree and don't leave my office until I pray and hit send.

Most of the staff has scattered for lunch, but Ms. Julia is still nearby. She has been peeking in on me all morning. I know she's unhappy about something. "The bakery equals joy," I repeat out loud. I'm working in a bakery—that's Joy. I'm not working on a trial— definite Joy.

Setting a goal to add true gestures of joy to each day was meant to train my mind to stop waiting for the weekend and enjoy each day. I remind myself to "Stop wishing away your days!" Stop bemoaning every unwanted task. Joy comes with the gift of each day. Don't forget to unwrap and enjoy. I open my door and step out into Joy.

"Why are we going to a food fair." Ms. Julia asks without pause. "Do we have to talk to people and play nice?"

My distraught look answered her question better than my words could manage to accomplish. "The vendor entry forms arrived yesterday. Did you read the info I left on your desk?"

"Of course, that's why I'm asking," she chimes back. "It's a lot of work. Are you wanting to have an oven or cooktop for demos?"

"Let's talk about it," I offer. "What does the team think is doable?" I've learned that just because Ms. Julia thinks something is a bad idea, the staff does not always agree. None of us has developed the courage to tell her she's turning into a grumpy old biddy. We all fear that such a comment may lead to a rolling pin to the head.

"Fine! We have staffing after lunch," she informs. "I will not say a word. Don't blame me if no one wants to go out mixing it up with food snobs."

"Customers—they're customers," I remind her. "Don't you want to meet the people who love what you make for them?"

"I work in a kitchen for a reason," she says defensively. "I barely like talking to you people."

"Oh, but we love talking to you," I joke. "Who would tell us how to behave if you didn't remind us?"

"Nothing would get done," she brags. "Without me—it's a tea party. You'd all bake in the morning and eat it all by lunch."

"Yes! We know," I confirm. "You also know I love competition. How would we know we're the best? You'll have fun—I promise."

We all could use another win. The lawsuit served as a wet rag on our enthusiasm for much too long. Getting out and showing off our hard work should be fun, and besides—I love to win. I attended this show last year, and I think our stuff is way better. The crowd favorite wins fifty-grand and gets a news spotlight.

I've considered reasons we may not win, but that version of reality doesn't stick. My reality remains focused on the win. Recipe creations, arguments before the court, winning a catering contract and finalizing a much needed contract for a client are all wins in a reality I first visualize and then conquer.

A food fair is just a distraction I hope will work to motivate us and impress *MajorMart*, but Ms. Julia is not wrong about the extra work and possible stress. Is Ms. Julia completely right? Why do we need to do a food fair? But what if we win? Now, see—that's Joy!

𝒯he food fair is still days away when I receive confirmation of my meeting with *MajorMart*. I never expected to hear from them so soon. Our meeting is tomorrow and now I panic.

"ℒily Guillory…"

"Yes," I reply as my name is called. Whitney arranged for me to meet with the West Coast baked goods rep for *MajorMart*. As I prepare my next words, a thousand scenarios begin racing through my mind. Who will we pick to hand out samples? Who will volunteer? Maybe we should all take turns—even Granna.

"Ms. Guillory, pleasure. I'm Scott Lands, Director of Baked Goods. We've tried your products and they are amazing. Also, we read up on you, your family, and the lawsuit. Quite a story. How's everyone getting along today?" Mr. Lands asks while escorting me through a large conference room door. He gestures for me to sit in the chair nearest to him.

"Hello, I'm Amy Cross, Director of On-site Marketing." a tall, imposing young lady states.

"Thank you for meeting with me. I'm honored to have this opportunity to tell you about our company and our products," I feel a slight shake in my voice which is very surprising. I speak for a living—daily. Maybe it's the "not a good businesswoman" comment Granna made that's haunting me?

"As an attorney, you should find that our supply agreements are standard and straightforward and shouldn't take you too long to sort through. You'll meet with Legal after this meeting." Mr. Lands explains.

"That's wonderful. Does this mean we're in?" I question with too much excitement.

"Absolutely, your product presentation was reviewed by our top staff and buyers, and everyone was quite impressed. Welcome to the *MajorMart* family!" they both say in unison.

I want to jump across the table and hug them both, but I quickly rethink that move.

"This meeting was mostly for us to meet with you in person and to introduce you to the team who will assist you with product placement. Our various in-store partners each have their own sets of rules. Welcome info and guidelines are all detailed here." Ms. Cross adds as she slides a two-inch binder across the table.

"Thank you both. Truly, this is life changing." As the words come out, I feel I'm being too mushy, but I don't try to suppress my gratitude. I think of mom, and my eyes begin to well. If only...?

"It's our pleasure. Take a moment, and someone from Legal will be in to escort you to your next meeting." Ms. Cross ends with a big hug, and Mr. Lands offers one as well.

I think of Uncle and his dedication to the bakery. I can imagine how proud he will be to see our products on store shelves. He will literally lose his mind when we make it onto Louisiana store shelves.

Sample tasting will surely become one of his new favorite hobbies. He will want to design new uniforms for our staff and come up with a new catchy welcome line. The standard "Would you like to try our tarts?" won't be good enough for Uncle. He's

NOLA born and raised. I'm just hoping he doesn't try to start a *Second line* through stores.

I'm anxious to call Granna and Uncle but decide to wait until I'm in my car so I can scream. Thinking of all we've lost, and all we've gained by never giving up weighs heavy. I begin to well up again as I pray. Then suddenly, the conference room doors swing open.

"Ms. Guillory, ready? I'll walk you over to Legal."

I hope she didn't see me crying. I'll lose all my negotiating power if I can't stop the waterworks. Get it together, woman. I am a partner and General Counsel for a new upcoming major national food brand. Ahhhaa! Look at me now!

I drive straight to Granna's to deliver her copy of *Much Ado About Pecan's* signed distribution agreement with *MajorMart Retailers*. I started this journey believing that opening bakery locations around the country was the best way for us to grow our business. My big-dreaming mind never truly imagined retail. I'm convinced Whitney was sent by my angels to save me from myself.

"It's done," I announce as I hand Granna the binder of documents from *MajorMart*. "Can you believe we actually got this done? I finally did something right—let me hear you say the words. 'Good job Lily!' You can do it."

"You do a lot right," Granna corrects. "I really like this display design. Who did this?"

"Me and Ms. Julia," I proudly reply. "I struggled for hours, and she walked in and laid everything out exactly as you see. She has a naturally artistic eye."

"I love Julia," Granna says. "She's one of my best discoveries."

"Yes, you also have a good eye," I add. "My business eye is on the rise, but my artistic eye is still in need of plenty of help."

"Keep making us all money, and we'll send you to art school," Granna jokes. "Look at your child—Lydia sings, acts, plays the piano. Does it all come from Adam?"

"She's in debate," I say. "That comes from me."

"Exactly, that's not her artistic side," Granna laughs. "Why don't you get one of those adult coloring books and meditate. Look on my desk. I think I have two or three from last Christmas."

"Granna, you are also a gifted artist. You write poetry and design beautiful, delicious pastries. I'm okay to know that my talents lie elsewhere. Mom wasn't especially artistic— she was talentedly kind, compassionate, and generous."

"Well...I hate to be the one to tell you, but you're also lacking in kindness and generosity," Granna enjoys her laugh at my expense.

"Thanks!" I say with a huge frown. "Should we call Uncle? Let's see if he can take a break for a quick video chat?"

"He can take a break," Granna replies. "He needs to take lots of breaks and slow down. I'm not sure who he can train to help? Luke and Will are not going to ever work at the bakery—maybe their children and your children?"

"We're building a legacy," I say. "One of these children will have the business talent and take us to the next level."

"The next level?" she questions. "What's that? *MajorMart* is plenty."

"Oh, Granna," I laugh. "The sky's the limit. We could go international. What about Paris Cafes? The French would love our pastries."

"The French don't need help with their pastries," she says. "We are trying to keep up with them. Haven't you been to Paris? Stop talking silly."

We share our news with Uncle, and I promise to visit soon to go over baking timelines. We still have lots of work to do to streamline our production, and we hope to grow without overwhelming our staff. Our Los Angeles kitchen will be expanded first to meet *MajorMart's* West Coast supply. I hope to soon secure the Southwest and Central stores. Getting Uncle on board with a larger New Orleans kitchen must come first.

If we have good first-quarter numbers, maybe they'll let me spend more money? I will need to call on my angels once again for the help.

CHAPTER TWENTY-ONE
Lily

Without the exchange, loss fails to exist

Sincere expressions of flattery are seldom wasted, and Cousin Kate's gestures directed toward me have undoubtedly achieved the goal she set to win me over and gain our trust.

She's convinced me to make an appearance at her campaign tailgate event. Not ever did I imagine I would agree to such a thing. But if I'm honest with myself, I'm curious to check out Kate in action and learn more about her family. I also need to see Uncle and properly celebrate our *MajorMart* miracle.

The flight into New Orleans now seems quicker and less exhausting. My guess is that I've now taken this flight so often it's beginning to feel like a part of my normal routine—like riding a bike. Adam has agreed to tag along, and the flight also does not seem to have bothered him one tiny bit. He travels a lot for work, so airplane rides are probably also like bike rides for him.

Kate's event is being held at a local park between the airport and downtown. The car service she arranged greets us as we exit the baggage area. Within minutes, we arrive without a moment to change our minds.

There's a surprisingly huge turnout and level of excitement. Outside events have remained the preferred new normal, and attendance is always much better because of the increased comfort level. Kate's face lights up when she notices us in the crowd. Adam and I chuckle and give each other a questionable look.

Is Kate extra chummy because it will help her campaign? I'm certain her ambitions win out over family love. Also, it will obviously help her campaign to promote family unity. Downplaying the fact that she sued the Black side of the family is what I have deducted as her true goal. I don't mind playing along. We are family, and that won't change regardless of the fact that they sued us.

Adam and I declined the offer to pose for any family group photos, but that didn't stop Kate from catching a few crowd shots of us chatting. I enjoy watching the crowd and seeing her campaign aids in action. Politics is also one of my great passions, but the visceral level of personal attacks has kept me from putting my name in the hat for any office. Supporting good candidates and advocating for important causes has been the best option for me. Maybe when my kiddos are adults, I'll give it another look.

"I really appreciate you coming and showing your support," Kate offers me the standard campaign greeting. "You know this lawsuit was never my idea, and I was technically not a party. Between us, I always thought it was madness and a waste of money."

"Thanks for that, Kate. The entire mess was a waste of time and money, but maybe we will find a Silver-Lining one day?" I leave her with the standard soft touch to her left shoulder and turn to speak to one of her campaign workers about the turnout.

"You're one of Kate's rich long-lost relatives, correct?" a perky stranger with press credentials hanging around her neck questions.

"I'm not sure what you mean?" I respond. After my television appearance started this whole mess, I know better than to make any comments to the press.

"I'm familiar with your family lawsuit," she adds. "It's obvious they were after your family's money. Who really cares about Pecan Butter?"

"Well, you seem to know a lot more than I do," I reply.

"Let me know if you would like to talk more," she says as she hands me her card. "You're a smart attorney. I'm sure you know to always follow the money. Bars took a big hit the last few years and political campaigns are expensive."

I take her card and walk away with a curious stare.

"You ready?" Adam asks. "I said hello and shook Kate's husband's hand. Someone grabbed a quick photo. We've served our purpose."

"Some reporter just implied that Kate's family is after our money," I laugh. I joke because I now know that compared to Granna, they are broke.

"You should know better than I do to not assume anything," Adam warns.

"Yes, I found that out the hard way," I say without disclosing details. We make a quick exit and wave goodbye to whomever is looking our way.

It's a perfect Louisiana day. The humidity is light, the sky is clear, and the Sun is bright with just the needed hint of warmth. An afternoon talking politics and an evening of football is my kind of day. The only thing missing is sugar, and we take care of that with a stop by the bakery.

Adam hasn't been to New Orleans in a few years, and I want him to see all the new things we've done with the bakery. I'm happy he joined me, but I know it was only because I was able to snag suite seats for the *Saints* game. Granna's estate attorneys invited us. It will be the first time we are all meeting face-to-face.

"Uncle, your favorite niece is here," I shout as we enter the busy bakery. "I also have a copy of the *MajorMart* package for you and Aunt Helen."

"Hello, mother of my favorite niece," he responds. "But Adam is definitely my favorite nephew-in-law." We all laugh and exchange tight hugs.

"Great to see you," Adam says. "We never get you out to California. I came specifically to see you."

"Sure, can I have your *Saints* tickets then?" After another long laugh, we all make our way to the front of the bakery to collect our treats. I pack roasted pecans and pecan bites and instruct Uncle to add them to my tab.

"GEAUX SAINTS!" We all yell as we exit for the *Superdome*.

We navigate through the crowds and snap selfies with a group of outrageous *Painted Saints Fans*. Hanging out with drunken, nearly naked, grown men covered in body paint is an experience we should all have just once.

We make our next few moves like the professional sports fans we are—quick moves to the left, then right, with a few strong arms, and we are through the crowd without a scratch. *Geaux Saints!*

We walk through the lower Plaza Level before taking the escalator up to the suite level. The lower levels are not for the humble *Saints Fan* and focused game watchers. *Saints Fans* who stand throughout most of the game screaming at the top of their lungs sit closest to the action. If you are not ready to go all in the entire game, sit up a level.

"Great idea to catch a game," Adam says. "I forget how much fun this city can be. It's still weird that you wanted to come for Kate, but the game is great."

"Yeah, it's weird," I agree. "I'm trying to figure her out, but so far—nothing. She seems sincere. We never really talked about the case or the bakery. Maybe she just really wants to make amends?"

"Naw, she wants something." Adam jokes. "When you figure it out, you owe me a Hundred."

"Sure thing, Dude!" I reply, "Stop taking pleasure in my family drama. Her idiot brother cost us lots of time and money. My brother has never given a second thought about the bakery. Kate's brother sits around waiting to receive royalty checks."

"Well, that's family," he adds. "Everyone has a few crazies."

Granna's attorneys welcome us and introduce us to their families. Their suite is large enough to hold thirty people with ample food and drinks. The firm's lead attorney looks to be around Uncle's age. His son also works for the firm and is there with his young children. I was warned by Granna to not talk business, and I complied. After claiming I'm not a good businesswoman, I don't want to give Granna any more reasons to doubt me.

The *Superdome* is overflowing with energy, and the *Saints* are using it to score touchdown after touchdown. The *Saints* typically keep us balled up in an anxious knot after every play. It's a rare pleasure to sit and enjoy the game without stressing about the clock.

With a twenty-point fourth-quarter game lead, the celebrating is unstoppable. *Saints* earn the "W," and the party is sure to continue throughout the night.

"Did I mention we agreed to go back and meet Uncle at the bakery?" I ask, knowing the answer is "No."

"What about hanging out and celebrating like normal people?" He responds. "Why are you trying to get me to work? I know what meeting Uncle at the bakery means."

"Don't be so negative," I offer. "You'll have fun. It's great people watching, and you'll get a chance to visit Uncle. He loves chatting you up about the State of America's relationship with the people."

"You've got jokes." Adam laughs. "A stroll through the *Quarter* with a few *Hurricanes* sounds much better."

"Give me one hour and then *Hurricanes*—promise," I beg. "We can sleep in tomorrow."

The bakery is busy as usual after a *Saints* game. Uncle skipped attending tonight's game, but every television in the bakery is always set on the game. We have a patio area that stays open until 2:00 AM on weekend nights. Roasted bags of pecans are popular with tourists. You can catch the smells of the bakery from a few blocks away.

"Lily, Adam, get in here," Uncle gestures. "Stop acting like customers. Help me get this line down. Did you love that game? We needed a big win. *WHO DAT!*"

Adam gives me the side-eye as he grabs the aprons Uncle had waiting for us. A family business is a *"family business."* Working for free without notice is expected.

"We'll start bagging more pecans," I propose. "Aunt Helen can open another register." Both Adam and I still have a slight buzz from the game and the adult beverages we enjoyed. Operating the register is probably not a good idea, and I'm hungry. The smell of roasting pecans is impossible to resist. We ate our first bag before sending more upfront to Uncle. Free labor and free food—standard family business protocols.

Being here with Adam makes me think of my childhood working in the bakery with Luke.

"Are you crying?" Adam asks as he snaps me out of my cloud. "Where did you go?"

"Thinking about summers working with Mom and Granna," I reply. "Wishing Mom was here to see all of this—her dream for us to all work together."

"Then smile, Lovey," he says. "Your mom is watching. You don't want her to think you are sad working to make her dream a reality."

"There you go again, calling me Lovey," I say. "You know she's the spoiled wife in *Gilligan's Island*?"

"There's a smile. Look, mom, we're living your dream," Adam shouts. "Thank you, mom."

"Ok, the line is down. What are you guys smiling about?" Uncle asks.

"Love, Uncle," I respond. "We love being here with you."

"Great," he says. "Come help me update the menu board for tomorrow." We comply and get back to work.

Uncle uses the Marchand name perfectly to highlight Granna's best sellers from her original bakery. "Uncle, I'd also like to include the Marchand name on the big box store pastry packaging like we do on the pecan butter and our L.A. stuff?" I say. "I'll send you the markups I've made."

"Errr...maybe? We use it here on the menu like a "Daily Special" list—*Marchand's Favorites*. It's not on any of our boxes, bags, napkins, or pastry packaging." Uncle's response is typical. He is the reality to my whimsy.

"I hear what you're thinking," I say. "Too many words are a waste. I know—you always say, 'no one is going to stand there and read a paragraph on the front of a package—keep it simple stupid' But...never mind. I get it."

"Lily, just show them what you want them to buy," Uncle directs. "Just because you know a lot of words doesn't mean you need to give us all of them at once."

"Ok, ok...well, let me see if I can design something you may like," I say. "Just keeping the dream alive. You know my mind never sleeps." Dropping an idea after the first "No" never happens with me. Uncle knows.

If you're trying to go national, stay with your brand," he advises. "You want people to recognize the *"Much Ado About Pecans"* logo. Adding the Marchand name will confuse people. Keep it simple and send it to me. I'll take a look."

"Will do!" I reply. The words *"I'm not a good businesswoman"* flash in front of me, and I accept the fact that today I should listen.

CHAPTER TWENTY-TWO
Lily

No greater goal is ever achieved

As I examine my reflection in the mirror, I wonder if what others see is somewhat close to what I see? My smile changed after mom. It took five years for my face to produce a genuine smile. Am I a good person? Am I a good friend? Are Kate and I friends? Why am I asking questions?

Before the thoughts have time to sink in, my ringing cellphone stops me, and Kate's name appears. "You will live a long time," I say as an answer. "You just popped in my head, and then you called. Why are you calling? I just saw you. Do you not have friends?"

"Can you video-chat and help me prepare for a television interview?" Kate begs. "You've been on national television. Help me, please!"

"You are just so inappropriate," I laugh. "Your mother seeing me on television led to this entire mess, and now you're asking me to help you with your television appearance?"

"Argghh, why do you always focus on the negative?" she relays. "I'm thankful to mom for seeing Mrs. Lilah's photo on TV.

We're family. The case is over, you won— let it go, and help me with my life."

I question if I don't quite trust Kate because her brother sued me or because I don't really trust anyone other than Granna, and look how that has turned out.

Can I talk to Kate about my husband and kids? Can I tell her about my sibling drama? I can't imagine it's anything she hasn't seen or heard before in the past? Her brother is a wacko scum bag—I'm sure she's experienced a lot.

"Fine!" I agree. "Next time, ask me in advance. I'm not a teenager."

"Ok, I'm connecting now," she says. "Look at my outfits and pick."

"Nothing green; OMG, you'll go viral. Blue is also tricky. Pick a one-piece dress or V-neck blouse with black flared pants and add 3-inch heels. Red, burnt gold, or orange are my favorites. What do you have?"

Kate flips her camera which provides me a full view of her closet. Her closet is smaller than mine, so I'm unnecessarily pleased. If she had rows of designer dresses and shelves of shoes and handbags, I would most likely have ended the call and told her to deal with her own non-problems.

"I have this red and this wine color. Black or nude pumps?"

"Nude, Kate. Really?"

"What?

"Wear the taupe shoes," she pouts out her lips, and then the light bulb goes off.

"Oh, Nude for who?" she realizes. "I've heard that before. See, I need you. What if I say something stupid like that on TV?"

Well...there it is. She needs Black Culture Training and I'm her tutor. Why am I so slow? See, I knew I wasn't racist. What next? Oh, Thanksgiving photos with the Black family for her website. Black friends don't use you for photo ops, but family will use you for just about anything. If I begin to view Kate as family, she will fit true to form. I'll check the *"Family Box"* for Kate.

"Kate, let me hear your talking points. Am I the only Black person you could find in a hurry?" I joke. "Who's on your staff? I can help you hire new staff and add a little diversity. You need it before a recall action is filed."

"Stop it, Lily, and help me!"

Giving Granna a tour of our new bakery setup seemed like a good idea when it popped into my head this morning. The *Garden Emporium* is only one mile away from the bakery, so I decided to use it as an excuse to get Granna in my car. My thought is that she will be in a better mood if she knows flower shopping is next on the agenda after our bakery stop.

"Lily, how much did this kitchen renovation cost?" Granna asks before she makes it past the doorway. I had given her a brief description of renovations during our ride.

"Not much more than we budgeted," I defend. "We needed a larger packing area. I'm working on a contract with a co-packer for when demand outgrows this space. Don't worry. I don't plan on spending any more money anytime soon."

The smell of fresh paint still lingers and has not yet been replaced with the smells of fresh-baked bread and pastries. The rows of sparkling silver ovens are followed by a basketball-court-sized room filled with stainless steel packaging counters.

"This all is very pretty, but it also looks pretty expensive. How much over budget?" she asks. "Not much more is not a number."

"It's a good move for us," I explain. "I know you think I can overspend, but this time I ran the numbers, and Uncle even agrees."

"I'm not thinking any such thing other than you answering my question, Lily," Granna demands. "How much of my money have you spent. I think you are trying to spend it up because you don't want me giving it away to the church. This stuff looks too shiny and too expensive. You couldn't find used equipment?"

"We'll be selling in major retailers," I say. "Don't you want us to use the best equipment possible?"

"My first bakery had all used ovens, and you know what—they worked just fine," she adds. "There's no need to buy new. You should also stop buying new cars. What's the point in that?" Granna continues her rant as she opens and inspects every new oven and cabinet.

There's a slight grin on her face as she turns and offers me her hand.

"Why are you talking about my car?" I question. "You said you liked it."

"Okay, my head-in-the-clouds grandchild," she laughs. "You did good. Now can you sit down and be still at least until my bank balance recovers?"

"Certainly," I respond even though we both know Granna's personal money was not used to remodel the bakery, but "ALL" company money is her money as far as she is concerned. Uncle and I may share ownership with Granna, but Granna has no interest in treating us as equals. She's the owner and we all know it.

"Turn on this new oven—the one right here," Granna instructs.

"Sure, Granna," I say. "Anything to make you happy."

"Well, if you would find your brother a wife so he can give me more great-grandchildren, I would really be happy," she laughs.

"I'm on it," I say. "Let me see what miracles I can pray up next."

"Since we are here, let's make a few rolls. Do you have fresh pecans? I want to take something different to *First Brunch*."

"You don't have to call it that anymore," I giggle. "I know it's your investment group. What's the name again… '*Rich Nana's*'—truly unbelievable."

"It's still *First Brunch*—the first Saturday of the month," Granna scolds.

"We cracked a bag yesterday," I say. "I'll text Ms. Julia and let her know we'll need to prepare more Monday morning," I explain as I hand Granna the prepped pecans. If I use them and forget to tell Ms. Julia when she gets here Monday morning, and there are no pecans, I will be in more trouble than I will be able to wiggle out of alone.

"Can you believe we spent the last year fussing over nothing more than this pile of pecans?" Granna laughs.

"No! It's too unbelievably strange to be true," I say. "Should we add more pecan products to our menu?"

Now that the lawsuit is over, we all seem to have gained a new sense of pride with fewer doubts about the future. Granna's worries never reached the level of mine nor Uncle's, but she had a few bad days as well. She loved her sister and her parents. Learning that parts of her family never completely accepted her was difficult to acknowledge, but today we are more grateful for the family love that remains.

"Lily, please. I don't have the energy for your silly talk. More products—why? Help me roll this dough, turn on a game and be quiet for half a second— Please!" Granna directs as she motions for me to turn on the television.

After remaining silent for at least ten minutes—more than her requested "half a second" I speak. "Granna, can I come to *First Brunch?* I'm only asking because I think it will help me become a better businesswoman."

"Nice try, but NO!" Granna answers. "No children allowed. We have that rule for a reason. You kids get educations and big fancy jobs, and you begin to believe you are the smartest person in the room. The answer is…NO."

"Well, that's so not true and so unfair," I explain. "You all don't feel guilty about not sharing your knowledge with your children?"

"I've given you the name of the investment firm I use; I've invited speakers to the church, and we all share information with our families," she replies. "The problem is you all don't listen. Now, listen and stop talking. What temperature did you set the oven?"

"Fine," I surrender. Helping Granna prepare pastries is always a delight. As a four-year-old, it was my unofficial summer camp, and I loved it. I was up with the Sun and darting for the kitchen as soon as I heard her footsteps. I put on my pink monogrammed apron Granna had given me for Christmas and began gathering the mixing bowls from under the cabinet.

Granna would always go straight for the kitchen window, open the curtains, and greet the day with a joyful "Good Morning World," before giving me my morning hug. "Rise and Shine my Beautiful Angel—Bakers must work while watching the Sunrise, Lily-bell." That was the name Granna called me when I was a happy young girl hanging onto her pants leg. Today, I'm just "Lily- please behave."

"I'm taking another trip to New Orleans," I explain. "Your estate lawyers have asked me to join them for a tour of *Cajun Made Foods*."

"Yes, I'm aware," Granna says with too much arrogance. "Hopefully, you will learn more about business valuations."

"Great, just awesome," I add with a laugh. "Anything else you suggest I learn?"

"See, exactly why you are not invited to *First Brunch*— know-it-all," Granna laughs, and I join in. I know she's right. Once again, she outsmarts me.

CHAPTER TWENTY-THREE
Kate

*Queens move diagonally, horizontally,
or vertically any number of squares*

I fear that protesting mom and Ryan's actions would lead to unwanted questions. My defense of people who have previously been strangers to us all would be difficult for me to explain. I'm good at hiding suspicious behavior. I'm a politician, but I'm not sure how much more I can get away with.

Mom's escalating dementia also renders her unable to assist with my attempts at thwarting Ryan's aggressive attacks even if she wanted to take my side. The ending to the lawsuit has returned some level of calm to my life, but now Ryan is questioning the *Cajun Made Foods* deal. I'm defenseless. I am once again alone.

The time I've spent with Lily has ignited the hopeful thoughts I previously fought to suppress. I'm beginning to allow space for the dreams I have long protected. Who is he—really? He has lived less than thirty miles away from me most of his life, and I kept an unknown distant watchful eye without intruding upon his life. The assumptions I've made about his identity must be true. He must be my son. I recognize his eyes. I'm not wrong, but I don't want to cause him pain. My grief should never become his burden.

The summer after my senior year of high school was supposed to be a time of joy and anticipation for the start of my promising future. Everything was lined up for me to start *LSU*. My dorm room was assigned, and my major was chosen. My giving birth was the only pending task not on my list of items I needed to complete.

Having a tall, sturdy frame was not always appreciated growing up, but now I was pleased because my full frame allowed me to conceal my growing belly. A sweatshirt and waist trimmer were all I needed.

By month eight, I realized I needed more help, but choosing the right person to trust was a much more complex problem to solve. Hiding my belly had really not been that hard. I estimated that within the next month, I would have a baby.

Thoughts of me giving birth ran rapidly through my head, but they seemed too foreign to truly be my life. For at least six months, I ignored the possibility of pregnancy. In month seven, I started feeling actual kicks, and I purchased a test. Then I knew for certain. A baby was coming—soon.

Graduation was also coming, and I needed a dresses—Senior Awards Night, Athletic Banquet, Prom, Graduation Ceremony. Each time mom questioned me about shopping, I picked a fight with her in order to avoid a shopping trip. I also requested to skip my parents hosting a big country club graduation party in my honor and asked to go new car shopping instead.

I picked out dresses on my own, and I was somehow able to make it through a week of celebrations and a two-hour-long graduation ceremony. I was still trying to figure everything out on my own, but my eighteen-year-old mind did not have the knowledge or experience to figure out most things. Grandma Rosey would offer me, *Saving Grace*.

"Grandma, I'm coming to visit you in my new car next week," I said, trying to sound like a normal giddy teen who had just received their first car. She had been in town for my graduation, and when I saw her, I immediately knew she was the best person to help.

"I'd love that, Katie-Rose," she responded. "Are you driving alone? What did your parents say?"

"I'll be fine," I replied. "It's only a two-hour drive. If you can drive here by yourself, I'm sure I will have no problem." We both laughed at the comparison and decided that I would be fine.

The following week, I announced to my parents that I wanted to spend the week with my grandmother. Telling them that I needed to get away and relax before starting *LSU* seemed reasonable. No one questioned my request, and I felt relieved by the thought of finally having help solving my problems.

The drive from my home to Grandma Rosey's in Lafayette was easier than I had predicted. I packed plenty of snacks and made the entire drive without stopping.

"Katie, I'm so proud of you," Grandma offered as she came out to help me bring in my bags. "You brought a lot of stuff. Are you staying the rest of the summer?" she inquired with a laugh but stopped when she saw the fear on my face.

"Let's go inside, grandma," I motioned. "There are some things we need to talk about."

Instead of trying to soften the news or use words to explain my condition, I raised my shirt and took off my waist trimmer. No words were needed.

"Well...okay," she expressed without concern. "Put your things away, and I'll fix us something to eat."

Grandma Rosey handled the news much better than I had imagined. Many dark scenarios had been racing through my mind. What if she told my parents? She was always a take-charge, confident source of stability for Ryan and me. Our parents were more focused on their social status than they were on raising children. Grandma provided us much needed attention and stability.

"I think I'm due soon, and I haven't seen a doctor," I revealed as I sat across from her at the kitchen table. Grandma made grilled cheese and salads—my favorite. Her fresh lemonade was also ready for us to enjoy. She always made a fresh pitcher whenever she knew we would be visiting.

"We'll go to my doctor and to the unwed mothers service center," she explained. "You've kept this secret for a reason.

Finding someone to adopt won't be a problem. Are we going to tell your mother?"

"I can't—she wouldn't approve of any of it," I proclaimed. "He's the star football player. He doesn't know. I haven't told anyone. Oh, he's also Black and going to *Bama*. I don't want to mess up his scholarship."

"Black, well, I guess I'm the best person you could have called," she giggled. "I happen to know a few things about taking care of mixed babies." I had no idea what Grandma Rosey was talking about, nor did I understand why she was laughing?

"Grandma, what are you saying?" I asked, confused. "And, what is so funny?"

"He's going to *Bama,* and you're going to *LSU*," she answered. "You're a match that's not meant to be."

We both laughed, and for the first time, I allowed myself to see past my mistakes and begin to hope. Grandma Rosey helped to save my baby and me. "I'm having a baby," I then said without feeling a sense of overwhelming despair.

The next afternoon I visited Grandma's doctor. The exam was a harsh experience filled with an astonishing level of pain. I set my focus on the ceiling tile patterns and counted the number of lines in each square—ten across and eight down.

Grandma Rosey was with me in the exam room, and neither she nor the doctor seemed bothered by my groans. I made this baby and kept my pregnancy hidden for eight months. Their expressions told me that my complaints about a little exam meant nothing.

"The baby is healthy and should arrive next week," the doctor informed. "Do you need me to schedule delivery?"

"No, I'll take care of that," Grandma confirmed. "The baby will be adopted."

Hearing the words "will be adopted" while sitting nearly naked on an exam table made it all seem more real and more frightening. My baby had been a secret, a problem I was determined to hide and solve on my own. Now, I see my belly as a baby—my baby.

"I want you to know that I've called my sister," Grandma disclosed during our drive back to her home. I knew she had a sister, but I didn't know anything about her—where she lived and why we've never met?

"Your sister?" I questioned. "Why? Does she live in Lafayette?"

"No," she responded sharply. "I am only telling you because I can see the worry in your eyes. You never have to worry about your baby. He will go to a good home and have a good life."

"He?" I questioned. 'Did the doctor tell you?" We had not spoken about the doctor's report. I didn't know that she was told my baby was a boy.

"Yes, it's in the report," she said while pointing to the section marked "sex."

"Why is your sister helping?" I asked. "No one can know."

"She will never tell a soul—that's not a worry you need to ever have," she assured. "I'm telling you because I won't be around forever, and if one day you have questions, you know where to look for answers."

That day, I didn't understand what she was trying to explain, but I trusted that she was doing what was best for my baby and what was best for me.

"What do I do about the father?" I wondered. "Does he have to know?"

"Don't take this the wrong way, but we are listing the father as unknown," she instructed. "It doesn't mean you've been sleeping around. It just means you are not sure, and that's all we are going to say about that."

Grandma Rosey called later that evening to tell my parents I'd be staying with her for a few weeks to help teach Summer Vacation Bible School. She discussed that I would be paid and that earning extra money for college was a smart idea. To my surprise, Grandma was also rather good at spinning a believable lie.

"The doctor said you'd deliver any day now," Grandma reminded. "How are you feeling?"

"The same," I replied. "I'm starting to feel more nervous, but that's it."

"Don't be afraid," she consoled. "I'll be with you the entire time. It will go fast. You are young and healthy—nothing to worry about. You will be up and back to normal in a few days."

Normal? I know she wanted to help me feel better, but "normal" is something I did not imagine my life would ever again become. If my baby wasn't Black, would I have wanted to keep him?

"Grandma, thank you for helping my baby," I said more out of concern for myself. "Thank you for finding him good parents."

"I've told you not to worry," she ordered with noticeable irritation. "This baby is my great-grandchild, and I owe him a duty as much as I owe one to you. He will have a fine life. You don't have to worry about the baby. Worry about yourself and how you will go home without your baby and get ready for college."

Her words described my reality perfectly. I would start college the following month.

Days passed quickly until the morning I awakened to the sounds of my own screams. I wasn't sure if I had rolled onto my belly during my sleep and had somehow caused the pain I was now feeling.

Walking to the bathroom and barely able to stand, I was bent over holding my belly. Grandma heard my struggle and helped me take the last few steps. She knew it was time. As I sat waiting for her to tell me what was next, she returned dressed and carried her nicest house robe for me.

The Sun was up and slightly covered by a morning haze, but I could see the hope it would bring. I kept my eyes locked on its brightness and also used its warmth to calm my waring belly. The pain had risen to a level I could no longer silently ignore.

Naming Lilah

Grandma grabbed my hand with one hand and steered the car with her other. She was well into her seventies, but her agility did not match her years.

I was placed in a room with a big window and couch for Grandma. She only left my side to fill her coffee cup. She rubbed my back, and we prayed to every angel we could remember.

"You made it," Grandma announced in relief as she welcomed her guest. The two exchanged a loving embrace and secret whispers. I could tell they were close but did not understand why. "This is my granddaughter, Katherine Rose."

"Lovely, such a joy to see you," she voiced gently. "I will always keep you in my prayers."

She takes my hand and gives it a squeeze as she offers a prayer. The two leave my room, and only Grandma returns.

"Was that your sister?" I questioned. "She looks nothing like you." Grandma ignored my words and returned to rubbing my back. Another question was never spoken.

My son arrived with the next day's Sun. For twenty-four hours, I prayed and asked for God's forgiveness. I felt the pain was punishment for my deception.

I slept the next twenty-four hours and was back home with Grandma Rosey before the following twenty-four hours would pass. I saw my son once. He had a round happy face and a full head of hair. A lingering kiss to his forehead was followed by a prayer I had written in my journal the day before he was born.

> *"May our God always protect you and send any harm aimed at you, my way. In Jesus' Name I pray, Amen."*

"Katie-Rose, how are your breasts?" Grandma questioned like she was asking what I wanted for dinner. "You may need to wrap them?"

"Grandma, why are you talking about this now?" I asked, embarrassed. We had been home two days, and I was starting to feel more like a teenager. Most of my time was spent either sleeping or eating. My body was beginning to again feel familiar, and my thoughts were returning to the more familiar. I began making a list of things I wanted to pack for my dorm room. Grandma Rosey had given me a large trunk that would hold nearly everything and would fit perfectly at the end of my bed.

"I want to make sure you are healed before you drive home," Grandma stated. "We'll call your mother tomorrow. She's asking about taking you to pick out bedding and towels."

"Yes, I do still need to shop," I replied. "I wasn't in the mood for shopping before, but now is the time. School starts soon."

Grandma Rosey had done for me more than I knew was possible. I came to her in trouble, and without question or condemnation, she helped me. My parents never did anything without pointing out how great they are or how undeserving I am.

As our time together neared its end, I craved more time to enjoy our new relationship. The past few weeks had shown me that I didn't know much about her as a person. I only knew her as my mom's mother. My opinion of her was that which was shown to me by my mom. I now see her as my Grandmother.

I convinced her to stay up late with me and watch a movie—*Titanic*. I knew I needed a distraction, and I felt Grandma Rosey did as well. We watched while cuddled up on her sofa with a huge bowl of buttered popcorn. We melted an entire stick of butter and poured it on top. I cried again at the ending. Grandma thought it was hormones, but I explained I'd seen it four times, and I cried each time. She thought I was ridiculous and went on to explain why she hated the ending.

"Jack could have been saved, and the necklace should have been sold," she concluded.

We debate the ending until I finally surprisingly begin to agree. The time I was allowed to share with Grandma Rosey was time I have always treasured.

The morning my son turned five days old I returned to my life as a teenager on her way to college. I remember every second on the drive I made that day. I haven't forgotten his face, his smell, his eyes. I wasn't sure if I ever would? I now know that answer is—No!

"Lily, have you arrived?" I ask.

"Yes, I'm on my way to meet my uncle before checking into the hotel," she responds. "Tomorrow, I have a meeting with Granna's attorneys. Do you want to meet me later?"

"I'd love to come by the bakery if that's ok?" I suggest. "It's still not weird for you guys, is it? I understand if you don't think it's a good idea."

"No, it's fine," Lily states. "I think everyone knows we are not getting rid of you easily."

"Thanks," I laugh. "I know you mean that as a compliment."

"Of course," she jokes.

I know my son won't be there, but his photos are on the walls. I snuck a selfie the last time I was there. One of his photos is next to a beautiful *Fleur de lis* painting. I'm sure everyone assumed I was taking a selfie with the painting.

The bakery is busy as usual, and Lily's uncle is out front chatting with customers. "Hello, Mr. Marchand. Good to see you again," I offer with a smile. He reaches out and gives me a welcoming hug.

"You can now call me EJ," he instructs. "You've passed the smell test. You're also probably Creole, but that brother of yours is not allowed around me unless he's with you," he lets out a big laugh as he walks away, but I know he's not at all joking.

"Is Lily around?" I ask as I look around the bakery.

"She's in the back," he shouts. "I'll grab her for you."

Lily bounces out from the back door with fresh bags of roasted pecans for us both.

"What's up, Kate?" she asks. "What do you have planned for me tonight. I took a nap," she leans in and gives me a big hug. I honestly believe Lily is beginning to like me—even if it may only be a tiny bit.

"I won't keep you out too late," I say. "And, I won't try to convince you to go by Ryan's."

"Perfect," Lily responds. "Give me a second to speak with my aunt. My nephew is coming later tonight, and I want to make sure I see him tomorrow before I leave."

Lily returns to the back of the bakery before her words completely register. My legs have literally frozen stiff as my mind searches for the best way to escape. Lily returns and immediately notices the terror on my face. Before either of us says a word, I turn, push through customers, and stumble, but catch my fall by grabbing the exit door. I can hear Lily calling my name, but I don't slow down until I make it to my car. Lily catches up, grabs me with both hands and demands that I stop.

"What happened?" she shouts. "You look horrified. Did someone say something about you voting against the jobs bill?" she asks too lightly to be serious.

"Lily, that's not funny," I say. "What if I was being attacked?"

"Well, what's wrong?" she questions while giving me a curious eyebrow raise.

"I thought I saw one of the protestors from Baton Rouge," I lie, but she seems convinced.

"You all may need to travel with security," Lily suggests. "This is a different time. Peaceful protests are turning into violent attack jobs."

"I'll look into it," I add. "You're right. I need to take things more seriously."

"Let me go grab my things, and I'll be right back," she explains before turning towards the bakery. "Don't move."

I try to relax and settle into the passenger seat of my car. My hands are shaking uncontrollably as I struggle to regain composure before Lily returns. I realize I have not thought through how my relationship with Lily would continue if our families grew closer. Knowing her was something I immediately felt compelled to pursue. I also felt that the lawsuit was a sign and that the time for me to find peace was nearing.

He's now twenty-three. Is Lily's nephew twenty-three? I know the answer is "yes." After years of allowing myself to stalk her family, what will Lily think? How will I even defend my actions to her?

I'm unable to form the words in my head in a way that makes me not seem like a criminally insane stalker. Maybe I'll talk about my kids and then ask her about hers? Would it then be natural to ask about her uncle's child? She has never once before mentioned him. Can I now tell her about my son? I feel my desperation growing as I consider telling Lily my truth. I'm desperate to say the words to someone other than myself.

CHAPTER TWENTY-FOUR
Kate

Kings move one square in any direction, so long as that square is not attacked by an enemy piece

Where is the best place for me to have the most important conversation of my life?

"*The Oyster House* is within walking distance," Lily announces. "Let's go there. We could use the walk, and I love their food."

"Sounds good," I say. The streets are busy, so that helps me avoid too many questions.

"I'm having a *Pelican Punch*," Lily adds. "It's light and fruity. Do you want one?"

"No, I'll have gin and tonic," I say. "Light and fruity will not work today."

"Are you up for dinner?" she poses with concern. "We can hang out tomorrow. I'm here until Monday. My nephew is in town, and he's singing at church Sunday."

My eyes buckle, and I grab my face with both hands. My reaction startles Lily, and she turns to check the room.

"Do you see someone here?" she says as she looks over her shoulder.

"No, it's not that," I answer.

Our drinks arrive, and I try to put away as much as possible before answering Lily's questions.

"What is it?" she asks. "Is it a Louisiana thing? A White thing? A crazy thing? What?"

"You are ridiculous and impossible to ignore," I reply. "Oh, you're an attorney. I shouldn't forget about that. It's your job to analyze and investigate. Well, can you also be my friend? Do you know how to just do that for a moment?"

I summon the waiter for my second drink and trust that the more I drink, the better I will be able to handle Lily.

"Well, the attorney in me knows you are not telling me the whole story," she explains. "Resisting is a waste of time. By the end of this meal, I will have figured out what you're hiding."

She's right. I need to tell her. Ryan may have put this ball in motion, but I think God agrees it's time for me to know the truth. He has to be my son. I know my grandma called her sister to help with the baby. She promised they would take good care of him and make sure he had a good life.

"I knew about you all before my mom saw you on TV," I blurt out, even to my surprise.

"What are you talking about," she utters, confused. "Knew about us how?"

"I knew about my grandma's Black sister," I explain. "I knew her name. I knew all your names. I visited her original bakery and even bought her pecan butter."

"How would you know, and your brother didn't?" Lily questions.

"I spent one summer with my grandma, and she called your grandma to help me," I say and wait for Lily to respond.

"Help...you...with what?" she speaks tentatively.

"I'm certain your first guess will be the correct one?" I say. "I went to my grandma's to hide a secret, and I needed her help. Ryan and my mother never knew why."

"What summer, when, how old were you?" she begins to interrogate.

"Eighteen—right out of high school," I explain. "I was a tall and chubby teenager. I was able to keep my secret hidden. I was less than two weeks away from giving birth by the time I made it to my grandma's house. She knew right away. My own mother saw me every day and noticed nothing."

"Wow!" Lily remarks. "Why are you telling me this today? What really happened earlier?

"I think your nephew is my son," I again let words slip out before I could change my mind. "I've been watching him since he was ten."

Our next round of drinks and appetizers arrive before Lily can process what I've said. I can see that she heard my words, but her blank stare does not provide much insight. Finishing my drink seems like the best option. I take my time with this one because I'm not sure if they will cut me off soon, and I can't make it through the rest of this evening sober. I'll stay out until my family is asleep and call a ride home.

"Lily, let me explain," I offer in an attempt to break the silence. "I must sound like a crazy stalker person, but I promise that's not the case. Just let me explain."

"Stop talking," she orders. "For months, I repeatedly asked you why you put forth such an effort to get to know me. I questioned why you tried so hard for us to get to know each other and become friends. I'm so silly! I thought you were acting as a double agent for your brother or wanted to promote family unity with your Black Family to help with your campaign. I'm so stupid."

Lily's reaction is not surprising. It took months before she even acknowledged my efforts. Trusting me did not come easily, and I always understood why. I'm not sure if I was her first White friend, but she is not my first Black friend. Will's father holds that role.

"Please, just give me an opportunity to explain," I beg. "I wanted us to become friends because of the loving, kind, smart, talented, loyal person I had the opportunity of getting to know this past year. I know you would never betray your family. I don't want anything from you other than friendship."

"Then, what was your plan?' she asks. "How did you see the first family Thanksgiving going?"

"It's not my fault this whole thing happened," I say in my defense. "I may never have said a thing to anyone. We're sitting here together now for a reason. I'm not sure where this goes next, but telling you today just happened. I couldn't have planned what happened today. You have to know that?"

"Sure, but now I know," she announces. "You also know that I'm not lying to my family."

"Yes, I understand," I say. "But your grandmother knows. I'm not sure about your uncle?"

"Knows what?" Lily responds agitated. "You don't know that Will is your son."

"He looks like his father, and he has my eyes," I make clear. "He's twenty-three years old. Your grandmother helped my grandma find a family to adopt my son. They were both there when he was born. The next day he left the hospital with your grandmother."

"You don't know that for sure," she argues. "Why wouldn't my grandmother tell me this when we all first met—when the stupid lawsuit first started?"

"Tell you what?" I answer sarcastically. "Oh, Will is Kate's biological son. Really, how would she have said that? Besides, we only met briefly in the hospital. I could hear them talking in the hallway, and my grandma told me to sign here…and that was that."

The memory of that day flooded back as fast as the words slipped from my lips. The white napkin in my lap was now covered with makeup and tears. Without another word, I escape to the bathroom. Looking in the mirror, I now see that I am changed. Saying the words "my son" out loud to another person in over twenty years has freed a long-trapped part of my heart.

Lily paid our bill and was waiting for me outside the bathroom door. "Let's take a walk," she suggests. "More fresh air is needed."

Neither of us says another word. She reaches over and gives me the hug of a concerned friend. I consider her my friend— not just because she's family, but because she has become my friend. I trust her, and I hope she also trusts me.

I order a ride home and we stand silent until it arrives. True relief has begun to rush over me for the first time since I was a pregnant teenager. I had rehearsed many different versions of this day— the day I tell someone about my son. None of those scenarios included me revealing my most sacred truth to a person who, one year ago, was a complete stranger.

Now that Lily knows, who should know next? Is it time for me to tell my husband? Should I tell my campaign? Who should know and when? I have many questions and no answers. Grandma Rosey is the one person that knows exactly what I should do, but she's been in Heaven for many years. Who on this Earth has the answers I need?

I arrive home and settle in my study to avoid waking anyone.

"Kate, who are you talking to?" my husband asks. "I thought you were on the telephone."

"No, sorry for rambling," I say. "There's a big vote coming up soon, and I was going over my argument." Sometimes I amaze myself at the speed at which I can come up with a good lie.

"Well, don't work too long," he responds. "It's late, and we have the *Tulane Medical* charity event."

I agree and close the door to my study behind him. I settle into my plush armchair and call Lily. There's no way I can sleep, and I'm sure she's also unable to sleep.

"Can we talk?" I ask. "Sorry to call you so late, but I'm finally able to sit still and think."

"I'm still, but I'm not sure what I think," she replies. "I'm supposed to meet my nephew for breakfast. There's no way I can do that. I'll make some excuse and catch an earlier flight."

"That's why I'm calling," I say. "What should we do next?"

"We—really?" Lily says, annoyed. "This cannot be a 'we' decide thing. I have to speak to Granna first. If she confirms what you are saying about Will, then I'll talk to Uncle. After that, I don't know?"

"You're right," I acknowledge. "I'm just overwhelmed by the flood of emotions I'm feeling right now. I don't know what I should do next. Should I tell my husband?"

"Kate, what does he know?" she asks. "Does he know you had a child and put him up for adoption?"

"I've told no one," I say again. "I really mean no one. Grandma Rosey and I never spoke about it again. I literally started college and acted like any other freshman who had spent the summer hanging out and vacationing with friends."

"Well, Kate—that's not something you just tell your husband after years of marriage," Lily advises. "You need to take time and sort through your own feelings. Next, you need to find out the truth about Will."

"I know you hope I'm wrong, but I'm not," I assure. "You're right. I need to slow down and take time to sort everything in my mind. Will you call me when you speak to your grandmother?"

"I will let you know when I can," she offers. "I cannot imagine how I'm going to ask my Granna about you and Will. If no one has spoken about this in twenty-three years, I'm terrified to be the one to speak. I'm the one to blame for the lawsuit and our business losses. Now, I'll be blamed for welcoming you into the family. Sorry."

"You don't have to apologize," I say. "The lawsuit was definitely not your fault, and we're related by blood. You didn't welcome me into the family. I am family."

I know Lily didn't mean to offend, and I have always known that considering me family is not as easy for her as it has been for me. I've known about her grandmother and uncle for years. She just learned about us twelve months ago.

"We both need to rest," Lily responds. "I promise to call you tomorrow night. Until then, please don't do anything crazy and try not to obsess the entire twenty-four hours."

"I'll take something and try to sleep," I say. "Thanks for your kind heart, Lily. I realize I have asked a lot from you. I'm the one who should say 'sorry' to you."

We end our call, and I try to sink deeper into my chair. I don't yet have the courage to leave this room. Now that I've allowed myself to speak about Will, I want to tell everyone I love. I'm aware that no one else will probably share my excitement, but nonetheless, I realize that a lot of what I'm feeling is now excitement.

I walk through every room in my house. I check all the doors. I look in on my three children. I wake our dogs and let them out into our backyard. If anyone sees me, they may call a doctor. I have so much anxious energy sitting still wasn't working, so I thought tossing a ball at Midnight with our dogs would help. After a few snacks, our dogs are wired and ready for the late-night challenge.

My cell phone rings, and my dogs run back towards our back door.

"I can't sleep," Lily announces. I was shocked she called again but grateful she did.

"I'm in the backyard with our dogs," I laugh. "I woke them up and made them keep me company. I'm sure they are thinking I've lost my mind."

"You have lost your mind," she jokes. "Can your neighbors see you? You know you have an election coming up soon?"

"You know, I almost forgot," I say. "What would I do without you?"

"What did I do for excitement before you came along?" she asks. "My dad's family is full of all sorts of shady characters, but you have definitely surpassed them all in the excitement category. Let me ask one more thing, and then I'm going to sleep."

"Anything," I respond.

"Was it always your plan to tell me your suspicions about Will?" Lily questions.

"Please trust me when I tell you—absolutely no," I reply. "It just happened. I was happy to officially meet you all, but I wasn't sure I'd ever say anything about Will. When your grandmother didn't mention meeting me at the hospital, I assumed she didn't think my grandmother told me they were sisters? I knew why your grandmother was there."

"Please go inside and get some rest," she orders. "We have a long day tomorrow."

"Thank you, Lily," I feel it necessary to say. I then comply with her orders and allow our dogs to return to their warm beds.

CHAPTER TWENTY-FIVE
Lily

No time is wasted if we resist

Seeing the things that are right in front of our faces we grow to learn are the very things we often fail to see. I didn't truly see Kate. Granna, I see nearly every day, and I never saw the secrets she held. Why does this moment make me again feel like such an idiot?

I left New Orleans early and made the excuse that my later flight was canceled, and I had to return for a client. I apologized to Will and told him we'd see each other soon. I arrived in Los Angeles before lunch and head straight to Granna's.

Seeing Uncle and Will before speaking with Granna didn't feel right—besides, I need time to process what I learned from Kate. I'm still not convinced she's right about Will. Maybe it's all just one big coincidence? Maybe it wasn't Granna she saw? Her baby could have been given to another family, and Will is not her son.

"Did you bring me back something great?" Granna asks, obviously wondering why I'm stopping by her house before going home.

"No, sorry," I say with a heavy voice. "Let's make tea. I have an unbelievable story to share, and I'm afraid to hear your response."

Granna has fresh croissants she baked this morning for breakfast. I add sugar to my tea and honey to my croissant. I need Jesus, the sugar, and the carbs to help me through this conversation.

Do I ask Granna if her sister asked her to help with Kate? Do I ask about Will? I mostly want to know if she's known about Kate this entire time and why she never said a word when we were all being sued by Kate's family? Forming the thoughts in my head makes it all seem more real and more frightening at the same time.

"What's on your mind, Lily?" Granna asks. "You're eating lots of sugar—something's wrong. Do you have some new silly business idea you want me to help you talk to EJ about? He hasn't gotten over the number you gave him for his kitchen expansion."

"No, it's personal," I say. "It's about Will."

"I spoke to him this morning," Granna says with joy. "He missed seeing you."

"Yes, I know," I reply. "I couldn't face him today before speaking with you."

"Me—why would you need to speak to me?" she asks, confused. "What have you done now?"

"Granna, stop blaming me for all our family problems," I object. "Yes, the TV spot caused the lawsuit, but it all turned out ok, and we gained a *MajorMart* deal. I think that makes up for all my other bad business moves."

"Then—what?" Granna asks. "What about Will?"

I'm struggling more than I had imagined, but the words spill out as gracefully as I can muster.

"Kate believes that Will is her son," I say. "She believes that she met you in the hospital—that her grandmother, your sister, called you to ask for your help with finding a family for her son."

"Well, I wasn't sure she had put that all together," Granna mumbles. "She was so young and troubled. I'm surprised she remembers meeting me. Rosey never introduced me as her sister. She never even spoke my name."

"Wait...is Kate right?" I ask. "What are you saying? Kate's grandmother told her she was asking you, her sister, for help."

"If I ever thought she knew, I would have warned you all," Granna defends. "EJ will be devastated. I told him she couldn't have known. Anyone could have adopted her son. Rosey never told her it was EJ."

"Maybe not, but she told her about you," I add. "Kate said her grandmother wanted her to know how to find answers if she ever needed them?"

"That sounds like Rosey," Granna confirms. "Why did she tell you, and why now?" Granna asks. "Did you tell her Will was adopted?"

"Again, stop trying to blame me," I demand. "I've never once spoken to her about Will. She came to the bakery last night, and I mentioned that Will was in town. She freaked out."

"Well, I guess she did?" Granna says. "If she thought Will was her son, she should have asked me. Why sneak around lying to all of us?"

"Now we know why she was always on our side during the lawsuit," I say. "I could have never figured out this was her true motive."

"We need to call EJ and speak to him alone," Granna orders. "He will be so angry with me. I did tell him not to worry about Kate. I never imagined she remembered me."

"You came to the hospital to get her baby," I explain. "Your face was burned into her brain. Don't you remember everything about the day my mother was born?"

"Stop asking me questions!" Granna yells. "I need to figure this out. How will I tell EJ?"

"Has Uncle always known Will's biological parents?" I ask. "Does Aunt Helen know? Did my mother know?"

The croissants are now gone, and we need more tea. My questions have worn on Granna, and she appears visibly shaken. I now feel that telling Granna the way I did, and her reaction is my fault. Maybe, I could have handled this better?

"Aunt Helen and EJ have known since day one," Granna informs. "No one else was ever told. We would never tell your mother. Her husband was unstable. Who knows what he would have done with the information?"

I cannot argue with Granna's comments about my parents, but what about me and what about the lawsuit? I make up a need to check in with the office and excuse myself to make a few calls. I put in my earbuds and listen to an audiobook. We both need a few minutes to process the moment. I truly regret not being gentler with Granna.

"Granna, would you like for me to call Uncle, or should you speak to him alone?" I ask after our thirty-minute timeout.

"Whatever you think is best is what we will do. If you want to wait until Will returns to school, that may be better. I won't say a word to anyone, and neither will Kate."

"No, I can't live with the weight," she says. "I need to let EJ know. Call him and ask him to call us when he is alone."

I follow her request without offering any more suggestions. Uncle's at the bakery and Aunt Helen is spending the day with Will. Granna asks me to repeat the details of our conversation and try to deliver the details as gently as possible.

Uncle quickly dials in for a video call, I repeat my words and wait for his response. It was not as I had imagined.

"I could tell," Uncle confesses. "Helen mentioned that she was sure she'd seen her at the bakery—*Marchand's*. And, she was just too jumpy...not White family meeting Black family jumpy, but I've got a secret I'm trying to hide jumpy."

"Maybe, you were also jumpy," I surprisingly defend Kate. "Weren't you nervous about meeting her as well?"

"Not really," Uncle explains. "Will's twenty-three. She had never said anything in all these years, and she has a political reputation to protect. Having a secret Black son may not go over well with her voters."

"So...when she came to the bakery to "Meet" you, you knew exactly who she was," I question. "Why even meet her?"

"Lily, calm down," Uncle replies. "Mama never wanted anyone to know that her sister asked her to take Will. After everything that has happened this year, you know what kind of people we are dealing with. You should understand our silence."

My frustration escalates and I seriously consider disconnecting our call, but Granna is sitting next to me. I just want to slam Granna's computer shut and pretend we lost Wi-Fi. Who are these people?

"We wanted to meet her and see if we could tell what she knew," Uncle clarifies. "I told mama she had to know—especially when the trial stuff started. It's not too hard a thing for her to figure out. Mama was there when Will was born. They saw each other."

"Will…he's named after your father?" I ask even though I know the answer. "William Elias Marchand— really?"

"Those are the names of his grandfathers," Granna answers. "William is a strong name. What else should we have named him?"

"So, who knows?" I ask again while turning to look at Granna. I trust her more than Uncle at this moment. Because of the nonchalant way Uncle has justified his reasons for meeting Kate, I don't think he cares to admit how things have now changed.

Will's biological mother is a family member we all know, and we are keeping it a secret. Granna and Uncle have been lying to me this entire time. We were fighting to keep our business intact, and neither of them thought it important to tell me, or at least Anastasia, that we are raising Kate's child!

"Me, Helen, and Mama—that's it." Uncle answers. "Your mother never knew. We didn't want her telling Lucas. He would have told all of Louisiana."

"Yes, Granna told me," I say. "Kate's mother was never told?"

"No, she was with my sister the summer she gave birth," Granna explains. "She had kept her pregnancy hidden the entire time. Rosey took her to an adoption center for unwed mothers in Lafayette, and they helped with the birth and adoption paperwork. EJ and Helen picked up Will two days after he was born and brought him home to New Orleans."

"I remember when we found out you adopted him," I recall. "I was in law school. We were all so happy that you and Aunt Helen finally had a child. Wow, I guess none of us ever thought to ask where he came from or who his biological parents were?"

"Why would anyone have asked?" Uncle says. "He was our son. You all never thought of him any differently, and you still shouldn't— and never call him Kate's son. And, never let him or Helen hear you call him that."

"Sorry, I understand," I convey. "He knows he's adopted. Has he never asked about his birth parents?"

"No! We had a talk with him when he graduated high school, and he said maybe later," Uncle reveals. "He's never again mentioned it. You know Will is drama free. He doesn't like conflict. That's your job."

"You both can keep picking on me if you want," I say. "I can take it. Kate is the one you should worry about."

"I'm not worried about anybody," Uncle responds. "My son knows all he needs to know."

"Well, Will may, but Kate doesn't," I say. "You must talk to Kate. She has been stalking you all for years—since *Marchand's* was open. She knows her grandmother asked you to help because her baby was half Black, and you are her grandmother's Black sister. OMG, Kate even pretended to not know her grandmother had a Black sister. I'm surrounded by liars."

"Now, you stop with the insults!" Granna reprimands. "Everyone was trying to do their best for Will and Kate. Look at you, Lily. I've seen you lie with a straight face more than I can count. You've been lying since you learned to speak."

"Ok, Granna—I get the point," I interject. "No need to put my character on trial."

"Let's all take a moment and calm down," Uncle orders. "Will and Helen will be back soon. You need to explain to him why you left before seeing him. I was surprised you left and told him something urgent must have come up. Well...now I know, and we can't tell him that."

"No, I blamed it on a work emergency," I clarify. "That should work. It's a good lie."

"Lily, if you say one more word about lying, I will hit you myself," Granna threatens. "Don't worry, EJ. Speak to Helen when you can, and don't worry about Lily. I'll make sure she stays under control."

Granna's threats are ignored because my mind has shifted back to Kate. Her confessing that she'd been watching Will since he was ten years old is shocking, but I could feel how heartbroken she was and how the words were difficult for Kate to share. My need to defend her is revealed once again.

"I'm not the enemy," I say. "I'm a part of this family, and whether you want to admit it or not, so is Kate. She's Granna's great-niece, and she knows Will is her son."

"I'm doing nothing—let her know," Uncle declares. "If Will ever wants to know his biology, we'll tell him and her then."

"We owe her something," I say lightly, trying to not cause more yelling. "I can't just act like we never had this conversation. Can I at least tell her you will let her know when Will asks?"

"Why do you feel the need to tell her anything?" Uncle says. "She's been kissing up to you for this very reason. She wants your sympathy and help to get to Will. She doesn't care anything about you."

"Please stop! You both are just being so ridiculous," Granna accuses. "Don't assume you know anything about Kate, EJ. She was a teenager who gave up her baby. There's a missing part of her that she's been trying to fill for over twenty years. Being friends with Lily probably helps. Either way, she's family, and I won't let you toss her aside when she's coming to us for help."

"Well, my son comes first," Uncle demands.

"I'm not asking you to say anything to Will, but you and Helen should talk to Kate," Granna orders. "Get it over with and go back to caring for your family. Lily, give him her number so they can call her today."

"Today!" Uncle pleads. "Why Mama?"

"I want this over," she instructs. "The more days it takes, the more we are all sitting around worried for no reason. We have more important things to do and to think about. I don't want to hear either of you bugging me about this for another minute. Get it done—now."

"Yes, Mama," Uncle relents. "I'll talk to Helen, and we'll call tonight."

$\mathcal{I}$'m relieved to arrive home and surround myself with the familiar, but patience was not with me. I did my best to try and not obsess about Uncle calling Kate. I'm relieved Kate will have her answers, but I'm not sure how I should feel about Uncle, Aunt Helen, and Will. Kate's not horrible, so knowing her may not be all that bad, but what do I know?

"Granna, any word," I ask, unable to wait for Uncle or Kate to call.

"Stop calling me," Granna insists. "I'm finishing my Bible Lesson for tomorrow. Don't you have something to do?"

"Yes, but I can't focus," I reply. "I tried watching a movie, but that didn't work."

"I haven't received my monthly sales numbers," she adds. "Go work on that—did I make any money last month? That's something you can worry about, young lady. Now, I'm hanging up, and don't call me back tonight."

Granna's so rude for a supposedly otherwise loving grandmother!

It's too early to call it a night, so should I have chocolate or wine? The worry will not leave, and I think it's trying to quietly find a home within my cellular membranes. Yes, that intertwined. I'm trying to *Let Go-Let God*!

My sedative of choice is usually wine, but I'd rather allot the calories to my chocolate budget. Chocolate is never far from my grasp. We have a jar on our kitchen counter, and I have plenty on my desk and in my handbag. Is there a support group for sugarholics?

I grab a piece of my favorite dark chocolate with almonds and decide to also have wine. Why not? My family's world has changed.

Oh, can I tell Adam? Should I ask Granna? Well…I'd just better let it go until tomorrow.

Just as I anticipated, Kate calls, not Uncle. He sent a text that he had made the call and that he would call and speak to Granna. I'm relieved he did at least send me a text, but I'm sure it's only because he did not want to hear my voice again tonight.

"Thank you so much, Lily—I can never tell you how much you have helped save my life." Kate cries before I can say hello.

"Kate, I'm still trying to understand everything," I explain. "I only spoke with my uncle and grandmother. It was all my grandmother. She thought my uncle should call and confirm what we all realized you had already figured out years ago."

"Please, thank your grandmother," she adds. "My grandmother was the only person I told. The father doesn't even know. I don't know how I will tell my family. Your uncle requested that I don't say anything until Will wants to know, so I'm not going to tell my family. I don't want them trying to find him."

"Ryan is going to lose his mind," I laugh. "You know your brother is a closet racist."

"He's not," she announces. "I wish you all would stop believing that. He's just misunderstood."

"Yeah, right," I say. "If we were White or all White, I should say, he probably never would have sued."

"No, not true," Kate defends. "He loves money. He saw an opportunity to double his monthly royalty checks, and he went full throttle attack."

We both laugh because we know Ryan surely loves money. His Love of family is still under review.

"You know I'm disappointed it took you so long to tell me about Will," I add. "We visited with each other many times and met each other's spouses. We drove in the car for hours to visit St. Francis. You talked the entire time but never mentioned having a child the summer after high school."

"I never told a soul other than Grandma Rosey," Kate continues. "I really didn't know how to tell anyone. I only told you because we have grown close, and you knew I was hiding something."

"Yes, yesterday was a mess," I agree.

"I covered my face like an idiot and ran out of the bakery," Kate says with a slight laugh. "Maybe I thought he would walk through the door and take one look at me and notice something? I guess that has been my dream all these years."

Listening to Kate's anguish showed me a person I never imagined she could become. She has strength, and that means she is not the unburdened, privileged softie I created in my mind. Kate is selfless, and there was never a time during the months I've known her that I would have imagined Kate as a selfless, strong, smart, empathetic, and multi-layered complex White Female Republican Louisiana State Senator. On the outside, she fits the standard societal mold. She's someone I would have never taken the time to get to know. That's my loss. I've probably missed many opportunities to know good people. Kate is a person that anyone would be lucky to call "friend."

CHAPTER TWENTY-SIX
Lily

Love's home is found by those who seek

"*I simply remember my favorite things and then I don't feel so bad...,*" I sing in concert with the strum of my smoothie blender. Everyone has left for the morning, so our dogs are my only audience.

After an amazingly good night's sleep, I'm well-rested with a calm feeling of peace. I cannot remember the last time I was my happiest. But, today is a law office day, and I am truly excited to show up. I'm not stopping for kolaches, nor am I bringing Granna's pastries. I'm going in with just me and my newly found gratitude for others.

Looking around my home, I finally accept that this is my life. I now know that I was afraid of life—losing it, losing loved ones. My love for life was being smothered by my fears. My husband, my children, my friends, and my entire family are all waiting for me to love and appreciate them. The tomorrow I'm chasing does not yet exist. The tomorrow that appears today was unimaginable the day before. My question now is, "what am I doing to respect myself today?"

As *Voltaire* so eloquently proclaimed, *"certainty is absurd."*

I decide to start with Love and Gratitude. I love my family—the ones I've known since birth and the ones I've recently come to know. I love the strength and loyalty I've witnessed in my friends and co-workers. I truly love this life.

"Have you calmed yourself down this morning?" Granna questions. I call her first this morning because I need to hear that she is doing well, and also because if she has more complaints about my behavior, I want to hear them now so that I can enjoy the rest of my day.

"I'm great," I profess as I grab my car keys and take another gulp of my smoothie. "I'm going to the office this morning and the bakery tomorrow."

"Good," she responds. "Keep yourself busy." My cell phone connects to my car, and I miss the rest of Granna's admonishments.

"Granna, have you imagined how different our lives would have been if Kate and I had grown up together?" I ask.

"Don't you have work?" Granna reminds. "I also need you to get me the profit reports for the third quarter."

"Just indulge me," I beg. "I won't mention Kate again this week—promise."

"You two make an odd pair," Granna observes. "Kate does remind me of Rosey—fun and unpredictable, just like her grandmother. Are you coming to yoga class tomorrow?" she asks, quickly switching the topic.

"Yoga, yes," I say. "It's helped us so much this last year. I avoided it for so long because my belly was always in the way.

Running helped with that, but the strength and flexibility I've gained is all yoga."

"Yes, I also love it," Granna adds. "I hired one of the teachers from the studio to give my group a private lesson. I can tell you these things now that you know I'm loaded."

"Granna—not funny, too soon," I complain. "You should not keep such secrets from me. I'm still not convinced you are not keeping other secrets."

"I'm an adult—your grandmother, not your child," she quips. "I don't have to tell you anything. Mind your own business. Snoop around Kate's business. That should give you enough to do. I know you have already started snooping around to find out more about Will's history."

"You're impossible," I conclude before saying goodbye. Granna was born in secrecy, and she seems determined to continue her life cloaked in a familiar veil of concrete secrecy.

Finola is nowhere to be found this morning. Her desk is uncluttered, which means she's not been in, and her assistant is also *M.I.A.* I open my curtains and admire the view as if it's for the first time. Moving into this office was a happy day. I remember feeling valued and important. I again welcome that feeling.

"Why are you here and here before me?" Finola shouts. I turn and run across my office to greet her like an excited three-year-old.

"I thought you decided to skip today," I say. "I'm so happy to see you."

"Are you feeling ok?" she laughs. "You should be tired of seeing me. Are you coming to work?"

"I am," I confirm. "I also want to offer a proper thanks to you all. I truly appreciate everyone for working so tirelessly for my family. I needed to say thank you with my presence."

"Does that mean you didn't bring food?" she questions.

"That's easy—I'll order lunch, but first, please accept my sincere thanks," I express while giving her another hug, and as if I had planned the day perfectly—four dozen sets of pink and white roses arrived for each member of our litigation team.

"Ok, George Bailey—Did you have a visit from your angel?" Finola jokes.

"Let me thank you today because tomorrow I may go back to acting like it's all about me." We both laugh at the probable reality of my future behavior.

Day two of my Love and Gratitude Tour is reserved for the bakery. Mondays are busy at the bakery with weekly order prep, so Tuesday was the best fit. The staff's thank you gift will take us away for most of the day. Our group consists of all full-grown adult people, but when asked what we should do to celebrate our wins and *MajorMart* deal—in unison, everyone blurted out "DISNEYLAND."

Even though I had recently spent the day at *Disneyland* with Ms. Gail, Joelle and Olivia, I'm just as eager as everyone else to enjoy another day of fun.

"I drove out to a souvenir shop last night and purchased matching t-shirts, hats, and string bags—we're ready," I announce as I hand out gift bags. Matching attire is a trick I use when visiting *Disneyland* without the kids. Matching t-shirts creates the illusion that we are a part of a family group and not just a bunch of adults skipping out on a workday. This judgment is probably something only I am making. No one else really seems to care.

"We also noticed the extra cash in Friday's paycheck." Ms. Julia says.

"Yes, Granna wanted you all to know how much she values each of you, and extra cash says it best."

"Amen!" Ms. Julia agrees, and the rest of the staff chimes in with the same.

There are a few orders due tomorrow, but the staff is working to have everything prepped and ready for an early pickup and delivery. "Let's meet at the front gate at 11:00 AM," I say. "Will that give everyone time to get your morning orders out? I can have a van pick everyone up here at 10:00 AM."

"Yes, that will work," Ms. Julia responds in agreement.

I'm the first one to arrive at the entrance gate, and my enthusiasm grows as I see the first of our group headed my way. Next, Finola arrives. She invited herself when I mentioned *Disneyland* yesterday.

"*Indiana Jones* roller coaster or *Space Mountain*—which one first," Finola takes a quick poll. "It's Tuesday, so there shouldn't be much of a line."

"*Indiana Jones*," I vote. "It's closer. Then we can hit *Splash Mountain*. Where's the fun if we're not walking around wet?"

Naming Lilah

"Can we all take this ride?" Finola jokes. "I don't need anyone passing out mid-ride. We're lawyers and bakers—there's not a doctor in this bunch."

"I prayed, so let's risk it," I say. "Ice cream for everyone if we all make it to the end in one piece."

The wait is short, the ride never disappoints, and we all exit with the smile of a five-year-old.

"How did you assemble this group of wackos?" Finola asks. "How lucky are we?'

"I agree, lucky," I say. "The credit goes to Granna. She hired most of the staff. She is gifted at picking out the good people from the duds—*Spirit of Discernment.*"

"Who has the app tracker on their phone?" Finola asks. "Let's pick something next with a short line. My legs are starting to reveal my age."

Three rides down, ice cream, and a *Dole Whip* later we all need a moment off our feet. Acknowledging that our minds are still operating at one-hundred percent but our bodies need time to recover is tough.

People our age accept the reality that the world of our adulthood is much smaller than the world we imagined as five-year-old geniuses. Days are shorter, and single years are grouped into categories…high school years, college years, 20's, 30's…what were you doing in the 90s? What most of us have now also realized is that one day you wake up shocked by the fact that you have lived over four decades. Decades!

I hope that our group of wackos is a group that has learned to look back on our decades with gratitude and marvel at all the fun we were able to pack into each of our days. Spending a day at the *"Happiest Place on Earth"* is just what we all need.

My drive home is peaceful. Traffic is light, and I listen to a jazz station. I mindfully choose to not think of tomorrow's to-do list. I also try to not think about how I can spend more of Granna's money. A family vacation home would be awesome. I stop myself before I begin to create more trouble.

As Granna often reminds us all…"God gives us everything we need to do everything we need."

Naming Lilah

Truth in Love

What we miss is shown each day,

To walk alone is bravery's test,

It's in the words we never say,

Love often gives us our meaning and our rest,

My time was never truly owned,

Our time was never truly seen,

We dance and frolic until hope is shown,

Our Love becomes ignored routine,

What matters most is both given and received,

Without the exchange loss fails to exist,

No greater goal is ever achieved,

No time is wasted if we resist,

Love's home is found by those who seek,

The impossible home filled with words we long to speak.

Lilah Cormier Marchand, 1968

www.ingramcontent.com/pod-product-compliance
Lightning Source LLC
Chambersburg PA
CBHW030248010526
44107CB00031B/1364/J